Occupational Injuries and Workplace Risks

Occupational Injuries and Workplace Risks:

Research to Improve Safety

By

Simo Salminen

Cambridge Scholars Publishing

Occupational Injuries and Workplace Risks: Research to Improve Safety

By Simo Salminen

This book first published 2023

Cambridge Scholars Publishing

Lady Stephenson Library, Newcastle upon Tyne, NE6 2PA, UK

British Library Cataloguing in Publication Data
A catalogue record for this book is available from the British Library

ISBN (10): 1-5275-2856-1
ISBN (13): 978-1-5275-2856-7

TABLE OF CONTENTS

PREFACE

Throughout my career of almost thirty years in research, I have explored occupational accidents and injuries, their characteristics and causes. My major motivation has always been that, in the end, this work is about preventing accidents from happening and preventing human suffering and loss of life. The value base of this target is generally accepted: Who would want accidents and injuries? Instead, there is often disagreement about exactly how safety should be improved in real workplaces.

Over the years, I have been engaged in various kinds of research work. At the very beginning, in 1988, I was recruited to a research group that investigated serious occupational injuries in southern Finland. Each investigation started with a visit to the site of the accident. My task was to interview the injury victims, their closest workmates and their boss. The other group members gathered information about the work task that had been going on at the time of the accident and any factors contributing to the injury.

Sometimes, I found the interviewing emotionally very hard. In one fatal accident, for instance, I learnt during the interview that the man whom I was talking to was not only the victim's foreman but also his father and the grandfather of his three-year-old son. All in all, this project allowed me to see the seamy side of working life from a close distance and realize that there are always real human beings behind injury statistics.

The traditional surveys and interview studies that I carried out later on were aimed at finding out the opinions and experiences of larger groups of people. For instance, young employees were asked how they saw the work safety knowledge they had acquired in vocational education match the real-life requirements in the workplace. In analysing occupational injury statistics, I found that fixed-term employment increases the risk of injury at work. The study with the longest time span was a ten-year project on hazards in work-related traffic. As a result of it, a special discussion method was introduced for improving traffic safety. During the most recent years, I have compiled several literature reviews, such as a review of seventy studies on occupational injuries among young people.

Constant changes in work methods and processes, and the advancement of technology create new work environments and new risks. There is always space for improvement in work safety. In this imperfect world, there is no such thing as perfect safety.

ACKNOWLEDGEMENTS

I wish to thank Leena Saarela for revising and editing and Lorna Pierce for proofreading the manuscript.

INTRODUCTION

In the early 1990s, in Finland, a deaf man was run over by a forklift truck in a factory yard as he was unable to hear the forklift truck behind him and the driver failed to see him because of a high load (Salminen 1997). This incident was included in the figures of the International Labour Organization (ILO) when it reported the number of occupational injuries around the world in 1994. That year, there were about 335,000 fatal occupational injuries globally (Takala 1999).

In 1998, the estimated number of non-fatal injuries was 264 million and that of fatalities 350,000 (Hämäläinen, Takala and Saarela 2006). In 2003, there were almost 360,000 fatal occupational accidents. Every day, more than 960,000 workers were hurt because of accidents (Hämäläinen, Saarela and Takala 2009).

The ILO updates on these estimates indicate an increase in accidents, injuries, and ill health. Recently, it was estimated that there are around 340 million occupational accidents annually worldwide. Moreover, the underreporting of occupational accidents, injuries and fatalities is giving a false picture of the real scope of the problem.

According to the ILO data, the construction industry still has a disproportionately high rate of recorded accidents, including falls, falling objects, collapses, being struck by heavy equipment, and being crushed under, between or even inside heavy objects or machinery.

Younger, older and inexperienced employees are particularly vulnerable in the workplace. As the population is ageing in developed countries, an increasing number of older persons are working and need special attention at work. Besides, immigrant and migrant workers face poorer working conditions than the native populations of developed countries.

In addition to human suffering, occupational injuries are a serious public-health problem. They also cause considerable economic losses. As the probability of accidents at work increases with any increase in safety hazards, all efforts to identify and control or eliminate such hazards are worthwhile, if not lifesaving.

In my studies on occupational safety, I have applied the traditional research approach, including accident and injury reporting, and analyses of the causes and risk factors for injuries. This book describes how employees' individual properties, such as gender, age, and health status, affect their risk of suffering occupational injuries. It also analyses the effects of different ways of organising work, such as precarious work and shift work, on risk rates. Further, it looks at the risk sources encountered by workers in a number of industrial environments, such as transportation, construction sites, manufacturing plants, and mines. Finally, it touches on more recent trends in this sector, i.e., migration and climate change.

PART I

EMPLOYEE-LEVEL RISK SOURCES

CHAPTER ONE

DOES GENDER MAKE A DIFFERENCE?

Gender can affect the occupational injury and safety risks in several ways. Differences in the participation of men and women in various occupations in the labour market can lead to differences in occupational exposures. Further, men and women working in the same occupations may not perform the same work tasks. Sociocultural factors and gendered expectations may also have their effect, as well as the biological and physical differences. Gender-differentiated data will be discussed throughout this publication. In this chapter, I will first discuss male risk-taking behaviour and then look at the gender differentiation of statistics in work-related injuries in the light of statistical data.

Risk-taking Behaviour among Men

The statistics of occupational injuries are dominated by men. In 2011, for example, it was found that men suffered 96 % of fatal and 76 % of non-fatal occupational injuries in workplaces across Europe, while they accounted for only 54 % of the labour force (Oortwijn *et al.* 2011). If we assume that men generally take more risks at work than women, risk-taking should be considered a special factor in male injuries. In the context of work environments, in particular, a major problem is that there are various ways to measure risk-taking.

For analysing risk-taking in occupational injuries in Finland, I developed a risk-point measure (Salminen 1997, 38) that was based on the definition of risk-taking as a voluntary and conscious exposure to danger. The measure was constructed as a Guttman scale in the following way:

0 = the victim failed to recognise the danger
1 = the victim recognised the danger but could not act otherwise
2 = the victim could have acted otherwise but acted in the normal way in the accident situation
3 = the victim worked in an irregular way

My analysis of ninety-nine serious occupational accidents in southern Finland showed that risk-taking played a role in 54 % of the accidents. The most important motives for taking risks were the saving of time and trouble, and the strain of timetables (Salminen 1994a). A questionnaire study we carried out among 228 Finnish forestry workers showed no significant relationships between risk-taking and accident frequency. The study also indicated that impulsiveness and neuroticism were related to risk-taking but not to accident frequency (Salminen, Klen and Ojanen 1999).

A comparison of Finnish forestry (n = 228) and construction workers (n = 45) showed that in both of these professional groups the workers with higher scores on external locus of control took more risks than workers with higher scores on internal locus of control. The forestry workers scored as having a more external locus than the construction workers (Salminen and Klen 1994).

Risk-taking has also been studied by Honkasalo (1991), who interviewed thirty-nine Finnish professional divers and found that they accepted risks as part of their work. For example, a certain length of time under water causes time pressure. Diving is primarily a male profession where craftmanship is valued.

Honkasalo (1990) also interviewed twenty-eight male welders at a Finnish machinery manufacturing plant. They connected risk-taking with being in a hurry imposed by piece payment. Besides, Honkasalo (1988) has claimed that risk-taking is more typical for men than for women. Risk-taking can also be seen as one way to resist the boss in a male culture.

Risk-taking is often related to young ages. Westaby and Lowe (2005) examined over 2,500 American youths and found that the risk-taking orientation was significantly related to work injury. Supervisory influence and co-worker risk-taking predicted the risk-taking behaviour of young workers.

Among 3,415 municipal employees in Birmingham, Alabama, risk-taking was associated with an increased risk of occupational injury. Risk-taking and injuries were related to the male sex (Forrester *et al.* 1996). Turner, McClure and Pirozzo (2004) published a systematic review of six case-control studies and one retrospective study, concluding that risk-taking was associated with an increased probability of sustaining an injury except in high-skilled sports. Among Australian drivers, a high level of risk acceptance was associated with an eight-fold increased risk of serious injury (Turner and McClure 2004)

A meta-analysis of 150 studies showed that males take more risks than females. The gender gap was larger in intellectual risk-taking and physical skills than in smoking. In the oldest age group, the difference between the genders was significantly smaller than in the age group of high-school students (Byrnes, Miller and Schafer 1999).

Arch (1993) argued that when faced with risk-taking situations males were more likely to see the situation as a challenge that called for further participation, while females tended to respond to a threat in ways that encouraged avoidance of risk. Knowles *et al.* (1973) found, with fifty-six American student nurses, that risk-taking was a single motivational trait or a tendency to approach or avoid risk situations.

Among male Danish ambulance workers and slaughterhouse workers, those with a traditional masculinity orientation reported less safety oversights and made more safety violations (Nielsen *et al.* 2015). Based on an analysis of sky divers, Lyng (1990) defined edgework as an activity where the subject gets as close as possible to the edge without going over it. Such edge workers had a high regard for their own abilities to deal with danger.

The most effective means of preventing risk-taking leading to accidents are better planning and putting in place work arrangements that prevent hurry, and rectifying the underestimation of hazards by workers. In addition, the commitment of the top management of a company to safety enables the entire safety culture of the company to support the elimination of unnecessary risk-taking.

Gender-differentiated Injury Statistics

Women are a minority in the occupational injury statistics compiled in Finland. Their proportion of injuries was 34.8 % (Statistics Finland 2015), while their proportion of all employed was 48.3 % (Statistics Finland 2018). On account of the minority status of women in occupational injuries, the official statistics often conceal the specific characteristics of female injuries. Perez (2020, 129) considers this to be due to data bias, whereby any increase in serious injuries to women remains unnoticed.

Our study with 1,681 Finnish employees (Salminen *et al.* 2017) showed no statistically significant difference between the genders in the frequency of occupational injury, although men were more often involved in injuries than women. My analysis of ninety-nine serious occupational accidents showed that women were less often involved in injuries than men (Salminen 1994b). Besides, women working on production lines, usually on a single machine in serial production, were found to have the highest incidence of serious injury (Salminen *et al.* 1992a). In service work, two out of three injuries happened to women (Seppälä 1993).

A review of fifteen studies showed that men were injured at work on average three times more often than women (Messing *et al.* 1994). Another review of sixteen studies (Salminen *et al.* 1992a) showed that the median relative injury risk for men was 3.3, while their median fatal risk was 13. The two reviews unanimously indicated that men were injured at work three times more often than women. With regard to fatalities, the gender gap was even larger.

In Boston, US, a study among new postal employees showed that women had an increased risk of occupational injuries (Zwerling *et al.* 1993). Among 24,000 American aluminium manufacturing workers, the risk of injury was higher for women in four out of five injury outcomes between 2001 and 2010 (Tessier-Sherman *et al.* 2014). It was only in the risk of lost-time injury that no gender difference was found. Among blue-collar employees in Quebec, Canada, no significant difference was found between the genders (Messing *et al.* 1994).

As regards fatal accidents in Taiwan, male workers had a significantly higher physical injury claims prevalence than female workers (Lin, Chen and Luo 2008). The same results were obtained in Canada (Essien, Trask and Feng 2022). Lindqvist, Schelp and Timpka (1999), in turn, analysed 677 work-related injuries in Motala, Sweden. They found that males suffered almost four times more occupational injuries than females.

In a study of 11,054 Spanish employees, it was found that men were injured more often than women although women had bad working conditions more often than men (Campos-Serna *et al.* 2012). Gyekye and Salminen (2011) showed, with 320 Ghanaian employees, that gender was not related to accident frequency. Berecki-Gisolf *et al.* (2015) analysed 254,704 compensation claims made in Victoria, Australia. They found that men had a higher rate of physical injury claims than women. Furthermore, an analysis of 31,438 injuries among Californian electric utility workers indicated that males had substantially higher injury rates than females. After an adjustment for occupations, job experience and age, female workers, however, had a higher injury rate (Kelsh and Sahl 1996). On the other hand, gender differences in the occupational accident mortality decreased between 1955 and 1998 in the US and Italy (Waldron, McCloskey and Earle 2005).

One interesting finding is from Dalton (1960), who showed that, among female hospital employees, more than half of occupational accidents occurred during menstruation or in the four days preceding menstruation. However, this result has not been confirmed since. Another study (Dunning *et al.* 2003) found that one out of four pregnant women had had a fall and one fourth of these falls had occurred at work. Walking on slippery floors, hurrying, and carrying an object or a child had contributed to two out of three falls.

In economic terms, injuries were more expensive to women than to men in the long term. Injured at work, women lost an average of 9.2 % of their earnings, while men lost only 6.5 % (Boden and Galizzi 2003).

The results of the above studies on injuries to women were contradictory. Some studies showed that men were injured more often than women while others indicated a higher frequency for women. However, it is hard to find jobs where men and women perform exactly the same work tasks, and some gender differences usually exist in all work tasks. Based on the Finnish Study on Working Conditions (1984) with 4,502 respondents, Kauppinen-Toropainen, Kandolin and Haavio-Mannila (1988) concluded that women often profit from performing the same sort of work as men, whereas men often profit from sex-segregated work.

Jensen *et al.* (2014) found that gender roles and expectations also impact occupational safety, and that gender is constantly produced and reproduced. For example, working-class men perform manual work, whereas women are employed in offices and shops. These stereotypes are also reflected in occupational safety, as men are expected to work in more hazardous environments. The analysis of Bauerle, McConagle and Magley (2016) showed that men had fatal injuries over 25 % more often than women, even when men and women were working in the same occupation.

CHAPTER TWO

YOUNG AND OLD AT HAZARD

The relationship between age and occupational injury has been studied intensively. The interest of researchers has focussed on young employees on the one hand and on older employees on the other. The reason is that middle-aged employees generally have the lowest accident frequency.

My extensive literature review of sixty-three studies on occupational injuries showed that young employees had a higher non-fatal injury rate than older employees. Moreover, of the forty-five review studies dealing with fatal occupational injuries, the majority indicated that older employees had a higher fatality rate than younger ones (Salminen 2004a). An earlier review of twenty-two studies had concluded that the injury frequency tended to decrease with age, whereas the age-related injury severity increased with age (Laflamme and Menckel 1995). Furthermore, Crawford *et al.* (2010) made a systematic review of 180 publications. They concluded that older employees had a reduced risk of injuries, while they had an elevated risk of fatal injuries. Later, Schwatka, Butler and Rosecrance (2012) reviewed twenty-two studies in the construction industry and found higher injury costs but lower injury frequency among older employees. These reviews unanimously showed that young employees had a higher injury frequency than older ones, whereas the injuries of older employees more often led to fatality.

Older employees are generally also more experienced workers. Previous experience protects from injuries in all age groups, which will be discussed in more detail later in this chapter.

Older Employees

Based on our study including ninety-nine serious occupational injuries in southern Finland, I found that the most typical accident risk of employees aged over 50 was getting run over by a moving vehicle (Salminen 1993). My later analysis of the same data set showed that the proportion of employees aged over 35 was higher in serious injuries than in all injuries (Salminen 1994b). According to the official Finnish occupational injury statistics, the injury risk to female employees aged over sixty-three was almost three times higher (5/100) than that of females aged between twenty-five and forty-four (2/100). In the manufacturing industries, the injury risk among male employees aged over sixty was almost two times higher (12.7/100) than among young employees (7/100) (Pukkila 1995). Later, it was shown, using the same data set, that the injury frequency of employees aged over sixty-three was 36 % higher than that of middle-aged employees (Salminen, Heinonen and Sysi-Aho 2016).

Accordingly, my conclusion is that, in Finland, the oldest employees have an increased risk of injury. Therefore, raising the retirement age from sixty-three to sixty-eight years, for instance, would lead to a slightly greater number of injuries and fatalities.

Between 2000 and 2006, the injury mortality rate for people over sixty-four increased by 3 % in the US. A significant rise in death rates occurred in motorcycle crashes, machinery, poisoning and drowning (Hu and Baker 2010). In the US, the fatality rate of employees aged over sixty-four was three times higher than that of younger employees. The four leading causes of death among older employees were machines, motor vehicles, homicides, and falls (Kisner and Pratt 1999). In the crops production agriculture industry in the US, the fatality risk involving tractors was almost double for employees aged sixty-five or older compared with employees in the twenty-to-twenty-four-year age group. Tractor rollovers, falls from moving equipment, and falls and vehicle collisions were typical fatalities of older farmers (Janicak 2000). In highway transportation, the fatality rate among employees over fifty-four was three times higher than that of employees aged between eighteen and fifty-four (Pratt and Rodriguez-Acosta 2013). On the other hand, looking at non-fatal occupational injuries in the US, injury rates for falls on the same level, fractures or dislocations, and hip injuries were higher for older than for younger employees (Layne and Landen 1997; Wuellner *et al.* 2011). Furthermore, Baidwan *et al.* (2018) analysed the US Health and Retirement Study from 2004 and 2014 of 7,212 employees over fifty. They found that the risk of work-related injuries was more than two times greater among those whose job included physical effort, lifting heavy loads, and kneeling.

In British Columbia, Canada, workers' compensation claims from 1997 to 2006 were analysed. Older employees reported more traumatic bone, nerve and spinal cord injuries, whereas younger ones had more open-wound injuries (Smith *et al.* 2013). In a study of 320 industrial employees in Ghana, older employees over forty had experienced fewer injuries than their younger colleagues (Gyekye and Salminen 2009).

One reason for the higher fatality rate of older employees is that they are more fragile than younger employees. Based on the Volvo Car Crash Registry, Brorsson (1989) indicated that the risk of fracture was more than three times higher among drivers or front seat passengers aged sixty-five to seventy-four than among those aged from eighteen to twenty-four and that the risk of fracture in the rib cage was nearly eleven times higher in the older age group. Employees over fifty-four were hospitalised after a fall injury more often than younger ones, although there was no difference in the risk of fall injury between the age groups (Layne and Pollack 2004). Furthermore, in Australia, heavy physical demands at work increased the risk of work injury among employees over fifty-five more than among younger employees (Smith and Berecki-Gisolf 2014). Older employees in New Hampshire, US, received more severe injuries than younger ones, but they recovered better because of longer workplace attachment and the healthy worker effect (Pransky *et al.* 2005). The latest meta-analysis (Peng and Chan 2019) showed that the risk of fatalities among older employees was twice that of younger ones, whereas the incidence of non-fatal injury among older employees was 5.8 % lower than that of younger employees.

One way to prevent injuries among older employees is to allow them to move from physically demanding to lighter work tasks. Another important way of prevention is to ensure that older employees can avoid work tasks that require swift reactions. In addition, due to their long work experience, older employees could be utilised as mentors to their younger colleagues as well as in occupational safety training.

Younger Employees

My analysis of ninety-nine serious occupational injuries showed that young employees hurt themselves more often than older ones when feeding or cleaning machines. Incautiousness contributed more often to injuries of young employees than to injuries to older ones (Salminen 1996). In a questionnaire study of 1,681 Finnish employees, those under thirty-five were involved in occupational injuries significantly more often than middle-aged employees (Salminen *et al.* 2017). The highest injury risk was found among young machine repairers and construction metal workers (Sysi-Aho 2013).

American adolescents working in convenience stores and gas stations were at risk of shooting, whereas those working in gas stations and restaurants had an increased risk of burn injuries (Runyan and Gerken 1989). In North Carolina, seventy-one adolescents under twenty died at work between 1980 and 1989. Over half of the fatalities involved a motorised vehicle, typically a tractor. For females, homicide was the leading cause of fatal occupational injury (Dunn and Runyan 1993). A total of 9,656 adolescents aged fourteen to seventeen were compensated for occupational injury in New York State from 1980 to 1987. The highest rates were seen in manufacturing and agriculture. The most dangerous occupation was unskilled labour (Belville *et al.* 1993). Based on a questionnaire study (n = 3,574) done in Wisconsin, Zierold and Anderson (2006) concluded that African American teens and Hispanic teens were seriously injured over two times more often than white teenagers. Although young employees had a higher injury frequency than middle-aged employees, their injuries were more often minor, and the costs of their injuries were lower (Miller and Waehrer 1998).

As part of the West Jutland Cohort study, 2,181 Danish adolescents born in 1989 were asked to report their work experiences. Approximately 5 % of working adolescents had been involved in an occupational injury. The risk of occupational injury was increased by heavy work, high psychological demands, and low social support (Rasmussen *et al.* 2011).

An analysis of 1,700 occupational injuries of British adolescents aged sixteen to eighteen showed that the most serious injuries occurred in situations that involved no normal work activity, e.g., during work breaks (Glendon and Hale 1986). The industries where Australian adolescents (fifteen to twenty-four years) were most often injured fatally were agriculture, forestry, and fishing, followed by the transport, postal and warehouse industries, and mining (Ehsani *et al.* 2013). An analysis of 317 work-related injuries of Italian youngsters revealed two groups of injuries: transportation injuries to lower extremities, and hand/wrist and head injuries (Aggazzotti *et al.* 2006).

At two hospitals in Aracaju, Brazil, 4 % of 917 patients aged five to seventeen had been injured at work. Transportation injuries and contact with tools and equipment were the main mechanisms of injuries (de Vasconcelos *et al.* 2010). In the Cusco Province, Peru, 97 % of 410 public night-school students had been injured at work during their lifetime. Higher income was associated with falls, and severe injuries with physical violence at work (Schlick *et al.* 2014).

Furthermore, an analysis of 19,547 Canadian adolescents showed that employees aged fifteen to eighteen reported more non-lost-worktime accidents, less safety voice, less safety compliance and more safety neglect than workers aged nineteen to twenty-two (Turner, Tucker and Kelloway 2015). One out of three Canadian adolescents reported that they worked at least part of the day without supervision. Young females worked more often without supervision or alone than young males (Lewko *et al.* 2010).

Young employees are not a homogenous group. Turner and his colleagues (2022) also criticise that studies include inconsistent definitions of young employees. In a Danish study of twenty-six young adults, the researchers (Nielsen *et al.* 2013) found five distinct groups: skilled workers, apprentices, sabbatical year workers, student workers, and school dropouts. They argued that exposure to an accident risk was not equally distributed among these groups. In my own review (Salminen 2004a), I found that young employees had a higher injury frequency than older ones and men were involved in injuries more often than women, which suggests that young men are a special risk group of occupational injuries. Based on their review, Richter and Jacobs (1991) recommended eliminating the worst working conditions and controlling hazards as the most important ways to decrease injuries among young employees.

As mentioned above, my studies in Finland have shown that working with machines is especially dangerous to young employees. Youngsters may not know how machines operate or they may underestimate the hazards caused by machines. One factor that clearly protects young employees is better guidance and control by older co-workers. Studies from Australia and Brazil indicate that young employees have many injuries in the transportation industry. This might be explained by the fact that young people often work in delivery tasks (e.g., delivering pizzas) and that they are also often prone to driving overspeed. Injuries in such transportation jobs are very difficult to prevent as the drivers are not under the immediate control of their employer.

Work Experience

Experience in the workplace is related to injury frequency. Young employees are often inexperienced, but not all inexperienced employees are young.

When examining ninety-nine serious occupational injuries in Finland, I found that the injury risk was highest for employees who had been working for their employer for less than one year. Their proportion of injury victims (31 %) was almost twice that of the entire working population (Salminen 1994b). Furthermore, the same data set indicated that new employees used hand tools for most of their working time or transported things from one place to another. Therefore, cuts caused by moving parts of machines and falls from a height were the most typical injuries for novice employees (Salminen *et al.* 1992b). In yet another study in Finland, we found the highest injury frequency among employees who had been working in the company for two to ten years (Salminen *et al.* 2017).

A study of 22,952 female employees in a French national railway company showed that female employees with shorter lengths of service had a higher risk of fall on the same level and fall to a lower level (Chau *et al.* 2014). Besides, Cellier, Eyrolle and Bertrand (1995) analysed the effects of age and tenure among French fruit and vegetable packing employees, who worked over nine million work hours. Novice employees had the highest injury and seriousness rates in all age groups.

In a study of 58,271 Italian employees, injury rates decreased with an increase in job tenure. Young employees had both the highest injury rate and the highest decrease with job tenure (Bena *et al.* 2013). In Mexico, there were 1,140 fatal occupational injuries in 2012. Employees who had worked on the same task for one to ten years had a 37 % higher risk of fatality than novice employees (Gonzalez-Delgado *et al.* 2015).

Kumar, Rathnakar and Kumar (2010) examined 416 employees of tile factories in Mangalore City, Karnataka, India. They found that employees who had worked in the company for less than five years were significantly more often involved in injuries (33 %) than employees with longer tenure (16 %). Among British bus drivers, experience was found to have the strongest effect on injuries in the first year of driving. Experience was more important than age in injury involvement (Dorn and af Wåhlberg 2008). An analysis of workers' compensation records and a labour force survey in Ontario, Canada, showed that lost-time injury rates were significantly higher for employees with shorter job tenure (Morassaei *et al.* 2013). Among Canadian adults, the work disability absence rate within the first two months on the job was over eight times higher than that of those who had spent more than twenty-five months on the job (Breslin *et al.* 2008). Burt (2015) concluded that new employees had an increased risk of injury during the first year of employment. He also gave several recommendations on how to improve their safety at work.

The first day in the workplace is the most critical for occupational safety. For example, the injury risk for a wood industry worker was over fifty times higher on their first day on the job (Larsson 1988a). An analysis of occupational injuries at small construction companies in Taiwan showed that 12 % of injuries occurred during the first day on the work site (Cheng *et al.* 2010). Accordingly, the employer or supervisor should focus more attention on the behaviour of new employees during their first day of work.

Age and tenure are, of course, interrelated. Novice employees are often young, but an older employee can also be a novice in a job. Blanch *et al.* (2009) studied 156 male employees of a plastic film factory in Barcelona. They found a significant association between age by tenure interaction and occupational injuries. In many studies, it was impossible to distinguish the effects of age from those of tenure.

To a degree, it is an open question, on the basis of the above studies, whether experience reduces the frequency of injuries. Most studies show that injuries decrease with experience while some studies reveal no such effect (Salminen 1997).

CHAPTER THREE

HEALTH AS A RESOURCE

Health is recognised as more than the absence of disease. My approach is to see health as a resource to support the capacity to function in the workplace. In the world of work, healthy employees are needed, but there is, of course, also space for people with disabilities. Unfortunately, occupational injuries impair employees' work capacity and, vice versa, health problems and disabilities expose employees to injuries.

According to the US National Health Interview Survey 1997–2011, employees with disabilities were more often involved in overexertion and falls than those without disabilities (Shi *et al.* 2015). It was also shown on the basis of the same survey that employees with disability had an elevated risk (OR = 2.39) of occupational injury compared to employees without disability (Price *et al.* 2012). The Health and Retirement Survey (n = 5,600) indicated that poor sight, poor hearing and other disabilities increased the risk of occupational injury among American employees over fifty (Zwerling *et al.* 1998). The Health and Retirement Study also indicated that both impaired hearing and impaired vision were associated with an increased risk of occupational injury among older American employees (Zwerling *et al.* 1996a).

Effects of Noise and Hearing Impairments

An early review based on five studies suggested that high noise levels may be associated with higher injury rates (Wilkins and Acton 1982). When Dias, Cordeiro and Goncalves (2006) compared 600 Brazilian employees involved in occupational injuries to a control group of 822 employees in the same age group (aged fifteen to sixty) but not involved in injuries, they found that employees exposed to noise at work had been injured two times as often as the control group.

Among 5,876 sawmill employees from British Columbia, Canada, an inverse-U-shaped trend was observed between noise exposure and occupational injuries. Cumulative noise over a very short period of time decreased the risk of injury, whereas noise exposure over a longer period (over ninety-one days) increased the risk of injury (Kling *et al.* 2012). Among 52,982 male employees in Quebec, a hearing loss of 20 dB significantly increased the risk of occupational injury. Noise exposure in the workplace was associated with 12 % of injuries (Picard *et al.* 2008). In their study, Moll van Charante, Snijders and Mulder (1991) compared injured Dutch shipyard employees with injury-free employees. They found no significant difference in posture control either in silence or during exposure to heavy noise.

Based on a review of fifteen studies, Palmer *et al.* (2008) found that hearing problems moderately increased the risk of injury. A computer-aided telephone interview with 150 farmers from Iowa showed that hearing loss in the better ear, hearing asymmetry, and poor self-reported hearing were among the risk factors for agricultural injuries (Choi *et al.* 2006).

Toppila, Pyykkö and Pääkkönen (2009) reported that impaired hearing may increase the risk of occupational injury because of reduced speech intelligibility and reduced capability to perceive the direction of incoming sound. In both Finland and the United Kingdom, poor hearing has been a contributory factor in fatalities. My study of ninety-nine serious occupational injuries included a fatality as a result of an accident where a deaf man was run over by a forklift truck in the yard of a factory as he was unable to hear the forklift truck behind him and the driver failed to see him because of a high load (Salminen 1997).

The conclusion to be drawn from these studies is that exposure to noise and hearing impairments consistently increase the risk of occupational injury. However, it is difficult to say what the thresholds are for hearing loss to affect occupational safety.

Vision Impairments and Eye Injuries

A review of ten studies showed little evidence of impairment of vision increasing the risk of occupational injury (Palmer, Harris and Coggon 2008). An earlier review of thirty-one studies revealed a positive association between falling and visual impairment in people over seventy-five and an association between visual acuity and hip fracture. In 2000, no studies showed a connection between visual impairment and occupational injury (Legood, Scuffham and Cryer 2002). In Quebec, however, Laberge-Nadeau *et al.* (1996) found that crashes of truck drivers were related to problems with binocular vision, whereas collisions of bus drivers were associated with hypertension. Later, they (Maag *et al.* 1997) showed that taxi drivers with binocular vision problems had more crashes than other drivers.

Based on the National Health Study carried out in Australia, 2004–2005, Lam (2008) concluded that the risk of occupational injury increased by 60 % among those who had any uncorrected or untreated vision problems and that the risk was 3.5 times higher for those with untreated macular degeneration compared with the healthy population. Davies *et al.* (2001) analysed 1,326 injuries and 1,504 employees, based on the Merseyside Accident Information Model, from Liverpool, United Kingdom. They found that wearing bifocal/varifocal spectacles increased the risk of missed step and, especially, problems with manual handling of loads at workplaces.

Lombardi and his co-workers (2005) compared 1,353 welders to 822 non-welders, based on data from a US workers' insurance compensation provider. One out of four injuries to welders were eye injuries. Almost all victims were male and 70 % of them worked in manufacturing. McCall, Horwitz and Taylor (2009) analysed workers' compensation data from Kentucky from 1994 to 2003 and found 10,545 claims of ocular injury. Men were injured three times more often than women and helpers and construction workers had a higher frequency of eye injury. Based on the 2002 National Health Interview Study (n = 28,913), the overall lifetime prevalence rate of work-related eye injuries was calculated to be 4.4 %. Men had eye injuries four times more often than women (Forrest and Call 2009). Bauza *et al.* (2013) identified 183 work-related open-globe injuries from the University Hospital in Newark, New Jersey. Males accounted for 97 % of the cases, their average age being thirty-five years.

An analysis of 420 patients at the Eye Clinic of Dicle University Hospital in Turkey showed that 13.1 % of eye injuries were due to occupational injury (Cakmak *et al.* 2004). An examination of 182 patients in the First Eye Hospital, Lublin, Poland, showed that 16 % of penetrating eye injuries were work-related agricultural injuries. Most injuries were due to repair and maintenance work (Mackiewicz *et al.* 2005).

Shaikh and Shaikh (2005) interviewed 208 welders in Islamabad and Rawalbindi, Pakistan. The most common injury was a foreign body in the eye. Woo and Sundar (2006) examined 133 patients with eye injuries who had sought medical treatment at the National University Hospital in Singapore. A typical victim of eye injury was a young, non-Singaporean male working with power tools in the construction industry. Furthermore, industrial eye-related injuries were studied in a retrospective analysis of 300 occupational injury victims with ocular trauma seen by Tan Tock Seng Hospital in Singapore (Ngo and Leo 2008). The patients were mainly young, non-resident men.

Ho and co-workers (2007) analysed 486 eye injuries in an academic medical centre in the city of Kaohsiung, Taiwan. Almost 40 % of these injuries were work-related, and men were injured four times more often than women. Later, they (Ho *et al.* 2008) found that occupational eye injuries were predicted by temporary employment and fewer than ten years of education. The highest frequency was shown for foreign body injuries.

Zghal-Mokni and his co-worker (2007) examined seventy-eight patients at an eye clinic in Tunis in 2000. About 9 % of these cases were due to occupational injury. The most common lesion was corneal superficial foreign body. Lamellar injuries (foreign bodies, chemicals) accounted for 92 % of the 105 eye injuries at an accident and emergency department in Scotland analysed by Thompson and Mollan (2009). About 31 % of these injuries were occupational eye injuries and those injured were male in 91 % of these cases. An analysis of 768 eye injuries at the Farabi Eye Hospital in Tehran, Iran, showed that 74 % of injuries were work-related. Most of the patients with work-related eye injuries were young men (Mansouri *et al.* 2010). Cai and Zhang (2015) examined 1,197 eye injuries at the Ninth People's Hospital of Chongqing, China, of which 43 % were work-related injuries. The most common diagnosis was foreign body on external eye.

To sum up, the effect of vision impairment on occupational injury was not consistently confirmed in the reviews dealt with above. Several studies based on data from eye hospitals in different countries showed that 9 % to 74 % of eye injuries (average 31 %) were work-related. Men injured their eyes many times more often than women, which is due to their differential work tasks—in the construction industry, for instance. Penetrating eye injuries can lead to the loss of sight, especially in developing countries. A foreign body in the eye was the most common diagnosis in work-related eye injuries. Victims of eye injuries wore safety glasses significantly less often than their colleagues without injuries (Okoye and Umeh 2002; Yu, Liu and Hui 2004; Blackburn *et al.* 2012).

Mental Health Problems

A review (Palmer, Harris and Coggan 2008) based on eleven studies showed mixed results on the relationship between mental health and occupational injury. However, the researchers concluded that employees with emotional problems might have a higher risk of injury at work. Cherry, Burstyn and Beach (2012) analysed 389,903 compensation claims from Alberta, Canada, over the 1995–2004 period. They found that employees with a recent history of mental health illness at the time of their first occupational injury were at a greater risk of a second injury. Furthermore, a questionnaire study of 7,979 adults from Cardiff and Merthyr Tydfil showed that psychotropic medication increased the risk of injury, especially among those with continuing mental health problems (Wadsworth *et al.* 2005). Among 120 patients with hand injuries in Taiwan, self-perceived mental health helped to decrease the number of days off work, whereas self-perceived physical functioning was negatively correlated to days off (Chen *et al.* 2012). Among 67,182 male Korean employees and 12,146 female Korean employees, neuropsychiatric impairment made returning to work and receiving a new job more difficult (Rhie, Jeong and Won 2013).

A questionnaire study among 2,882 French employees indicated that depressive symptoms were related to occupational injury (Chau *et al.* 2011). A secondary analysis of workers' compensation claims in British Columbia—102,997 men and 53,882 women—showed that depression was higher among women than men and peaked in the middle age groups (Smith *et al.* 2014).

In a Canadian social enterprise, Lysaght *et al.* (2011) compared 255 employees with intellectual disability to 320 employees without such disability. Employees with intellectual disability had almost three times less occupational injuries than the comparison group. When a health risk appraisal survey of 8,563 employees in a large American manufacturing company was carried out, attention deficit hyperactivity disorder (ADHD) was diagnosed in 1.9 % of the employees. ADHD was associated with a 4 % to 5 % reduction in work performance and with double the risk of occupational injury (Kessler *et al.* 2009).

My conclusion is that there seems to be weak confirmation of the relationship between mental illness and occupational injury. One study confirms the association between depression and occupational injury. Further studies are needed on all these issues.

Musculoskeletal Symptoms

Palmer, Harris and Coggon (2008) reviewed six studies on musculoskeletal problems related to occupational injury. Most of these studies showed that self-reported arthritis increased the risk of occupational injury. Based on the National Health Interview Survey, from 1985 to 1994, Zwerling *et al.* (1997) found a 34 % higher risk of occupational injury among employees with arthritis compared to healthy employees. The Lorhandicap Group examined 2,888 employees in the Lorraine area in northeastern France. Musculoskeletal disorders almost doubled the risk of occupational injury (Chau *et al.* 2008). Bunn and his co-workers (2006) made a staged communication and educational intervention to prevent musculoskeletal injuries at the International Truck and Engine Corporation factory in Springfield, Ohio (n = 3,417). This intervention reduced work-related injuries by 75 % and the days lost per employee by up to 50 %. The programme also improved the company's communication and relationship with local physicians.

Merely tentative conclusions can be reached on the basis of these studies. Musculoskeletal problems may increase the risk of occupational injury. Maybe falls could be mentioned as a typical injury for employees with such problems.

Epilepsy

Based on four studies, Palmer, Harris and Coggan (2008) concluded that epilepsy raised the risk of occupational injury by 1.5 to 2.5 times. Zwerling *et al.* (1997) found a 1.56 times higher risk of occupational injury among employees with epilepsy compared to healthy employees. In Brazil, an epidemiologic association was found between epilepsy and occupational injury based on 858 records in the Epidemiologic and Technical Security System Nexus (Lunardi *et al.* 2011). More research is needed to provide a more solid basis for assessing the relationship between epilepsy and occupational injury.

Diabetes and Obesity

A review of three studies showed that diabetes may be associated with occupational injuries (Palmer, Harris and Coggon 2008). Based on the National Health Interview Survey, of 195,284 employees, Sprince *et al.* (2008) found no significant association between diabetes and occupational injury. However, an increased risk of occupational injury was found among those with untreated diabetes or with long-term sickness. Dionne *et al.* (1995) followed 1,198 truck drivers in Quebec for more than four years. Drivers with diabetes were more often involved in injuries than healthy drivers. Among 71,001 Taiwanese employees, amputations of the lower extremities increased the risk of diabetes by over seven-fold (Lin *et al.* 2010).

A review of eight studies showed that obese employees had more frequent sick leaves than their colleagues (Schmier, Jones and Halpern 2006). Based on the review of twelve studies, Pollack and Cheskin (2007) concluded that obese employees had an elevated risk of occupational injury. Froom *et al.* (1996) followed 3,801 men working in twenty-one industrial plants in Israel over two years. Both the body mass index (BMI) and ergonomic stress independently predicted involvement in multiple injuries, whereas employees in the highest BMI index group with a high ergonomic stress had a 4.6 times higher risk of injury compared to the lowest BMI group. Pollack and her co-workers (2007) examined 7,690 employees at a US aluminium company and showed that the risk of occupational injury was doubled in the highest obesity group. In particular, this group had injuries to the leg or knee. The Lorhandicap Group showed that obesity (high BMI) was associated with occupational injury among employees over forty (Bhattacherjee *et al.* 2003; Chau *et al.* 2008).

Poston *et al.* (2011) examined 478 male firefighters from the Missouri Valley Region. Firefighters with class II or class III obesity had five times more days off work due to injury than their colleagues with class I obesity. A prospective cohort study of 69,515 Finnish public sector employees showed that obesity was associated with occupational injury. Bone fractures, dislocations, and injuries to lower extremities were especially related to obesity (Kouvonen *et al.* 2013). Based on the fourth Korea National Health and Nutrition Examination Survey of 8,261 employees, Kim and his co-workers (2013) concluded that an abnormal waist circumference was related to occupational injury. Males, managers, professionals and administrators had an elevated risk of injury. Lin, Verma and Courtney (2013) analysed the National Survey of Youth (1979) of 8,941 subjects. Obesity was associated with a 25 % higher risk of occupational injury, and obese employees had a 29 % higher risk of sustaining injuries. Koepp, Snedden and Levine (2015) reviewed 8,581 medical reports of employees in the Idaho National Laboratory in Idaho Falls. They found that obese employees more often had slip, trip and fall injuries than their colleagues with normal weight. Contusions were more common in women, whereas men suffered strains more often. An examination of 442 manual material handlers from three large American companies showed that body mass index, percentage body fat, aerobic power, smoking, and sit-and-reach flexibility were associated with occupational injury (Craig *et al.* 2006).

The above studies seem to suggest that diabetes increases the injury risk to some extent, especially when untreated. Besides, the studies unanimously indicate that obesity increases the risk of occupational injury, especially injuries to the lower extremities.

Medication

Based on a review of twenty-two studies, Palmer, Harris and Coggon (2008) concluded that the connections between medication and occupational injuries were mostly attributable to drugs with sedative potential. Also, regular use of psychotropic drugs increased the risk of occupational injury among French employees (Bhattacherjee *et al.* 2003; Khlat *et al.* 2008).

Frequent use of fatigue drugs doubled the risk of injuries among employees from northeastern France (Chau *et al.* 2008). Among the inhabitants of Cardiff and Merthyr Tydfil, Wales, the use of tricyclic antidepressants was related to injuries at work (Wadsworth *et al.* 2005). Karsh *et al.* (2000) compared 1,223 American employees who were using drowsing medication and had been involved in an acute occupational injury (e.g., falls) to 1,202 controls also using drowsing drugs but without involvement in acute injuries (e.g., strain injuries). The risk of acute occupational injury was over two times higher among drowsing medication users and especially for younger employees.

Among 166 patients treated at the Alice Ho Miu Ling Nethersole Hospital in Hong Kong, occupational injury had caused chronic pain in one out of three patients. They were also more often involved in litigation than other patients (Lee *et al.* 2005). Further, it was found among 1,850 patients of an American rehabilitation centre that dependence on opiate pain medication increased the risk of failure in returning to work after occupational injury (Brede, Mayer and Gatchel 2012). Self-evidently, the use of drugs weakens concentration at work and increases the risk of occupational injury.

Brain and Head Injuries

Brain injuries are often a consequence of occupational injury. Traumatic brain injury was identified in 45 % of 488 work-related fatalities in Ontario from 1996 to 2000. Employees with brain injury were more likely to suffer falls than their healthy colleagues (Tricco *et al.* 2006). In 2004, based on data from the Ontario Workplace Safety and Insurance Board, 1,006 traumatic brain injuries were identified. "Struck by object" was the most common mechanism and the highest injury rate was found in the transport and storage industries (Colantino *et al.* 2010). Liu *et al.* (2011) found 435 employees with mild-moderate traumatic brain injury in Ontario from 1998 to 2001. One out of five injuries occurred in the construction industry, and a fall from elevation was a risk factor for brain injury. The National Electronic Injury Surveillance System identified 586,600 work-related traumatic brain injuries in the US between 1998 and 2007. There were 4.3 injuries per 10,000 employees, and the highest rates were found among the youngest and oldest employees (Konda *et al.* 2015). Among 581 patients of traumatic brain injury in an Abu Dhabi hospital, 10 % of injuries were work-related injuries. All of them occurred to male migrants and two thirds were falls (Salem *et al.* 2013).

Eggensperger *et al.* (2006) found forty-two patients with occupational maxillofacial fractures from the University Hospital in Berne, Switzerland. Farm and forestry employees carried a 127-fold and construction employees a 44-fold higher risk of maxillofacial fractures than service and office employees. An examination of 103 patients with maxillofacial fractures due to work injury at the Department of Oral and Maxillofacial Surgery in Nara Medical University, Japan, showed that 96 % of patients were male. Most of the injuries occurred in the construction industry, and the most typical injury was struck by a thrown object (Yamamoto *et al.* 2011). Among 2,110 patients with maxillofacial fractures in the Division of Maxillofacial Surgery, San Giovanni Battista Hospital, Turin, Italy, 6.3 % of the injuries were work-related. Construction employees were most often the victims, and the injuries were often due to falling objects (Roccia *et al.* 2013). Kica and Rosenman (2014) identified 318 work-related skull fractures in Michigan between 2010 and 2012. One out of three facial fractures happened to women, and health care and social assistance was the most common industry for these to occur.

After Occupational Injury

One important research topic is returning to work after brain injury. Radford and her co-workers (2013) examined ninety-four victims of traumatic brain injury in a teaching hospital in Nottingham, UK. One year later, 15 % more victims of traumatic brain injury working with a specialist in vocational rehabilitation returned to work compared to victims who received the usual care.

Franceschini *et al.* (2011) conducted a telephone interview with 403 Italian patients of traumatic spinal cord injury. About 42 % of the patients had returned to work after injury, although two out of three subjects reported a worsening in their employment level. Kurtaran *et al.* (2009) investigated 192 Turkish patients with spinal cord injury. Only 14.6 % of them returned to work. Those who returned to work had a higher education, a workplace before injury and used a bladder-emptying method.

An analysis of 59,526 claims of Australian WorkSafe in Victoria showed that 79 % of injury victims returned to work during the two-year follow-up period. Return to work was slower among older victims (Berecki-Gisolf *et al.* 2012). Hepp, Moergeli *et al.* (2011) examined eighty-five victims of serious occupational injury in the Division of Trauma Surgery at Zurich University Hospital, Switzerland. The injury severity and coping abilities of patients predicted the number of sick leave days. Subjective feeling of sickness was associated with occupational injuries among 1,693 patients at two Danish emergency departments (Østerlund *et al.* 2017).

Factors related to failure to retain work were examined in a study of 1,850 patients of chronic disabling occupational musculoskeletal disorders in Texas. These factors were older age, female sex, non-working status at discharge, extreme disability at admission, and antisocial personality disorder (Brede, Mayer and Gatchel 2012).

Based on the Medical Expenditure Panel Survey, Shi *et al.* (2015) showed that American employees with a persistent disability had a higher occupational injury frequency and higher medical costs. In New Zealand, 2,626 employees with injury were recruited to the Prospective Outcomes of Injury Study. Three months after injury, 27 % of them reported that they were not working. Low income, physical work tasks, temporary employment, and obesity were predictors of not working (Lilley *et al.* 2012).

In Florida, a "welcome back" path to reemployment after an occupational back injury provided workers with a sense of being valued by their preinjury employer. With all different paths, females were less likely to be currently working, whereas white males were more likely to be employed in skilled jobs (Strunin and Boden 2000).

A Cochrane review of pre-employment medical examination was based on seven studies with 5,872 participants and two studies with 2,164 participants. The results showed that a general medical examination failed to reduce sick leaves, while a task-focused examination dropped sick leaves and injuries by 37 % (Mahmud *et al.* 2010). Lalic (2009) assessed the effects of occupational medicine for 5,800 employees in Littoral-Mountainous County, Croatia. The number of occupational injuries dropped from thirty-two in 2008 to twelve in 2009. The author concluded that occupational medicine was more efficient in assessing sick leaves than family practice with a general practitioner.

In Finland, injury victims are entitled to early part-time sick leave with modified work tasks and reduced work hours to help them to remain in work and return to full-time work. Viikari-Juntura and her co-workers (2012) found, in a study with sixty-three patients, that early part-time sick leave may shorten the total sickness absence during the following twelve months by about 20 %. In the US, transitional work is an individualised and progressive programme that returns an injured employee to his/her own job with minimal interruption to employment. In Ohio, the programme reduced loss of workdays by 11 % besides having many indirect positive effects like increased productivity (Dunning *et al.* 2008).

As can be judged from the studies discussed in this chapter, sickness can increase the risk of occupational injury even if it would not lead to any absence from work. For example, impairments of vision or hearing are no reasons to be without employment. Therefore, additional attention should be paid to the safety of people with such impairments in workplaces. On the other hand, proper treatment of sickness can be one way of preventing occupational injury. For example, keeping diabetes under control decreases the risk of injury. In such ways, employees with a health problem can continue in employment.

CHAPTER FOUR

SUBSTANCE USE AND SMOKING

This chapter deals with the effects of the use of alcohol and drugs and smoking on accidents and fatal and non-fatal injuries in the workplace. The topic has been studied quite extensively in many countries. Findings from these studies will be discussed below.

Alcohol Consumption

Alcohol consumption can have negative impacts for both employees and employers by increasing occupational injuries. A review of emergency room studies showed that, in ten out of seventeen studies, injured employees had both had positive alcohol tests and been intoxicated over the legal limit more often than non-injured employees (Cherpitel 1993a). Another review showed that in six out of eleven studies injured employees had drunk alcohol just before the injury significantly more often than non-injured employees (Cherpitel 1993b). In still another review of nine studies, eight of these studies indicated a positive association between alcohol use and occupational injury (Stallones and Kraus 1993). Furthermore, Webb and Fresta (1994) reviewed six Australian studies on the relationship between alcohol drinking and occupational injury. Two of them showed a significant positive association, whereas no significant relationship was found in the remaining four studies. Based on several studies, Emery (1986) concluded that at least 20 % of industrial injuries were alcohol-related and that this may be an underestimate. However, Smith and Kraus (1988) reported based on eight studies that alcohol contributed to only 3 % to 4 % of occupational deaths. Also, Webb and her co-workers (1994) found twenty-nine studies on the relationship between alcohol and work injuries. Problem drinkers were 2.7 times more likely to have injury-related absences than non-problem drinkers. Earlier, a critical view had been presented by Feinauer (1990) concluding, on the basis of a review of thirty-one authors' work, that our knowledge on this relationship was quite limited. He stated that the empirical research before his article had been "based more on guesswork and conjecture than on scientific analysis." I hope that the later studies have overcome these problems.

In Finland, the effects of alcohol consumption on occupational injuries were studied, particularly in the 1970's. Lahelma (1974) examined 959 fatalities in workplaces in Finland between 1965 and 1969. He found that 5.6 % of the cases were related to alcohol. Later, Honkanen and Ottelin (1976) tested blood alcohol from 182 injury victims at an emergency department in central Finland. Alcohol was involved in 9 % of industrial injuries. Honkanen and Visuri (1976) tested 1,012 injury victims at the emergency department of the University Central Hospital in Helsinki. Alcohol in the blood was found in 19 % of industrial injury victims, and alcohol was involved even more often (28 %) in falls in workplaces and during commuting.

After the 1970s, the relationship between alcohol and occupational injuries was no longer studied in Finland. One reason for this was that alcohol consumption in workplaces was then believed to be under control as a constant consumption of alcohol by an employee at work was defined to constitute a reason for terminating the employee's contract. The attitudes towards the use of alcohol in the workplace have also become more negative over the last few decades in Finland. However, the Central Organisation of Finnish Trade Unions (SAK) stated on its website on 6 November 2019 that two out of three employees' representatives reported having noticed alcohol-related problems in their workplace.

A Norwegian study showed that 5.1 % of seventy-eight occupational injuries examined were alcohol related (Kristensen and Christiansen 1980). Lings *et al.* (1984) examined 5,439 patients who had suffered occupational injuries at two emergency departments in Århus, Denmark. In only 2.0 % of the victims, the blood alcohol concentration was above the legal limit.

Hingson, Lederman and Chapman Walsh (1985) interviewed 1,740 employed adults in four New England states. They found no significant association between alcohol drinking and occupational injuries but drinking over five drinks daily almost doubled the risk of injury. Copeland (1985) examined 147 occupational fatalities in Miami, Florida, and found that 7.3 % of the victims had been under the influence of alcohol. Lewis and Cooper (1989) analysed 207 death certificates and 196 autopsy reports of victims of work-related fatalities near Houston, Texas. Alcohol was involved in 13.3 % of fatalities, and a positive drug screen result was found in 17.4 % of tests. Of the 2,805 employed adults who participated in a telephone survey in the US, about 15 % had suffered impairment in the workplace due to alcohol (Frone 2006). Based on the National Electronic Injury Surveillance System (NEISS), Trent (1991) found that only 0.01 % of all work injury victims were alcohol intoxicated in US emergency rooms. Alcohol was ten times more often a factor in non-work injuries than in work injuries.

Holcom, Lehman and Simpson (1993) divided 1,054 municipal employees in Texas into a high (technical, protection, etc.) and a low (official, professional, etc.) job-risk group. Employees in high-risk jobs with injuries were more than three times more likely to use alcohol or drugs than injury-free employees. In the low job-risk group, there was no relationship between alcohol or drug use and injuries. Dawson (1994) analysed the 1988 National Health Interview Survey involving 29,192 American adults. Drinking five or more drinks of alcohol every day almost doubled the risk of occupational injury. Based on the National Health and Nutrition Examination Survey, with 8,477 subjects, Leigh (1996) found no significant relationship between total alcohol use and job hazards. However, heavy beer drinking was strongly correlated with fatality rate in the US. Further, Zwerling and his co-workers (1996b) analysed the Health and Retirement Study of 7,089 Americans aged fifty-one to sixty-one. Alcoholism increased the risk of occupational injury by 68 %, whereas five or more drinks daily elevated the risk of injury over four times. Chen, Baker and Li (2005) compared 5,549 victims of fatal injury to 42,698 civilians in the US. They found that current drinkers had a 38 % higher risk of death from falls than non-drinkers. Plurad and his co-workers (2011) analysed the National Trauma Data Bank of 31,028 Americans. Alcohol ingestion was not significantly related to work-related injuries, but it was related to complications in recovery after work injury. Li and his co-workers (2005) analysed 313 pilots of general aviation who had crashed fatally. Alcohol was found in the blood of 11 % of the pilots, and a majority of the crashes had occurred at night.

Alleyne, Stuart and Copes (1991) analysed 459 death certificates from between 1979 and 1986 in Alberta, Canada. Alcohol was involved in 10.7 % of the deaths. Based on the General Social Survey of 10,385 Canadians, Wells and Macdonald (1999) showed a relationship between alcohol consumption and work injuries.

In the Spanish National Health Survey, 11,016 men aged sixteen to sixty-four were interviewed. Approximately 17 % of their occupational injuries could be attributed to alcohol consumption. The proportion was higher among young and middle-aged men than in older men (Gutièrrez-Fisac, Regidor and Ronda 1992).

In Britain, one of the earliest studies on this subject was done in the Birmingham Accident Hospital Burns Unit, where White (1977) compared twenty-eight male patients who had contributed to their burn injury to twenty-eight other male patients who had not contributed to their injury.

Consumption of alcohol per week was almost double in the contributory group. This applied to younger age groups (fifteen to thirty-four) but not to older age groups.

Kurzthaler and her co-workers (2004) examined 1,611 patients in the Innsbruck University Hospital, Austria, of whom 18.9 % had work-related injuries. Alcohol played a role in men's injuries more often (13.3 %) than in women's injuries (1.8 %). However, alcohol was less involved in work injuries than in other injuries. In the Forensic Medicine Department at the University of Medicine in Katowice, Poland, 301 autopsies of occupational injury victims were done between 1992 and 2001. Alcohol was involved in 7 % of fatalities (Rygol, Kabiesz-Neniczka and Olszowy 2004).

Hollo, Leigh and Nurminen (1993) analysed 1,737 work-related fatalities in Australia between 1982 and 1984. Alcohol was involved in 16 % of fatalities. Single, separated or divorced employees had more often used alcohol before their injury. Watt *et al.* (2004) examined 488 patients at an accident and emergency department in Queensland, Australia, and compared them to 488 population controls. Any alcohol drinking in the six hours prior to injury doubled the risk of injury. McNeilly *et al.* (2010) found 355 work-related deaths in Victoria, Australia, between 2001 and 2006. Alcohol was present in 7 % of these deaths.

Bamberger (2005) made a survey of 762 male employees in manufacturing and service occupations in Israel. Problem drinking was related to the number of critical incidents at work. The Lorhandicap Group (Bourgkard *et al.* 2008) analysed mortality before the age of seventy among 4,268 French employees. Alcohol abuse doubled the risk of death before the seventieth birthday. Wang and his co-workers (2010) made a survey of 2,050 farmers in Heilongjiang Province, China. Current drinkers had a 77 % higher risk of occupational injury. Using a random sample of 569 Israeli employees, Biron, Bamberger and Noyman (2011) found a positive correlation between substance use and job hazards. Kifle and his co-workers (2014) made a survey among iron and steel employees in Addis Ababa, Ethiopia. They found that employees drinking alcohol during three working days had a three times higher risk of work-related injury than sober employees.

A meta-analysis of fourteen studies from seven different countries (n = 17,708) showed that alcohol contributed to the risk of both injury and violence when alcohol consumption was measured at emergency rooms. When asked about alcohol drinking six hours before the injury, 6 % of all victims reported having been drinking, whereas alcohol was found in the blood in only 2 % of injury victims. The risk of violence was considerably higher: 28 % of victims had alcohol in the blood and 43 % had drank six hours before the incident. Alcohol played a significantly higher role in men's injuries than in women's injuries (Cherpitel, Ye and Bond 2005). Zaloshnja *et al.* (2007) estimated that alcohol-involving injuries annually cost employers over 28.6 billion dollars, of which 3.1 billion dollars are due to job-related injuries.

The studies discussed above show almost unanimously that drinking alcohol increases the risk of occupational injury. Alcohol has been found to be a contributory factor in between 0.01 % and 17 % of injuries. It has also been found that the impact of alcohol increases with the amounts consumed. It is, thus, important that employers and employees have a negative attitude towards drinking and being intoxicated in the workplace.

Drug Abuse

The relationship between drug abuse and occupational injury has been studied widely. Kaestner and Grossman (1998) analysed data from the National Longitudinal Survey of Youth of fourteen-to-twenty-year-old subjects. They found that drug use was positively related to occupational injuries among young males, whereas no systematic relationship was found among young females. Pollack *et al.* (1998), in turn, analysed substance abuse among 7,895 construction employees in Washington State, US. The analysis showed that employees with a substance abuse diagnosis had a 39 % higher risk of job injury, while substance abusers aged between twenty-five and thirty-four had occupational injuries almost two times more often than non-users. Furthermore, Miller, Lestina and Smith (2001) analysed 1.5 million healthcare claims from employees of seventy large American corporations. Alcohol and drug abusers had a four times higher risk of hospitalisation for injury than sober employees. Spicer, Miller and Smith (2003) made a case-control study with 26,413 hourly employees in an American transport company. The study indicated that problem substance users were 61 % more often involved in occupational injuries than non-users. Also, Frone (2004) found that both overall and on-the-job substance use was associated with a higher rate of work injuries. A questionnaire sent by Shipp and her co-workers (2005) to 3,265 high school students with jobs in South Texas showed that using alcohol, marijuana, cocaine, inhalants and steroids increased the risk of occupational injury, and the risk consistently increased with increased use.

A positive drug testing result was found in 9.0 % of decedents of fatal occupational injuries in Miami (Copeland 1985). In Innsbruck, Austria, benzodiazepine use was not related to work injuries (Kurzthaler *et al.* 2004). On the contrary, cocaine or crack use was related to work injuries among 882 Ontario adults and especially among young employees (Macdonald

1995; Macdonald, Wells and Lothian 1998). Cannabis and illicit drugs were both involved in 8.5 % of occupational fatalities in Alberta (Alleyne, Stuart and Copes 1991). Further, cannabis or amphetamines were involved in 6 % of work-related deaths in Victoria, Australia (McNeilly *et al.* 2010). Cheng *et al.* (2013) examined 432 drug-poisoning deaths in Utah in 2008–2009, of which 145 had been in work-related injury. Decedents of work-related injury had used pain medication more often than decedents that had never suffered work-related injury.

The above studies show almost consistently that drug users have a higher risk of occupational injury. Only one study (Kurzthaler *et al.* 2004) out of the twelve studies showed a non-significant relationship between drugs and injuries. All in all, drugs caused 6 % to 9 % of work-related fatalities.

Some countries (Uruguay, Canada, Colorado) have approved the recreational use of cocaine. This type of drug use may also spread to workplaces. Drug use is more difficult to notice than alcohol use. Drug testing can be used in recruiting new employees, but it is very expensive to test all employees on daily basis. However, some airline companies, for instance, have a zero tolerance for drugs.

Drug Testing

Drug testing is one way to attempt to prevent drug use at work. It has been especially used in the health checks of new employees. In 1996, about three out of four American companies reported using pre-employment drug testing (Bryan 1998). According to the Finnish representatives of employees, drug testing was applied to all employees in 11 % of workplaces and to some of the employees in 18 % of workplaces (SAK 2019).

The Southern Pacific Railroad started drug tests from urine in 1984. The human-factor train injury ratio dropped from 22.2 in 1983 to 3.2 in 1987 (Taggart 1989–1990). Zwerling, Ryan and Orav (1990) carried out a urine drug screen of 2,537 new employees in the Boston postal office. Both marijuana-positive and cocaine-positive employees had a higher risk of injuries than drug-free employees. Gerber and Yacoubian (2002) examined forty-nine American construction companies that carried out drug testing. The injury rate in these companies was reduced by 51 % in two years. A large American company with 1,791 employees carried out a urine drug test on average 1.68 times per year. Doubling the testing rate reduced the occurrence of injuries by over half (Ozminkowski *et al.* 2003). A drug-free workplace programme including a drug test was initiated in 261 companies in Washington State. The overall injury rate in all industrial groups declined by 27 % in four years (Wickizer *et al.* 2004). Elliot and Shelley (2006) divided 507 employees of a large American company into 334 drug-test positive and 173 self-referred employees. The drug-test positive employees had a significantly higher injury rate than the self-referred group. A Portuguese railroad company tested alcohol and drug use at random among 3,801 employees. Testing reduced the risk of occupational injury especially among white-collar employees (Marques *et al.* 2014). Waehrer *et al.* (2016) analysed workplace anti-drug programmes carried out in 1,405 US establishments in 1988. Drug testing reduced minor occupational injuries by 15 %, whereas no significant reduction was found in lost-time injuries.

Beside the studies discussed above, there are also studies showing a non-significant relationship between drug testing and injuries. For example, Normand, Salyards and Mahoney (1990) made a urine test for marijuana and cocaine. No relationship between drug testing and injuries was found, whereas the positive test group had an almost 60 % higher absence rate. Feinauer and Havlovic (1993) found no significant reduction in the injury rate after pre-employment drug testing at forty-eight Wisconsin companies, whereas post-accident drug testing reduced injuries in comparison to the pre-employment testing. Drug screening had no effect on injury occurrence either in testing new employees or in testing after the injury (Dell and Berkhout 1998).

These contradictory results (eight positive, three negative) are in line with a review made by Pidd and Roche (2014). Based on twenty-three studies reviewed, they concluded that evidence for the effectiveness of testing is "at best tenuous." There are no studies with a randomised control method or trial. The studies conducted have many methodological problems: an inappropriate study design, a limited number of subjects, and failure to control for potentially confounding variables. Better studies are required although conditions in workplaces may restrict the possibility to use a controlled study design. Zwerling (1993) has suggested historical controls instead of randomised studies.

Tobacco Smoking

Smoking is not as obvious as a risk factor for occupational safety as alcohol drinking. Five out six studies reviewed by Sacks and Nelson (1994) showed that smokers had a 1.4–2.5 times higher risk of occupational injury than non-smokers. Leistikow *et al.* (2000) found four cohort studies with eight populations from the US, the UK, Norway and Sweden. Current smokers had a 51 % higher risk of accidental death at work than those who had never smoked. The death risk of the heaviest smokers was two to four times higher than that of the non-smokers.

Naus *et al.* (1966) distributed a questionnaire to 1,500 machine employees in Czechoslovakia. Among smoking men, 31 % had been involved in an occupational injury compared with 25 % of non-smokers. Among women, the proportions were 19 % and 8 %, respectively. Calle Yuste and Lardon de Guevara (1973) examined 364 employees from a Spanish ceramics factory. Among men, smokers had been involved in an occupational injury more often than non-smokers. Among women, the number of injury cases was too small to compare. Ryan, Zwerling and Orav (1992) made a prospective, controlled study of 2,537 postal employees in Boston. Smokers had a 40 % higher risk of occupational injury than non-smokers. The mean absence rate of smokers was 5.43 % compared with 4.06 % for non-smokers. It was also found that American employees in dangerous jobs were disproportionately often also smokers (Leigh 1996). Tobacco smoking was not related to occupational injury among older American employees (Zwerling *et al.* 1996b). Macdonald, Wells and Lothian (1998) showed with a household survey of 882 Ontario adults that the risk of occupational injury among current smokers was two times higher than among non-smokers. Nakata and his co-workers (2006) made a survey of the 2,302 employees of 244 Japanese small- and medium-sized companies. Current and former smoking men had an almost two times higher risk of occupational injury than men who had never smoked. In women, the effect was non-significant. The Lorhandicap Group showed that current smokers had a 76 % higher risk of premature mortality than non-smokers among employees in northeastern France (Bourgkard *et al.* 2008). In Great Britain, among 1,115 male Royal Marine recruits, the injury risk of the smokers was almost twofold compared with the non-smokers (Munnoch and Bridger 2007). Based on the 2011 Korean Working Conditions Survey of 12,507 manual employees, it was found that passive smokers were more often involved in occupational injury than active smokers. The lowest prevalence was found among those who had never smoked and were not exposed to tobacco smoke (Kim *et al.* 2015).

The studies discussed above showed consistently that smokers have a higher risk of injury than non-smokers. In most of the studies, the risk was found to be double. However, these epidemiological studies failed to demonstrate any mechanism between smoking and occupational injuries.

One possibility is that there is the same personality type behind both tobacco smoking and injury. It has been shown that extroverts smoke more often than introverts. They are also involved in injuries more often than their introvert colleagues.

Another possibility is that smokers may become nervous just before a break during which they are allowed to smoke. Their attention to work tasks may be weakened when they are thinking about the break and a cigarette. This type of situation, of course, exposes them to injuries.

Theoretically, it is also possible that an injury happens during tobacco smoking. The employee's attention is then focussed on smoking. In Finland, for example, this is a very rare situation because smoking is strictly prohibited in the workplace.

On the whole, the research evidence presented in this chapter seems to indicate that alcohol, drugs and tobacco considerably increase the risk of occupational injury. Therefore, if employees are not able to stop their use of stimulants, they should be guided towards only using them outside of their work hours.

CHAPTER FIVE

THE SLEEPY EMPLOYEE RISK

In Finland, the average sleeping time decreased by 4 % from 1972 to 2005. The proportion of seven-hour sleepers has increased, while the proportion of eight-hour sleepers has decreased. Sleep complaints have increased, especially among middle-aged employees (Kronholm *et al.* 2008).

A meta-analysis of twenty-seven studies with 268,332 participants showed that sleep problems increase the risk of occupational injury by 62 %. Approximately, every eighth injury was attributed to sleep problems (Uehli *et al.* 2013a). Another meta-analysis, which was based on fifteen studies, showed that excessive daytime sleepiness, sleep apnoea and acute sleepiness were associated with modestly increased accident risks (Zhang and Chan 2014). Philip and Åkerstedt (2006) showed in their review that shortened sleep was a major cause of injuries in industry and transport. This connection is much better established in transport than in other industrial areas. A Spanish review showed that the obstructive sleep apnoea-hypopnoea syndrome was not related to workplace injuries (Egea Santaolalla and del Campo Matias 2015).

In Sweden, Lindberg *et al.* (2001) received 2,009 answers to their questionnaire on daytime sleepiness; the answerers reported 345 occupational injuries. Male snorers with excessive daytime sleepiness had a two times higher risk of occupational injury than their colleagues. Åkerstedt *et al.* (2002) analysed a data set of 47,860 subjects including 166 fatal injuries. Sleeping difficulties increased the risk of fatal injury by 89 %. Later, Carter *et al.* (2003) compared professional drivers and general drivers. Among professional drivers, snoring and sleep apnoea were not related to injuries, but sleep debt increased the risk of traffic accidents in leisure time, during commuting, and at work. Further, Hägg, Torén and Lindberg (2015) conducted a survey among 4,320 female employees in the Municipality of Uppsala. Persistent insomnia symptoms increased the risk of occupational injury. My co-workers and I (Salminen *et al.* 2010) examined 48,598 Finnish public-sector employees and found that disturbed sleep increased the risk of occupational injury among men. Among women, difficulty in initiating sleep was related to occupational injuries.

Chau and his co-workers (2004a) made a survey to 880 male construction employees in the region of Meurthe-et-Moselle, France. Sleep disorders were related to the moving of objects at the site. In a later study, they (Chau *et al.* 2004b) found that sleep disorders doubled the risk of occupational injury. Sleep disorders were a problem, especially among plumbers, electricians and civil engineering employees. When they (Chau *et al.* 2004c) examined French railway employees, they found that sleep problems increase the risk of injury.

Tzamalouka, Papadakaki and Chliaoutakis (2005) interviewed 317 professional truck drivers in Crete, Greece. Less hours of sleep increased the risk of crash involvement. Vennelle, Engleman and Douglas (2010) gathered survey answers from 677 bus drivers in Edinburgh, Scotland. Drivers with serious sleeping problems had accidents and near-accidents more often than other drivers. Uehli and her co-workers (2013b) examined 180 patients at the emergency department of a Basel hospital, Switzerland. Employees sleeping less than six hours per night had a five times higher risk of work injury than those sleeping eight hours. Later, they (2014) showed that older age, short sleep duration and long working hours enhanced the risk of work injuries. Torzsa and his co-workers (2011) found that loud snorers had a higher risk of traffic and work injuries than non-snorers. Catarino *et al.* (2014) interviewed 714 truck drivers in Portugal, which had one of the highest road traffic fatality rates in Europe. Drivers with a high score on the Epworth Sleepiness Scale had both near-injuries and injuries more frequently than other drivers. Papalia and co-workers (2012) made a survey of 253 Italian drivers of public transport. Drivers with an obstructive sleep apnoea syndrome were injured more often than other drivers. A total of 647 physicians from ten different countries gave a questionnaire to 5,293 subjects. It was found that insomnia increased the risk of car and home injuries but decreased the risk of work injuries (Léger *et al.* 2014).

In Argentina, Pérez-Chada and his co-workers (2005) asked 738 long-haul truck drivers from Buenos Aires about their sleep problems. Frequent snoring, daytime sleepiness, and reporting of sleepiness at the wheel were associated with injury risk. Excessive daytime sleepiness was related to the motor vehicle injuries of one group of 260 male truck drivers in Brazil (Souza, Paiva and Reimão 2005) and of another group of 300 male truck drivers in Brazil (de Pinho *et al.* 2006). Further, Rey de Castro, Gallo and Loureiro (2004) examined 238 bus drivers in Peru. Among them, tiredness and having the eyes drop shut while driving was strongly associated with injuries.

In Quebec, Canada, 953 French-speaking adults participated in a study concerning insomnia. Drivers with insomnia symptoms were involved in injuries two times more often than other drivers (Daley *et al.* 2009). Based on data from the Canadian Community Health Survey Cycle of 69,584 subjects, Kling, McLeod and Koehoorn (2010) found that trouble sleeping was associated with work injury. This association was highest with men in trades and transportation and women in processing and manufacturing jobs.

In the Rocky Mountain region of the US, DeArmond and Chen (2009) examined 143 certified nursing assistants in long-term care facilities. A high level of workplace sleepiness was associated with low levels of safety behaviour. In addition, workplace sleepiness increased the risk of occupational injuries. Choi and co-workers (2006) surveyed 1,345 adults in Iowa. Sleeping less than 7.5 hours increased the risk of injury by 61 %, but snoring and daytime sleepiness were no predictors of injuries. Heaton, Azuero and Reed (2010) examined 756 farmers from Kentucky and South Carolina. Stopping breathing while sleeping and problems staying awake in the last month increased the risk of farm injury. Based on data from the America Insomnia Survey, Kessler and his co-workers (2012) analysed the results of 4,991 employed Americans. Employees with insomnia had a two times higher risk of injuries than their colleagues. Based on the US National Health Interview Survey, Lombardi *et al.* (2012) examined the results of 101,891 employees. Usual daily sleep duration and body mass index were independent predictors of occupational injury. In particular, a daily sleep shorter than seven hours elevated the risk of injury. Johnson and his co-workers (2014) analysed the results of 778 American road, rail and airplane operators. Sleep disorders doubled the risk of accidents and near-misses. Stutts *et al.* (2003) interviewed 312 drivers from North Carolina who had been asleep in the car at the time of the crash and 519 drivers who had not been identified as having been asleep. Drivers with sleep-related crashes were more likely to work multiple jobs, night shifts and have other unusual work schedules. They had also slept for fewer hours the night before. Graves and Miller (2015) analysed the results from a survey of 4,144 working teens in the Washington State. Reduced school-night sleep was associated with increased work-related injuries.

In Israel, Lavie, Kremerman and Wiel (1982) investigated 1,502 industry employees. Employees with excessive daytime sleepiness had occupational injuries more often than other employees. Melamed and Oksenberg (2002) examined 532 non-shift daytime employees in Israel. Employees with excessive daytime sleepiness had a two times higher risk of occupational injury than their colleagues.

In Japan, Suzuki *et al.* (2005) studied 4,407 nurses from eight large general hospitals. Excessive daytime sleepiness was related to occupational injuries and especially to needlestick injuries. In addition, Nakata *et al.* (2005) distributed a self-administrated questionnaire to 2,903 employees in the Saitama area. Difficulty in initiating sleep, sleeping poorly at night, insufficient sleep and insomnia were associated with a significantly higher prevalence of injuries. Later, they (2006) showed that insomnia symptoms increased the risk of occupational injury.

Among 4,331 bus/truck drivers in Thailand, a strong relationship between crashes and drowsiness was found (Leechawengwongs *et al.* 2006). Fidan *et al.* (2007) examined 316 male long-distance truck drivers in Turkey. Snoring was related to the number of injuries. Amra *et al.* (2012) made a survey of 931 professional drivers in Shahrekord, Iran. Drivers with apnoea were involved in car accidents two times more often than their colleagues. In Taiwan, Chiu and co-workers (2014) analysed data from the 2005 Taiwan Social Development Trend Survey of 36,473 subjects. Early morning awakening and nonrestorative sleep increased the risk of occupational and leisure-time injuries. Based on the same dataset, Chen and Wu (2010) showed that excessive daytime sleepiness was associated with traffic and falling injuries. In Saudi Arabia, BaHammam *et al.* (2014) interviewed 1,219 drivers face-to-face, of whom 35 % were professional drivers. Young age, feeling very sleepy and having at least one near-accident caused by sleepiness were predictors of traffic injuries. In Australia, Howard *et al.* (2004) made a survey of 2,342 commercial vehicle drivers. The sleepiest 5 % of drivers were involved in crashes and multiple crashes two times more often than other drivers. Later, Dorrian *et al.* (2006) analysed the logbooks of twenty-three Australian nurses. Short sleep time predicted errors and near-errors at work.

A few reasonable conclusions can be drawn from these studies, which were conducted in almost all continents of the world. As many as forty-six of them showed that sleeping problems increased the risk of injury in general and the risk of work injury in particular. Only two studies (Egea Santaolalla and Léger 2015) found a negative relationship. Excessive daytime sleepiness was the problem mentioned most often in the studies. It can also be noticed that there were gender differences in sleeping problems. Doi and Minowa (2003) found that Japanese women suffered excessive daytime sleepiness more often than men. However, gender was mentioned in only a few of the studies, although many of them concerned male-dominated professions (e.g., truck and bus driving). Four of the studies were focused on men and two on women.

There is at least one obvious factor that explains impaired sleep: stress. The anticipation of high demands on the next workday was found to cause stress in particular (Åkerstedt 2006). On the other hand, insomnia patients regarded work as the primary source of insomnia (Henry *et al.* 2008). An American study (Knudsen, Ducharme and Roman 2007) showed that work overload was related to poor sleep quality. Role conflict and repetitive work tasks were associated with difficulties in initiating sleep. Among Swedish women, adverse psychosocial factors (i.e., demand, control and emotional support) increased the risk of poor sleep (Nordin *et al.* 2005). Sexual harassment at work increased sleep problems by 3.5 times among Korean employees (Park *et al.* 2013). Hillman *et al.* (2006) calculated the economic costs of sleep disorders in 2004. The total price was 7,494 million dollars, of which work-related injuries accounted for 1,956 million dollars. These costs represented 0.8 % of Australian gross domestic product. The Body Mass Index (BMI) can be a first-line screening method for excessive daytime sleepiness (Dagan *et al.* 2006).

One special case of sleep problems was due to changes associated with daylight saving time. Barnes and Wagner (2009) showed that, based on a database with 576,292 mining injuries, the change to daylight saving time increased injuries by 6 %, with an increase of 68 % in days of work lost per year compared to days with no change. Their other study indicated that during the night of the time change employees slept on average forty minutes less than during other nights. In Ontario, Canada, daytime saving time involved no increase in work injuries immediately after the change. The same result was obtained after the autumn change (Morassaei and Smith 2010). In Finland, no increase in occupational injuries was associated with daylight saving time (Lahti *et al.* 2011). In Minnesota, US, the effect of daylight-saving time was not related to crashes the next morning (Huang and Levinson 2010). Thus, three out of four studies revealed no increase in occupational injuries as a result of daylight-saving time. Maybe employees and drivers are able to adjust their behaviour to the transitions into and from daylight saving time.

CHAPTER SIX

CAN STRESS LEAD TO INJURY?

A review of twenty studies consistently showed that stress was significantly related to occupational injury. The odds ratios varied from 0.3 to 4.6 (Johnston 1995). Later, Clarke (2012) conducted a meta-analysis of forty-five studies and 60,240 subjects. Hindrance stressors were associated with higher levels of occupational injuries and near-misses.

Based on the 1958 British Birth Cohort study, with 11,405 subjects, it was found that psychological distress had a short-term effect on injuries. Injuries to drivers increased the risk of limiting illness (Li, Roberts and Power 2001). High job strain was the most important risk factor for occupational injuries among 874 German nurses (Nolting *et al.* 2002). In Spain, Julià *et al.* (2013) conducted a prospective cohort study of 10,667 employees. Stress was not related to occupational injuries among men, while lack of organisational support was associated with injuries among women. High psychological demands, verbal abuse, and low predictability were the psychosocial risk factors for occupational injury among 20,079 French women, whereas low reward, physical violence, and bullying were risk factors among 26,883 men, according to the SUMER study by the French Ministry of Labour (Lesuffleur *et al.* 2015).

Stress and injuries have also been studied in the Nordic countries. Rundmo (1995) examined this relationship with 915 employees working on Norwegian offshore installations. Employees who had suffered injuries experienced more stress than employees who had avoided injuries. In Denmark, Glasscock *et al.* (2006) received 310 questionnaires from farmers. Higher levels of stressors and stress symptoms as well as poor safety behaviour predicted occupational injuries. The combination of high levels of stress symptoms and poor safety behaviour was related to an exceptionally high risk of injuries. Among 5,111 Finnish hospital employees, psychological distress was not related to occupational injuries. However, low decision latitude, low skill discretion (only for men), and highly monotonous work were additional stress factors for both genders (Salminen *et al.* 2003). Another Finnish study with 16,385 forest employees showed that highly stressed subjects were more often hospitalised due to occupational injury than participants with low stress (Salminen *et al.* 2014).

In the US, Stuart and Brown (1981) tested a stress measure called College Schedule of Recent Experience with 163 undergraduate students. They found a significant relationship between stress and injuries, and subjects who experienced a high amount of stress suffered injuries more often than subjects with a low level of stress. A survey of sixty-eight American construction employees showed that occupational stressors like job control, responsibility for the safety of co-workers, safety climate, training and job uncertainty were related to occupational injuries (Abbe *et al.* 2011). Wilkins and Beaudet (1998) analysed the National Health Survey conducted in Canada with 9,023 employees. Job strain was related to work injuries among women, whereas high physical demands increased the risk of injury for both genders.

The relationship between stress and injuries has also been examined in Asia. In a Japanese manufacturing company, 139 blue-collar employees completed a content questionnaire. Among female employees, high job demands were related to work injury, whereas work stress was not related to injury among males (Murata, Kawakami and Amari 2000). At the oil offshore installations of the South China Sea, 561 employees completed a questionnaire. Safety, physical environment, family life, and feeling isolated were perceived stress factors among Chinese oil employees (Wong *et al.* 2002). Later, Kim *et al.* (2009) completed a follow-up survey with 1,209 employees in Incheon, South Korea. Men with high job demands and high job strain had an increased risk of injury, whereas among women, in addition to earlier factors, low decision latitude was associated with injuries. In Iran, Soori, Rahimi and Mohseni (2008) examined 608 male employees in the Iran-Saipa car manufacturing company. Job stress was higher among employees with injuries compared to employees who had avoided injuries. Job stress was responsible for 12 % of occupational injuries. Kiani *et al.* (2011) received a questionnaire from 189 employees of the Isfahan Steel Company. Perceived job stress was measured by the Job Stress Questionnaire and was found not to be related to injuries but to incident reporting rate.

In Australia, Savery and Wooden (1994) conducted a questionnaire study of 1,425 employees from sixty-one workplaces. Stress contributed strongly to injury involvement. Low, Griffith and Alston (1996) interviewed, via telephone, 919 farm workers in New South Wales, Australia, who were involved in 425 injuries. Perceived stress was associated with injuries as well as age, previous injuries, body mass index, hours of sleep and daytime drowsiness. Later, Hilton and Whiteford (2010) conducted a survey of fifty-eight large Australian companies with 60,556 employees. Moderate and high psychological distress increased workplace injuries and failures and decreased workplace successes.

In the city of Botucatu, in southeast Brazil, Cordeiro and Dias (2005) interviewed 108 victims of occupational injury. Stressful life events such as being a victim of assault, not having enough food, non-occupational fatigue and environmental problems were risk factors of injuries. At a Mexican textile company, 277 employees participated in an interview study. Work stress was directly related to work injuries, use of alcohol at work, and negative job climate (Garcia *et al.* 2006).

The above studies on stress and injuries concern fifteen different countries. With the exception of Spain, all of them indicate that stress perceived by employees increases their risk of injury. Further, women are more prone to the effects of stress than men, which can be seen in its association with work injuries in studies carried out in Germany, Spain, France, Canada and Japan.

It is worth remembering that work injuries can be prevented by reducing employee stress. Clarke and Cooper (2004) have presented a number of stress reduction tools, ranging from stress management by employers to individual-level measures. These methods, however, still need to be developed further, as stress, and its effects on work injuries, seems to be on the increase.

CHAPTER SEVEN

CULTURAL DIFFERENCES AND GENETICS

Many cultural factors may affect the risk of injury at work. Cultural differences in safety attitudes can play a critical role in how workers respond to hazards, for instance. Language skills are essential for effective communication in multicultural work environments. In this chapter, I will, first, describe our research project on whether occupational injury rates vary between Finnish- and Swedish-speaking people in Finland. Secondly, I will review a few studies carried out in multicultural workplaces. Thirdly, I will present some studies on the influence of genetics and environment on injury involvement.

Language Differences

Finland is a bilingual country, i.e., it has two official languages, Finnish and Swedish. Swedish is spoken as a first language by just over 5 % of the population of 5.5 million. The Swedish-speaking minority mostly lives in the southern and western coastal areas of Finland.

In our research project on the relationship between language group and occupational injury, we, first, analysed three independent statistical data sets and found that Swedish-speaking employees were injured at work less often than Finnish-speaking employees. The difference between the language groups was consistently between 30 % and 40 % in favour of Swedish-speaking employees (Salminen *et al.* 1996; Salminen and Johansson 2000). The difference could not be reasonably explained by any statistical biases or demographic variables (Johansson and Salminen 1999).

Then, to test this result, we compared fourteen Finnish- and Swedish-speaking companies (the management and a majority of employees spoke the same language) that operated within the same industry. They also used similar technologies and had approximately the same number of employees. The comparison indicated that the injury frequency was 21 % lower in the Swedish-speaking companies. In addition, these companies scored higher in cooperation and flow of information. Their machines were newer and better protected. Also, their employees had received safety training more often (Johansson and Salminen 1999; Salminen and Johansson 2000). All in all, the Swedish-speaking companies consistently performed a little better than the Finnish-speaking companies.

Finally, we compared safety climates in the Finnish- and Swedish-speaking companies. The safety climate questionnaire was developed by Seppälä (1992). In the total variables of safety climate, no significant differences were found between the language groups. Based on single items, however, Swedish-speaking employees attached greater importance to collective safety, whereas Finnish-speaking employees put more emphasis on their personal responsibility for safety (Salminen and Seppälä 2005).

Our research project was based on a theory of symbol systems developed by Strømnes (2006). According to this theory, there are systematic differences in the formation of mental models between people speaking languages belonging to different language groups. Swedish is an Indo-European language, while Finnish belongs to the Ural-Altaic languages. As a consequence, the lexical markers in Finnish (case endings) and in Swedish (prepositions) refer to totally different structural spatial relations. Another difference between these languages is the grammatical tense: while Swedish has a future tense, Finnish lacks it. This could be seen as one reason why Swedish-speaking employees seem to plan the work before starting, whereas Finnish employees tend to start the work without thinking it through in advance (Salminen and Johansson 2000).

The better results of the Swedish-speaking population in Finland have also been explained by their minority status (Suominen *et al.* 2000). The idea is that a minority group can take better care of its members because they are fewer in number. Moreover, the strain of the majority group drives the members of the minority group to seek support from other minority group members.

Differences in personality traits can also explain the wide gap in the injury frequency between Swedish- and Finnish-speaking employees. A comparison of Finnish-speaking people in Turku and Swedish-speaking people in Stockholm showed that the Swedes were more achievement-oriented, whereas Finns were more nurturant (Daun, Mattlar and Alanen 1989). The achievement-orientation of the Swedish-speaking employees can also be reflected in their better attitudes to safety.

Other bilingual countries include, e.g., Belgium and Canada. As far as I know, the differences in the injury frequency between different language groups in these countries have not been studied. However, the Finnish example suggests that the majority language group, in particular, could benefit from the experiences of the minority group. One exception is the study by Vela Acosta, Sechrest and Chen (2009), who taught safety knowledge in both English and Spanish to Hispanic farmworkers in the US. They found significant improvements in safety knowledge and safety risk perception after the training.

Multicultural Workplaces and Safety Attitudes

The construction of a bridge (Øresund Link) between Sweden and Denmark might have been an opportunity to compare injury frequency in two countries. However, the researchers (Spangenberg *et al.* 2002) only carried out a safety campaign for the Danish employees. They received promising results, with a decrease of 25 % in the injury frequency. In addition, an interview study of Swedish and Danish construction employees indicated that Danish employees were tougher in their safety attitudes than their Swedish colleagues (Grill, Grytnes and Törner 2015).

An analysis of fatal work injuries in twenty-two European countries (Reniers and Gidron 2013) showed that power distance (a dimension used by Hofstede) was positively related to fatal injuries, whereas individualism was inversely associated with fatal injuries. Håvold (2007) sent a questionnaire to 2,558 seafarers who were from ten countries and worked for Norwegian shipping companies. He found that high power distance, high uncertainty avoidance, and high individualism were positive for safety.

Strauch (2010) insisted that cultural factors can lead to injuries. He used some transportation injuries as examples. Cultural factors played a role, especially during high-workload and high-stress operational phases. International ships with seafarers from different cultures working together were a case in point.

A study of 608 seafarers working from the port of Kaohsiung in Taiwan showed that Taiwanese seafarers stressed uncertainty avoidance, whereas their Filipino colleagues leant more towards power distance. The results obtained by Lu *et al.* (2012) suggested that fewer human failures occur when power distance is low, and collectivism and uncertainty avoidance are high. On the other hand, Grön and Knudsen (2012) concluded, based on their review of the literature, that the fact that Filipinos had reported less injuries than Danish seafarers was not due to the ethnic or national background. They insisted that it was their minority status that explained the national differences.

Casey, Riseborough and Krauss (2015) examined 562 employees working for a multinational oil and gas company in the Timor Sea, Australia. Employees from southern Asia had more negative relationships, including supervisor production pressure and willingness to report errors, than Anglo employees. In addition, Jing, Lu and Peng (2001) wrote that authoritarianism is the most important cultural factor, explaining more than half of the variance in accident rates. Based on their review of studies from six different nations, Mearns and Yule (2009) concluded that management commitment inside the company is a more important determinant of behaviour at work than national culture. On the other hand, Starren, Hornikx and Luijters (2013) argued that it is difficult to achieve a shared safety climate in multicultural teams.

Genetics and Environment

The effects of genetics and environment on injury involvement can be analysed by examining twins. A genetic effect would be seen to exist if the injury involvement of monozygotic twins was higher than that of dizygotic twins. In other cases, environment would be seen to have a greater influence on injury involvement than genetic factors.

A research group (Salminen *et al.* 2018) examined 955 Finnish twins born between 1983 and 1987 and aged from twenty to twenty-four at the time of the study. Within-twin correlations in monozygotic and dizygotic twins suggested that genetic effects play no role in injury involvement. An older data set included 12,428 twins born between 1930 and 1957 and aged from thirty-three to sixty. The best-fit model for females showed a heritability of 25 %. For men, the heritability was 22 %.

An earlier study was conducted in England and Wales among 1,116 families with same-sex five-year-old twins born in 1994 and 1995. Environmental factors explained 86.4 % of the injury variance. The dizygotic correlation (.49) was actually higher than that for monozygotic twins (.29), showing that genetic factors had no effect (Ordoñana, Caspi and Moffitt 2008). The Virginia Twin Study of Adolescent Behavioural Development was a cohort longitudinal study of 1,400 twin pairs aged from eight to seventeen. Girls showed significant genetic effects in unintentional injuries, whereas shared environmental effects were found among both boys and girls (Rowe, Simonoff and Silberg 2007).

A review made by Schulte *et al.* (2012) indicated that genetic factors alone are unable to explain the variance in occupational injuries. However, when combined with occupational risk factors, these factors can increase the risk of injury. For injury prevention, the results of these studies are promising: if the influence of environment on injuries is greater than that of heritage, it is possible to prevent injuries by doing safety work.

PART II

ORGANISING WORK IN THE WORKPLACE

CHAPTER EIGHT

PRECARIOUS WORK CAREERS

Precarious work is a concept that does not have any universally accepted definition. According to the ILO, it includes temporary or fixed-term employment, part-time employment and various other nonstandard forms of employment, such as agency work, subcontracting, casual or on-call work, seasonal work, home-work and self-employment. The related concept of job insecurity can be described as an employee's uncertainty about the continuation of their job. The varying terminology has been somewhat problematic in analysing the studies on the health and safety effects of nonstandard forms of work. In the review below, the terminology used in each individual publication has mostly been retained.

Temporary Work in Finland

In Finland, 15.8 % of work contracts are fixed-term contracts (Statistics Finland 2020). Women work in fixed-term employment more often than men (Tilastokeskus 2007). Based on the official statistics of occupational injuries in Finland, Tarvainen (1999) found 417,047 employees who had been employed on a work contract of less than six months. These employees had a 10 % higher frequency of injury than permanent employees in the manufacturing industry and in the metal industry their frequency of injury was 15 % higher. Later, based on the official Finnish statistics of occupational injuries, Hintikka (2011) showed that temporary employees had a higher risk of injury than permanent employees. The effect of temporary work was most typically to be seen in manual work in the production and construction industries.

However, Notkola and Vänskä (2000), who analysed the Work Conditions Study of Statistics Finland, found that temporary employees had fewer injuries than permanent employees. By utilising a data set concerning people born in northern Finland in 1966, Pekkarinen and Anttonen (2000) found that women in fixed-term employment had a higher rate of occupational injuries than permanent employees overall. Furthermore, Saloniemi, Virtanen and Koivisto (2004) showed in a study with 1,127

Finnish blue-collar employees that fixed-term employees had an increased risk of physical strain at work but only in the construction industry. Saloniemi and Salminen (2010), who analysed three large data sets in Finland, reported that, in two data sets, fixed-term employees had a lower injury rate than their colleagues in permanent employment, whereas one data set showed the opposite result.

Kivimäki *et al.* (2003), who analysed a data set of 26,592 men and 65,759 women from ten Finnish towns, found that the overall mortality of temporary employees was 1.2 to 1.6 times higher than that of permanent employees. A change from temporary to permanent employment reduced the overall risk of death. In a review of thirteen studies compiled in Finland, seven studies showed a higher risk of occupational injuries among temporary employees, although their sickness absence was lower (Virtanen *et al.* 2005).

Thus, the results obtained in Finland failed to consistently indicate that fixed-term employment increases the risk of injury.

Temporary and Other Precarious Work Globally

In their review of ninety-three studies, Quinlan, Mayhew and Bohle (2001) found eighty-one studies showing that precarious employment was associated with occupational injuries. Koranyi *et al.* (2018) picked up seventeen articles from 471 original titles. Ten studies reported a positive association between precarious employment and occupational injuries, four reported a negative relationship, and three showed no significant association. Thus, the researchers stated that the results for temporary employment were inconclusive.

Størseth (2006) analysed a self-reported questionnaire of 729 Norwegian employees. Job insecurity was directly associated with risk-taking and safety.

Based on Spanish data, Guadalupe (2003) argued that a pure contractual effect increased the risk of occupational injury of fixed-term employees by 5 %. Later, Benavides *et al.* (2006) analysed a data set from the Spanish Ministry of Labour and Social Affairs, including 3,616,064 non-fatal and 3,000 fatal injuries. Temporary employees had an almost threefold risk of non-fatal injuries and a two and a half times higher risk of fatalities compared to permanent employees. The authors suggested that lower job experience and knowledge of workplace hazards explained these differences.

Based on an Italian insurance data set, Fabiano *et al.* (2008) showed that temporary employees were involved in injuries 4.4 times more often than permanent employees. Also, their injury severity was twice as high as the overall value. Also, in Italy, Ciarapica and Giacchetta (2009) used neuro-fuzzy networks to analyse 1,960 occupational injuries during the period from 2002 to 2006. Males were involved in injuries 1.7 times more often than females. Temporary employees were injured 1.2 times more often than permanent employees.

Bellamy and Aneziris (2015) analysed 3,261 injuries of temporary employees and 20,447 injuries of permanent employees in the Netherlands. They found that, for example, in the construction industry, temporary employees fell from the roof and died sixteen times more often than permanent construction employees.

Wrench and Lee (1982) analysed injuries in a textile company with 1,297 mostly female employees in Birmingham, UK. Most of the injuries to day employees occurred on Mondays and Tuesdays, whereas in piecework most of the injuries occurred on Fridays, just before the pay day. The Workplace Employee Relations Survey of 1998 included interviews with managers from 2,191 British workplaces. Robinson and Smallman (2006) showed that, based on this data set, temporary contracts increased the injury rate in the manufacturing industry, whereas temporary employment decreased the injury rate in the service sector.

The analysis of industrial deaths among 79,822 male asphalt employees in eight European countries indicated that there was an increased risk of mortality due to external causes among short-term employees. However, no support was found for the hypothesis that asphalt employees were at an increased risk of occupational fatality (Burstyn *et al.* 2004).

Based on the Canadian National Population Health Survey in 1994 and 1995, Cole, Ibrahim and Shannon (2005) analysed the data of 2,806 employees. Women suffered work-related repetitive strain injuries two times more often than men. High job insecurity almost doubled the risk of strain injury.

Probst and Brubaker (2001) examined 237 food-processing employees in the northwestern part of the US. High perceptions of job insecurity were associated with decreased safety motivation and compliance, which, in turn, were related to higher levels of workplace injuries. In the southwestern part of the US, Probst, Jiang and Graso (2016) conducted a survey of 212 copper miners. Job insecurity was related to higher levels of occupational injuries, whereas leader–member exchange attenuated that relationship. Park and Butler (2001) analysed a data set from the Minnesota Department of Labor and Industry, including 13,323 injuries to contingent employees and 10,600 to permanent employees. Contingent employees were involved in injuries four to seven times more often than permanent employees. The researchers explained this difference by the hazardous work tasks of the contingent employees, who were also younger and less experienced than permanent employees. Based on the National Health Interview Study, from 1997 to 2011, Marucci-Wellman *et al.* (2014) analysed the injury risk of 268,615 American employees with 7,492 injuries. On average, 8 % of employees had several jobs at the same time. Multiple job holders were involved in injuries both at work and during leisure-time more often than single-job holders.

In an Indian fertilizer-producing factory, Saha *et al.* (2004) compared the 419 temporary employees to the 307 permanent colleagues. The rate of no-time-loss injuries of temporary employees was 1.2 to 3.5 times higher than that of permanent employees. With lost-time injuries, the rate for temporary employees was from 1.7 to 4.3 times higher than that for permanent employees. Later, the same research group (Saha *et al.* 2005) studied the injury statistics of 764 employees in an Indian chemical factory. The injury frequency for temporary employees was 6.7 times higher and the severity rate 7.4 times higher than those for permanent employees.

Workplace Violence and Suicidal Thoughts

In their review, Quinlan, Mayhew and Bohle (2001) found three studies suggesting that organisational downsizing increased occupational violence. Mayhew and Chappell (2007) reported that precarious jobs increased the risk of occupational violence, especially among taxi drivers and employees in fast-food restaurants.

According to James *et al.* (1990), there were 102 violent incidents over a period of fifteen months in a general hospital in London. Temporary nursing staff experienced violence more often than permanent employees. Violent patients were young, had been admitted compulsorily and were less often depressed than those without violence. In Australia, Mayhew and Quinlan (2000) indicated that precarious employees had a higher risk of violence in child-care centres and transport compared with permanent employees. A study involving face-to-face interviews with 304 Australian adolescents working in 132 outlets of a multinational fast-food chain showed that seven out of ten adolescents were precariously employed. Almost half of them had experienced verbal abuse, while physical assault occurred in only 2 % of cases (Mayhew 2004). According to Salminen and Saloniemi (2010), however, fixed-term employees did not meet violence at work more often than permanent employees.

Moreover, nonstandard types of employment, including temporary work, increased thoughts of suicide. Based on the Korean National Health and Nutrition Examination Surveys of 13,632 employees, Lee and Ha

(2011) found a 1.3 times higher risk of suicidal ideation among temporary employees. Their more insecure work situation caused increased stress and suicidal ideation.

The majority of the studies considered in this chapter support the claim that temporary employment increases the risk of occupational injury compared with permanent employment. This conclusion was supported in six out of the eight studies conducted in Finland, eight out of the nine studies in other European countries, and all of the seven studies conducted outside of Europe. Also, earlier literature reviews have been in favour of the conclusion that temporary workers have injuries at work more often than others. It has also been found that temporary workers experience violence more often than the permanently employed.

It should be kept in mind that differences in the legislation of different countries may lead to differences in the status of temporary workers. This concerns immigrant and migrant employees in particular. The risks of subcontracting for employees is dealt with in Chapter 12 on the construction industry.

In my view, there are three major reasons for the higher levels of workplace injuries and violence among temporary employees compared with the permanently employed. First, temporary workers are mostly young and inexperienced. Therefore, they may be too shy to ask questions, for instance. Second, they have had less time than permanent workers to gain a thorough knowledge of their work environment. Third, they are less efficiently informed of any changes in work practices and communities than others. It is noteworthy that temporary workers need job orientation even if they had previously worked in the company.

CHAPTER NINE

SHIFT WORK: DAY AND NIGHT

Shift work is a system in which employees work for different agreed periods during the day and night. Under a fixed shift system, working time can be organised in two or three shifts: the morning, afternoon and/or night shifts. Under a system of rotating shifts, workers are assigned to work shifts that vary regularly over time.

Shift work is often used for economic reasons in order to ensure an efficient use of costly equipment. However, it is known to lead to increased levels of occupational injuries. Therefore, it has been studied extensively all over Europe and elsewhere.

Folkard and Tucker (2003) concluded, on the basis of the five studies reviewed, that the risk of injuries increased by 18 % during the afternoon shift and by 30 % during the night shift compared with the morning shift. Therefore, the researchers recommended that a long night shift should include frequent rest breaks to improve safety. My own calculation based on four studies (Salminen 2010) showed that the risk of occupational injury during night shifts was 15 % lower than during morning shifts. Another calculation, based on five studies, confirmed this finding (Salminen 2016).

Pokorny, Bloom and van Leeuwen (1987) examined 944 injuries among bus drivers in the western part of the Netherlands. The injury risk in the early morning shift (between 5 a.m. and 10 a.m.) was higher than in the afternoon (between 12 noon and 5 p.m.).

In Wales, Smith, Folkard and Poole (1994) analysed 4,645 injuries in a large engineering company of 4,250 employees. Employees working the night shifts were involved in injuries more often than employees in the day shifts. During the night shifts, injuries in self-paced work were more often serious compared with the morning shifts.

Working on offshore platforms is a special case of shift work because employees stay for two to three weeks at the platform without going ashore. Parkes (1999) sent a questionnaire to 1,354 employees working on seventeen North Sea oil and gas installations. Job type and shift work were strongly related to work-related injury. Those in construction work in particular had an excess risk of injury. Based on a data set from the Rogaland Research Institute in Norway, Lauridsen and Tönnesen (1990) found 3,229 injuries at offshore drilling sites. A higher injury rate was noticed during the night hours from midnight to six in the morning. Rotating shifts also increased the risk of injury. Wagstaff and Sigstad Lie from Norway (2011) analysed fourteen high-quality studies from a total of 6,889 references. These studies showed that both shift work and long working hours doubled the injury rate. Shift work that included nights substantially increased the risk of injuries. Parkes (2012) analysed twenty-four studies in her review of shift work on North Sea oil/gas installations. Offshore night work increased the risk of injury, especially the risk of serious injury. On the other hand, Fossum *et al.* (2013) concluded, based on a review of twenty-nine studies, that the relationship between injuries and shift work in the offshore petroleum industry was inconsistent; employees adapted to night work within a week or two.

Based on the Danish Labour Force Study of 1999–2013, Larsen *et al.* (2017) examined 23,495 injuries to 150,438 employees. Night work increased the risk of occupational injury significantly and was linked with injuries among women to a greater extent than men. Ott *et al.* (2009) compared 14,128 rotating shift employees to 17,218 employees working in day shifts at the Ludwigshafen site of BASF in Germany. Shift employees experienced occupational injuries more often than daytime employees. Injury declined over time and increased with age. Garbarino *et al.* (2004) found an excessive risk of crashing among 1,195 Italian shift-working police drivers. Napping before the night shift decreased the injury risk by 48 %.

Kantermann, Haubruge and Skene (2013) studied 578 injuries to 730 shift employees in a steel factory in Belgium. Employees on the morning shifts had a higher injury rate than those on the evening and night shifts. The researchers mentioned two reasons for this result: the early starting time (6 a.m.) and more labour-intensive shifts.

In the US, Dembe *et al.* (2006) examined the effect of nonstandard shift schedules on occupational injuries based on the National Longitudinal Survey of Youth (1987–2000) of 12,686 employees. An excess risk of injuries was found for evening shifts, night shifts, and rotating shifts. Levin, Oler and Whiteside (1985) examined injuries in a paint production company with 1,691 employees working in rotating shifts. The incidence rate of night-shift employees was 25 % higher than that of day-shift employees, the difference being particularly great during the last three hours of the night shifts. Gold *et al.* (1992) sent a questionnaire to 878 hospital nurses in

Massachusetts and 635 of them responded. Nurses working in rotating shifts were more often involved in injuries than nurses working on the day shift. Rotators also crashed more often while driving to home or work. Hopcia *et al.* (2012) analysed 533 injuries among 502 hospital employees and 502 controls in Boston. Injury incidence was two times higher for those working consecutive (twenty or more) shifts. Also, three or more twelve-hour night shifts increased the risk of injury.

Glazner (1996) examined 171 injuries of 447 fire fighters in the northeastern US. She found that 92 % of injuries occurred at the fire scene. During the night shift, the fighters were injured more often than during the day shift. Violanti and his co-workers (2013) examined the injuries of 419 police officers in a Buffalo police department. During the night shift, the injury risk was higher than during the day or afternoon shifts. The largest difference between the night and other shifts was noticed in injuries causing a ninety-day absence.

In Canada, Wojtczak-Jaroszowa and Jarosz (1987) analysed 676,389 occupational injuries in Ontario. They found that the highest injury frequency occurred around noon, just before the lunch break. Although the number of injuries was lowest during the night, the injury frequency slightly increased between 2 a.m. and 4 a.m. Based on the 2003 Canadian Community Health Survey (n = 135,573), it was estimated that 630,000 Canadians had experienced at least one occupational injury. Among employees in shift work, there were significantly more injuries than among daytime employees, for both women and men (Wilkins and Mackenzie 2007).

Wong *et al.* (2014) analysed longitudinal panels from the Survey of Labor and Income Dynamics of 19,131 Canadian employees. Moving from day to nonstandard shifts, or vice versa, or working in nonstandard shifts only increased the risk of occupational injury. The effect of shift work on injuries was stronger for women than for men (Wong, McLeod and Demers 2011). Later, they (Wong *et al.* 2015) examined the National Population Health Survey of 9,541 Canadian employees. Employees with a nonstandard-shift schedule were involved in injuries more often than daytime employees. The elevated risk of injuries was noticed among male, young and less educated participants.

In Australia, based on a data set of 1,020 work-related fatalities between 1982 and 1984, Williamson and Feyer (1995) found that, compared with day shifts, the number of fatalities during night shifts was more than double—in proportion to the number of people at work at this time. Behavioural factors influenced fatalities most in the early morning (between midnight and 6 a.m.).

In Queensland, Australia, Loudoun and Allan (2008) examined 3,201 injuries to adolescents under twenty. Among both females and males, adolescents were involved in injuries several times more often than adults on night shifts. Further, Smith *et al.* (2013) found, from the Multipurpose Household Survey of 2009–2010 including 6,927 Australian women and 7,340 men, that the injury risk for shift work was higher among women than among men. Women with dependent children suffered from injuries related to shift work more often than women without small children.

In New Zealand, a cross-sectional analysis of 15,687 blood donors indicated that rotating shift work with nights increased the risk of work injury, whereas no increase in the risk of injury was found in permanent night-shift workers (Fransen *et al.* 2006).

The relation between shift work and injury has also been studied in Asia. Nag and Patel (1998) examined 3,470 fatal and non-fatal injuries in eleven textile factories in Ahmedabad, India. The highest rate of injury was found in the morning shifts, while the injuries were more dangerous in the night shifts. More injuries occurred on the pay day than during other days.

Halvani, Zare and Mirmohammadi (2009) compared 137 shift employees to 130 non-shift employees in the Iranian Industrial Mining Group. Shift miners with injuries suffered fatigue more often than shift employees without injuries. Sanati *et al.* (2010) studied 836 injuries in a factory of synthetic fibres in Iran. A sharp rise was noticed in the first three hours of the day shift. Exposure to smoke, fire and flames, or transport injuries were more likely to occur in the second half of a shift.

Park *et al.* (2012) analysed the Korean Working Condition Survey of 2006 of 7,075 employees. Shift workers had occupational injuries two times more often than other employees. Rey de Castro *et al.* (2010) sent a questionnaire to 1,000 registered nurses in the Philippines and 655 of them responded. Non-day shift and working mandatory overtime (over forty hours per week) were significantly associated with occupational injury. Based on the Taiwan Social Development Trend Survey in 2005 (n = 18,794), Chiu and Tsai (2013) showed that those working on evening and night shifts, or day and evening shifts experienced more injuries than other employees. Employees working day and evening shifts had a higher risk of minor injury than those working daytime only. Ong *et al.* (1987) found 921 occupational injuries among 1,000 employees at an iron and steel mill in Singapore. The injury frequency was lower during the night shift than during the morning shift.

Gander and Signal (2008) examined 2,685 participants of the Sleep Heart Health Study, who were aged from thirty-seven to ninety-two. Among those aged from fifty to sixty, sleep loss was, on average, 3.5-fold higher compared with the other participants. Accordingly, it was recommended that fatigue and sleep loss should become a standard part of the medical assessment of older shift workers. However, Folkard (2008) concluded in his review that it was unproven that older employees had a greater risk of injury on the night shift. A Finnish study showed that, with a shift-schedule evaluation tool with ergonomic recommendations, it is possible to reduce occupational injuries (Shiri *et al.* 2023).

Monk and Wagner (1989) analysed 457 injuries during the night shift at the Lake Superior iron ore mining region in the US. They found a huge increase in injuries during the Sunday night shifts. Obviously, the two days off at the weekends may loosen night employees' grip on work tasks, i.e., the social disruption at weekends may explain this effect better than biological factors.

In order to improve the design of shift systems, Knauth (1996) presented the following five recommendations based on earlier studies:

- Reduce nightwork as much as possible.
- Avoid an early start for the morning shift.
- Avoid quick changeover to diminish the risk of injury.
- Prefer forward rotation.
- Allow long workdays (over eight hours/day) only if the workload is suitable.

I very much agree with Knauth on his recommendations. In addition, it should be remembered that shift work increases the risk of injury more among women than among men. Mothers of small children, in particular, are at risk. The risk of injury is smaller if the employee is allowed to take a nap before a night shift.

CHAPTER TEN

LONG WORKING HOURS

Long working hours refer to working hours exceeding the regular weekly working time. Excessive working increases the risk of occupational injury. In my review of twelve studies (Salminen 2016), I found that a ten-hour working day increased the risk of occupational injury by 15 %. When the number of hours at work increased to twelve hours, the risk of injury increased by 38 % compared to an eight-hour workday.

Bendak (2003) from Saudi Arabia conducted a review of forty-nine studies concerning twelve-hour workdays. The extra four hours at work increased fatigue, which then increased the risk of injury. Knauth (2007) collected 105 studies on the effects of extended working hours. Nine of these studies showed an increase in injuries during long working hours, whereas four studies indicated a negative relationship. Furthermore, in five studies, no significant effects were found. Matre and others (2021) completed a meta-analysis based on twenty-one selected studies. They concluded that working over twelve hours per day or over fifty-five hours per week increased the risk of injury. However, the level of evidence was low.

In Germany, in 1994, 1.2 million occupational injuries were found to have occurred in the ninth hour at work. When the job started at a later time, the relative injury risk increased dramatically after the eighth hour at work (Hänecke *et al*. 1998).

In the US, a great number of studies have been conducted on long working hours. Johnson and Sharit (2001) studied the change from an eight-hour to a twelve-hour shift in an American manufacturing plant with 350 employees. The subjects preferred a twelve-hour shift because of a better subjective feeling toward health and social family life along with the longer free time between work periods. There was no significant change in the number of occupational injuries. Based on the National Longitudinal Survey of Youth of 1979, Dong (2005) showed that over fifty hours at work per week and shift work increased the risk of occupational injury among construction employees. Vegso and co-workers (2007) examined the effect of extended working hours on injuries in five American primary metal production plants with a total of 6,895 employees. Those who worked over sixty-four hours per week had an 88 % excess risk of occupational injury compared to those who worked forty hours or less per week. Allen, Slavin and Bunn (2007) conducted a survey of 2,746 American employees in May and September 2001. An excess risk of injury was found among employees who worked over sixty hours per week. Based on the National Longitudinal Survey of Youth, Dembe, Delbos and Erickson (2009) examined 545 injuries to healthcare personnel. The greatest injury risk was noticed for healthcare employees working at least sixty hours per week. Support personnel had a higher risk of injury than physicians and nurses. Based on the US National Health Interview Survey, with 96,915 respondents, Wirtz *et al.* (2012) showed that working over forty hours per week increased the risk of occupational injury among women but not among men. Later, the same research group (Arlinghaus *et al.* 2012a) showed that, based on the same database, each ten-hour increase in weekly working hours increased the risk of injury by 14 %. Short sleep duration is another independent risk factor.

A Canadian synthetic yarn manufacturing company with 247 employees changed from eight-hour to twelve-hour workdays. Overall injury rates were reduced among those working on the twelve-hour shift, but injuries outside the working hours increased. The change decreased injuries for males but not for females (Laundry and Lees 1991).

In Asia, long working hours are frequent. Based on the 2004 Occupational Safety Survey in Korea, Kim *et al.* (2009) analysed injuries in 1,866 small-sized manufacturing companies with a total of 65,921 employees. Those working over fifty-four hours per week suffered occupational injuries three times more often than those working less than forty-four hours per week. Shift work was not related to injuries. Further, in Korea, Im *et al.* (2012) interviewed 1,576 injured employees and 1,500 of their colleagues as a control group. Working over sixty hours per week increased the risk of occupational injury to the extent that it was almost four times higher than for those working the standard forty-six weekly hours. Employees with a temporary employment contract also had an excess risk of injury.

Rest Breaks

The purpose of rest breaks is to compensate for the tiredness caused by long working hours. Rest breaks also serve to refresh the thinking of employees.

Tucker, Folkard and Macdonald (2003) examined the effect of rest breaks on injuries at a car assembly plant in the UK with 2,224 employees.

Two hours of continuous work was followed by a fifteen-minute break. The injury risk during the last half-hour of each work period was doubled, and it diminished immediately after the break. There were significantly more injuries on the day shift than on the night shift.

Later, Tucker *et al.* (2006) studied 4,645 injuries among 4,250 shift employees in a large engineering company. In addition, they interviewed 407 victims of hand injury in sixteen clinics in New England, US. The risk of injury increased from the first to the second half-hour following a break but then remained relatively stable. A sharp decline in injuries was found at the very end of a shift.

In the US, Arlinghaus *et al.* (2012b) interviewed 306 employees who had fallen from a ladder. Employees without rest breaks had worked a median of 3.0 hours before injury, whereas employees with a rest break over thirty minutes had worked a median of 6.8 hours before injury.

In eleven Chinese hospitals, 703 victims of severe occupational injury were examined (Lombardi *et al.* 2014). Employees without breaks had worked a median of two hours before injury, whereas employees with rest breaks had worked over five hours without injury.

Based on the fourth Korean Working Conditions Survey of 25,439 employees, Park, Lee and Lee (2019) concluded that the risk of work-related injuries increased for employees without sufficient rest breaks, whereas the risk was not significant among those with sufficient breaks.

Folkard (2008) reviewed studies on the effects of rest breaks from seven different databases. Regular rest breaks helped to control the accumulation of the risk of injuries over a prolonged performance. Short intensive work periods without rest breaks increased the risk of injuries. Napping was an effective way to improve alertness on night shifts.

PART III

WORKER HAZARDS IN INDUSTRIAL ENVIRONMENTS

CHAPTER ELEVEN

MANUFACTURING PLANTS AND SHIPYARDS

Manufacturing industries produce goods through a combination of human labour, equipment, chemicals, tooling, and similar systems. Of the different types of manufacturing industries, this chapter focuses on metal, automobile and textile manufacturing plants and shipyards in terms of occupational injuries and fatalities. All these industrial work environments have their specific types of safety hazards.

An analysis of ninety-nine serious occupational injuries in Finland showed that thirty-four of the victims were injured by the cutting and pressing parts of machines and that slips were typical accidents in various production tasks, whereas errors in the assessment of danger were typical in machine repair tasks (Salminen *et al.* 1991).

Larsson (1990) examined 735 injuries in the Swedish metal industry in 1986 and found that cutting machines and saws caused two out of three injuries. Larsson and Björnstig (1990), in turn, found 1,785 injuries in the town of Umeå, Sweden. Over half of the injuries had occurred in the manufacturing industry and about 8 % in trades and health services.

Webb, Redman and Sanson-Fisher (1992) analysed 1,740 injuries at a large metal manufacturing company in Australia. The most common types of injuries were soreness and pain, lacerations, superficial injuries, and foreign body in the eye. Injuries occurred most often on Mondays.

Concalves and Dias (2011) interviewed 662 employees of a Brazilian metallurgic plant, 166 of whom were involved in injuries over a period of three years (2004–2006). Almost half of them were boilermakers and were exposed to intense noise over 90 dBA.

Kifle and co-workers (2014) asked 444 iron and steel employees in Addis Ababa, Ethiopia, about their work injuries. One out of three employees had been involved in injuries, and the most general causes of injuries were splitting and flying objects, hit by falling objects, and machinery. Also in Ethiopia, Gebretsadik, Kumie and Gebremichael (2017) asked 484 employees from the Mugher Cement Factory about occupational injuries. Every tenth employee had been involved in an injury during the last year, and the most common causes of injury were machinery, splintering objects, and falls.

Safety Management

Workplace safety management systems are policies, procedures and plans that aim to systematically manage safety and help minimise the risk of occupational injury. The Participatory Behaviour Modification Programme (Tuttava) is a workplace improvement method originally developed by Jorma Saari (1992) in Finland. It aims at general organisation in the workplace, consisting of the following eight phases:

(1) Select team members: department manager, supervisor, employees' safety representative and two to four employees from the department.

(2) Prepare housekeeping rules. They should be positive, generally accepted, simple, use action verbs, and easy to measure.

(3) Develop an observation checklist to measure the rules. From each observation area about 100 observations are gathered, e.g., whether the waste container is full or not.

(4) Make baseline observations weekly for a few weeks.

(5) Organise a discussion session about the housekeeping rules for everyone.

(6) Carry out feedback observations weekly and show the results by means of a housekeeping index on a chart on the wall.

(7) Carry out the technical and organisational improvements.

(8) Organise a closing seminar and define future actions.

Laitinen, Saari and Kuusela (1997) tested this method in a metal workshop of the Finnish State Railways with about 300 employees. Over a period of two years, the average housekeeping index increased from 57 % to 89 %, and it also remained at a high level. Furthermore, during a follow-up period of three years, improvements were observed in working conditions and the psychosocial work environment (Laitinen *et al.* 1998).

Another Finnish observation method, Elmeri, includes twenty-six observation items in the following seven groups:

- safety behaviour
- order and tidiness
- machine safety
- industrial hygiene
- ergonomics
- walkways, and
- first aid and fire safety.

When this method was used in safety inspections in sixty metal companies, the safety index correlated significantly with the injury rate (Laitinen *et al.* 1999b). A subsequent analysis of the same data set showed that metal companies with the poorest safety indexes had an injury rate almost twice as high as the best companies (Laitinen *et al.* 1999a). Räsänen, Laitinen and Rasa (2009) also observed 261 employees from sixty metal companies in southern Finland. The results showed that younger and older employees received greater benefits from hygienic work environments than middle-aged employees.

Laitinen *et al.* (2013) used the Elmeri method in carrying out five observation rounds in 126 metal and mechanical engineering companies with 23,399 employees. The index was highly significantly related to the total injury rate (-0.512).

Furthermore, Hyytiäinen and Saarela (1990) examined 674 employees from a Finnish shipyard and a metal factory for lower back injuries. They analysed the injury reports and conducted surveys and a safety analysis. They found eleven lower back injuries, the highest risk factors being incorrect heavy lifting and prolonged work postures. As a result, a new safety regulation was given for Finnish metal presses. In order to examine the implementation of the regulation, Suokas (1993) sent a questionnaire to 120 metal companies, of which sixty-seven answered. The number of safer two-hand control systems rapidly increased and the number of press injuries decreased. Nenonen (2011) showed that almost half of all fatalities in the Finnish manufacturing industry occurred to external employees, who were typically making preparations or installations.

As early as the 1970s, Smith, Anger and Uslan (1978) studied behavioural modification among 20,000 employees in American shipyards. Four out of five supervisors succeeded in decreasing the number of eye injuries. The decrease that occurred in experimental groups was seven times higher than in control groups. Reber and Wallin (1983) developed and observed thirty-seven safety rules for 107 employees of a farm machinery manufacturing company in the southeast of the US. The lost-time injury rates were inversely related to baseline performance.

Welsh, Luthans and Sommer (1993) tested US-based behavioural management systems among ninety-nine Russian textile employees. They found that extrinsic rewards and behavioural management increased productivity significantly, whereas a participative technique decreased performance.

In the US, Ray and Frey (1999) observed a light engineering factory with 500 employees. Work groups with a higher observed safety index had a lower injury rate than groups with a lower observed safety index.

The fact that behavioural modification has been studied widely in the metal industry can be explained by this sector having large companies manufacturing products rather similar in kind. Therefore, they offer steady conditions for experiments as well as production, thus, enabling experiments of several weeks.

These early safety management and observation methods have subsequently been followed by many other similar methods in Finland and elsewhere.

Injuries from Cranes and Forklift Trucks

In Finland, it has been evaluated that 30 % of all occupational injuries are due to materials handling. More than half of these occurred in manual operations (Häkkinen 1982). Crane injuries accounted for 1 % of all occupational injuries.

Collins *et al.* (1999b) studied 916 powered industrial vehicle injuries at fifty-four automobile manufacturing plants. The most typical causes of injuries were pedestrian accidents, collisions with other vehicles, and a driver mounting a vehicle. Of the nonfatal injuries, 41 % resulted in an employee missing their work. Jones and Switzer-McIntyre (2003), in turn, found 352 falls from a non-moving vehicle. The most frequent sites of injuries were the back of a truck or trailer, the step of a truck, and at the cargo being transported. Strains/sprains, contusions and fractures were the major injuries.

Häkkinen (1978) examined a sample of 100 crane injuries. The priority areas of prevention in crane injuries were found to be lifting gear, the dismantling of cranes, and the overturning of cranes. Later, the researcher (Häkkinen 1993) found that crane injuries had decreased during the decades preceding his study. However, new types of injuries were found as crane drivers now controlled their crane at the floor level more often.

Using the OSHA data, 1985–1995, Shepherd, Kahler and Cross (2000) analysed over 500 crane fatalities. Two out of three crane fatalities were caused by mobile cranes, while the next most frequent crane types involved in fatalities were aerial lifts and tower cranes.

Among the ninety-nine serious occupational injuries that occurred in southern Finland, one fatality happened when a drunken driver fell with a forklift truck from the platform of a warehouse (Salminen 1997). Another fatality caused by a forklift truck was the death of a deaf man (already mentioned in Chapter 11).

Based on the OSHA data set for September 1984, Swartz (2000) showed that loading-dock accidents caused one third of injuries and half of them occurred when the employee was in a trailer. Almost one third of injuries occurred while unloading a vehicle. The researcher (Swartz 1998) also showed that, based on the OSHA data set, tip-over injuries caused one fourth of all forklift truck fatalities. Operator inattention, overturn, and unstable load were the main causes of industrial forklift truck injuries.

Collins *et al.* (1999a) found 1,021 fatalities with forklift trucks in the US from 1980 to 1994. The most common circumstances of deaths were forklift truck overturns, pedestrian struck by forklift, and worker crushed by forklift. Furthermore, Collins *et al.* (1999c) examined 171 forklift collision incidents at eight manufacturing plants in the US. Half of the collisions occurred when a pedestrian was struck by a forklift; restricted aisle width doubled the risk of collision.

Trafford Park in Manchester is one of the largest industrial park sites in England. During an eighteen-month period, there were sixty forklift truck injuries, whereby drivers injured their hands and other employees injured their forefeet (Williams and Priestley 1980). Based on Supplementary Data Systems, in 1983, Stout-Wiegand (1987) showed that forklift truck operators, warehouse workers and material handlers were the occupations most often involved in forklift truck injuries.

In Australia, 2 % of the 1,278 work-related fatalities in 1982–1984 were caused by forklift trucks. A huge majority of them were crush injuries (Mandryk *et al.* 1996). Larsson and Rechnitzer (1994) found 1,267 injuries and fifteen fatalities by forklift trucks in Victoria, Australia. The most general types of injuries were hit by forklift, fall from forklift, and overexertion.

At two manufacturing sites in Victoria, Australia, forklifts were separated to their own gangways. This reduced forklift and pedestrian interaction by one half. Speed limits and seat belts further improved safety (Horberry *et al.* 2004).

About 1 % of injuries and 5 % of all fatalities in German industries involved a fork-lift truck. Three out of four of those injuries were mainly caused by a driving error and one fourth by unauthorised driving. In one out of three fatalities, the forklift had tipped over sideways (Dicke 1997).

One major problem with forklift trucks is the limited visibility from their cab, especially if the load makes it difficult for the driver to see in front them. Separating forklifts and pedestrians to their own gangways is an effective way of increasing safety, particularly with automated forklift trucks.

CHAPTER TWELVE

CONSTRUCTION SITES

The construction industry is recognised as a sector with a great contribution to the economy of a country. Relating to building, repairing, renovating, and maintaining infrastructure, it is one of the most hazardous industries worldwide.

Safety Measuring and Inspection

The nature of work at construction sites (such as working at height and moving large volumes) and the required tools and equipment make the consequences of any accidents serious or even fatal. Reliable methods are needed for risk assessment and safety inspection.

One of the methods for assessing workplace conditions for occupational safety and health comprises an analysis of job loads and hazards. This Finnish innovation has four stages: identification of hazards, assessment of significance, suggestions for preventive measures, and follow-up. Occupational safety and health personnel and worker representatives use this method together to solve problems at construction sites (Mattila 1989). With the method, the participants managed to produce a higher number of preventive measures, in addition to which the organisational climate and safety could be improved (Mattila and Kivi 1991).

Mattila and Hyödynmaa (1988) applied a behaviour analysis approach at two Finnish construction sites to examine its effectiveness in improving occupational safety in the building sector. The injury rate was lower, and injuries were less serious at the experimental site than at the control site. The finding was later confirmed by a study in the veneer industry (Mattila 1990).

Mattila, Hyttinen and Rantanen (1994), in turn, observed fifteen site managers and sixteen other first-line foremen with the Operant Supervisory Taxonomy and Index (OSTI). The most effective foremen spent more time communicating with employees about non-work-related topics. They also had more discussion with their employees than the bureau supervisors (Hyttinen and Immonen 1994). Furthermore, based on the same data set, the researchers (Mattila, Rantanen and Hyttinen 1994) reported that the higher the safety index was, the lower the injury rate was. They also emphasized that management support was an essential element in ensuring safety.

Safety inspection is one way to improve safety at construction sites. A further Finnish innovation, the TR measuring method, is the same kind of safety management method for construction industries as the Tuttava method, discussed in Chapter Twelve, is for the manufacturing industries. The TR method is based on observations made by occupational safety inspectors, comprising twenty-seven items to be observed divided into seven groups:

– safety behaviour
– order and tidiness
– machine safety
– industrial hygiene
– ergonomics
– gangways, and
– first aid and fire safety.

A safety index is obtained by observing each item and marking it either "correct" or "incorrect," depending on whether the criteria of occupational safety are fulfilled or not (Laitinen *et al.* 1998).

When safety inspectors monitored 305 construction sites, with an average of 144 observations per site, the injury rate at the sites with the highest safety index was three times lower than at the sites with the lowest safety index (Laitinen, Marjamäki and Päivärinta 1999). Furthermore, when a supervisor and the employees' safety delegate made safety rounds once a week at two construction sites, the safety index at both sites rose by about 20 %, while the most visible change was an improvement in order and tidiness (Laitinen and Ruohomäki 1996).

Earlier, however, Cooper *et al.* (1993) had applied a psychologically based technique, reporting even better safety indexes (35 %) than those obtained by the "all-or-nothing" TR-method.

With the TR method as a measuring tool, a safety contest was organised between construction companies in southern Finland between 1997 and 2000. The safety index rose from 68 % before the competition to 88 % after the competition. It was estimated that 4,000 occupational injuries and three fatalities were prevented (Laitinen and Päivärinta 2010). Nykänen and his co-workers (2020) evaluated virtual-reality-based safety training and participatory human factors safety training with 119 Finnish construction employees. The virtual-reality-based training improved safety motivation more than mere lectures. The safety motivation after the human factors safety training was not significantly different from the conditions without this virtual training.

Auld *et al.* (2001) found that on-site safety inspections had no effect on injuries in the Alberta construction sites. However, the number of fatalities decreased at the sites. Mikkelsen, Spangenberg and Kines (2010), in turn, developed "Safe Workplace," a Danish version of the TR method and tested it in the Copenhagen Metro construction site. They found that the relative risk increased with the number of safety indicators that had been violated. In Hong Kong, the safety index at construction sites rose from 86 % to 93 % when a behaviour-based approach was used (Choudry 2014). Austin *et al.* (1996) observed seven American roof employees' safety performances and found that the intervention increased the safety index from 55 % to 80 % for work on the roof.

Europe, North America, Australia

As the construction industry contributes significantly to the Finnish national economy, many studies have been conducted on occupational safety in that sector. In 2014, the Finnish construction industry had the second highest injury frequency, after agriculture (Salminen 2014). In 2014, the injury frequency in this sector (sixty-three) was, thus, considerably higher than in many other sectors (such as transport and warehouse, forty-three) (Tynkkynen 2019).

Niskanen and Saarsalmi (1983) examined 215 injuries at Finnish construction sites and found that relatively more injuries occurred at sites for blocks of flats than for terraced houses. Niskanen (1985) reported that the incidence rate was four times higher among reinforcement employees than among painters. In minor injuries, the difference was fivefold. Niskanen and Lauttalammi (1989) analysed 422 injury reports from Finnish construction sites. The most hazardous phase in construction work was framework building, its proportion of injuries being 64 % at office and public building sites, 44 % at high-rise apartment-house sites, and 55 % at industrial sites.

The town of Kostomuksha in the former Soviet Union was built by Finnish construction workers from 1977 to 1985. The injury rate at this site was almost double (260 injuries / 1,000 employees) that of Finnish sites (126–149). However, injuries in this over-the-border project were less serious (Pekkarinen and Anttonen 1989).

Among the ninety-nine victims of serious occupational injuries in southern Finland, thirty-five victims worked in the construction industry.

They were better educated than victims from other industries. Falls from a height were the most typical injury at construction sites (Salminen 1995). Material handling caused one third of construction site injuries. These injuries were more often serious than other type of injuries at construction sites (Perttula *et al.* 2003).

A Finnish-driven Cochrane review (Lehtola *et al.* 2008) analysed 7,522 titles related to the prevention of injuries in the construction industry. Of these, four interrupted time-series studies and one controlled interrupted time-series study met the inclusion criteria. Among these, a safety campaign study and a drug-free-workplace study showed that both of these methods of injury prevention reduced the level and trend of construction injuries, whereas legislation was not effective in preventing such injuries.

Fredin, Gerdman and Thorson (1974) examined 321 disabled employees and seventy-four fatalities in the Swedish construction industry. Falls from a height, falls on the same level and falling objects were the main types of injuries. Over half of the victims had a piece-work contract.

Kines, Spangenberg and Dyreborg (2007) examined injuries at the Copenhagen Metro construction site in the 2000–2001 period. Sprains and strains accounted for one out of three injuries, whereas fractures caused the greatest proportion of long-term absences.

Based on data from the Spanish National Institute of Safety and Hygiene at Work, Camino Lopez *et al.* (2008) found 1,630,452 construction injuries between 1990 and 2000. Age, type of contract, time of injury, length of service in the company, company size and day of week related to the seriousness of injury. Later, Arquillos, Romero and Gibb (2012) analysed 1,163,178 construction injuries with the same data set. The results showed that the severity of injuries increased with age, that more fatalities occurred in larger companies, and that four out of five injuries involved employees with less than three-years' experience in the company.

Frickmann *et al.* (2012) examined 782 injuries at the construction site of the University Emergency Centre in Bern, Switzerland. Being hit by a moveable object was the most general injury type, and fracture was the diagnosis in over half of the injuries. Construction employees over sixty suffered more severe injuries.

Thuret *et al.* (2007) analysed a cohort of 12,788 French male construction employees over twenty-six years between 1974 and 1999. There was an increased risk of accidental falls, especially among skilled employees in roofing-installations and among unskilled masonry employees.

Larsson and Field (2002) examined construction injuries in Victoria, Australia. The major severe injury type was fall. The problems causing injuries were mainly related to equipment and tasks, and the risks of different occupational groups varied to a large degree.

Kumar (1991) analysed construction injuries (n = 58,903) in Alberta, drawing on data from Statistics Canada. Roofing, sheet metal and concrete work had the highest number of lost-time claim rates, whereas the most common cause of injury was overexertion, and the most frequent nature of injury was sprains and strains. The majority of lost-time injuries were experienced by employees below the age of thirty-five.

In the US, quite a few studies have been conducted on the occurrence of occupational accidents at construction sites. Culver, Marshall and Connolly (1993) analysed 359,765 construction site injuries in ten states from 1985 to 1988. The most usual injury types were sprains and strains, cuts and fractures, while the body parts that were hurt most often were back, lower extremities, and fingers. The injury rate decreased substantially as the length of service increased. Courtney, Matz and Webster (2002) analysed 35,790 construction industry claims to a workers' compensation insurer in 1996. The most frequently occurring types of injury were lower back pain, foreign body in the eye, and finger lacerations. Hinze and Russell (1995) showed that, based on the OSHA's database, falls, being struck by an object and shocks were the most general causes of fatalities in the US construction industry. Hunting *et al.* (1999) made a trade-specific analysis of 2,791 injured construction employees at the George Washington University Emergency Department. The results showed that eye injuries were typical among plumbers, falls from ladders among electricians and plumbers, falls on the same level among iron workers, electrical exposure, of course, among electricians, and amputations among carpenters. Thus, work tasks determine the types of injuries. Based on the National Health Interview Survey with 24,144 construction workers, Brown, Brooks and Xiuwen (2021) showed that an elevated risk of occupational injury occurred among younger, male, not college-educated, and blue-collar employees. In the Oregon construction industry, male and younger employees had the highest injury rate but injuries to older employees caused higher medical costs (Yang *et al.* 2020).

In New South Wales, Australia, the injury rate in the construction industry was more than double that of the all-industry average. The most frequent agencies of injuries were machinery and equipment and chemical substances, while the majority of diseases consisted of hearing losses (Ore 1992).

Asia, South America, Africa

The construction industry is the most hazardous industry in Kuwait, as 42 % of work-related fatalities occurred at the country's construction sites in 1996. The most general types of injuries were falling from a height, falling from wooden scaffolding, and objects falling from height, while the leading causes of injury were labour turnover, inadequate safety procedures, and improper cleaning (Kartam and Bouz 1998).

In Turkey, Colak, Etiler and Bicer (2004) examined 153 construction fatalities in the Kocaeli Province. Falling down from a height, vehicle accident and electrocution were the main causes of death.

In the South Delhi district, India, 145 construction employees died at the site between 1996 and 2002. The most common types of injury were falling from a height, being trapped inside a falling building, and being hit by a falling object. Ethanol was involved in 16 % of deaths (Rautji, Lalwani and Dogra 2005).

Ling, Liu and Woo (2009) found that forty construction fatalities had occurred in Singapore between June 2006 and May 2008. Falling from a height and being struck against objects were the main types of injury, whereas plastering and roofing were the most hazardous work tasks.

Wong (1994) examined 122 injured construction employees in Hong Kong. Falling from a height was related to injury severity, and safety hazards were identified in the work environment in 68 % of cases. A lack of formal education and safety training were risk factors of injury as well as current smoking.

In South Korea, Jeong (1998) found 3,028 fatalities and 125,929 non-fatal injuries in the construction industry from the official national statistics. The most typical injury was falling from a height, and the leading injury type was fracture. Older and temporary employees were victims of injuries and deaths more often than others.

Xia *et al.* (2000) reported 235 fatalities in the new development area near Shanghai, China, from 1991 to 1997. The main fatality antecedents were falls, collisions, being struck by/against something, electrocutions, and excavation cave-ins. Zheng *et al.* (2010) conducted a survey of 1,260 male construction employees in the cities of Wuhan and Maanshan in China. Collisions, cuts and falls were the most general types of injuries. Smoking and heavy alcohol drinking had no effect on occupational injuries, whereas safety education and depression were factors related to construction injuries.

Cheng *et al.* (2012) analysed 1,542 construction injuries in Taiwan. The main types of injuries were falls and collapses of objects, and males were victims in 96 % of the injuries.

In Indonesia, Ramdan *et al.* (2019) examined 105 employees at a hotel building site. Young and inexperienced employees who worked long hours and had less occupational health and safety knowledge experienced occupational injuries more often.

Based on the files of the National Insurance Institute in Israel, Pines, Halfon and Prior (1987) reported that falls, collisions with foreign bodies and falling objects were the main types of construction injuries, while contusions and open and superficial wounds were the most general natures of injury. Employees over sixty-five years had the highest risk of injury. Yanai *et al.* (1999) found 147 fatalities had occurred in Israel from January 1996 to July 1998. Two out of three fatalities occurred at construction sites and one out of five were industrial injuries.

Al-Sari and Al-Khatib (2012) sent a questionnaire to 349 construction employees in the southern West Bank of Palestine. Five out of six employees perceived their job as risky but one third had not experienced any work injury. The main causes of injuries were carelessness, lack of safety measures, and stress due to excessive overtime hours.

In Ilam, Western Iran, 387 construction workers were examined. The incidence rate was 8.2 injuries per 1,000 employees and 71 % of the injuries were fractures. Slipping and falling was the most important injury event, and the lack of surveillance by employers was an important factor related to injuries (Moradinazar *et al.* 2013). Khosravi and his co-workers (2014) conducted a review of fifty-six studies concerning construction site injuries. Based on a content analysis, they classified these studies into eight categories. The review stressed the contribution of distal factors like society, organisation, and project management to reducing such injuries.

Sarmiento-Salinas and his co-workers (2004) compared 385 Mexican construction employees who were involved in injuries to 385 injury-free employees. The differential factors in these groups were: age from 16 to twenty years, eventual insurance, and no training for the job.

Irumba (2014) analysed injuries at 201 large construction sites in Kampala, Uganda. The incidence rate was 37.97 per 1,000 employees and the fatality rate was 84.0 per 100,000 employees. Mechanical hazards were related to machines, and the most typical hazards were falling objects and falls from a height.

Risk Factors and Risk Groups

Studies concerning specific risk factors and risk groups in the construction industry are abundant in the US. McCann (2003) identified 339 personnel lift deaths from the CFOI database, 1992–1999. Falls, collapses and electrocutions were the main causes of death, and boom-supported lifts, suspended scaffolds, and scissor lifts were the main types of equipment involved. Later, McCann (2006) examined 253 heavy-equipment-related and truck-related deaths from the CFOI data. Rollovers were the main cause of death for heavy-equipment operators and struck by trucks for maintenance employees. Struck-by injuries caused one out of four fatalities in the OSHA data. The materials involved in these injuries were wooden wall, concrete block wall, and soil (Hinze, Huang and Terry 2005). Hinze and Teizer (2011) found 659 visibility-related fatalities among 13,511 OSHA-investigated cases in the US. Blind spots, obstructions and lightning were the most common factors contributing to vision-related fatalities.

Memarian and Mitropoulos (2013) examined 141 incidents in a large American masonry company over a period of three years. Overexertion, being struck by objects and contact with objects were the most frequent incident events, whereas block laying, material handling and scaffold erection were the main phases of work related to injury. Labourers had a significantly higher injury rate than masons.

Furthermore, Suruda, Smith and Baker (1988) analysed 306 construction fatalities due to trench cave-ins based on OSHA investigations from 1974 to 1986. Most of the deaths occurred in shallow trenches, young employees and those in small companies being the most at risk. Suruda (1992) examined 129 deaths in construction painting in the US. The main causes of death were electrocutions and asphyxiation from solvents, and the risk of death was the highest in companies with fewer than ten employees.

Based on the National Traumatic Occupational Fatalities (NTOF) data from 1990 to 1994, Chen and Fosbroke (1998) showed that the highest fatality rate was among electrical-power installers, structural-metal employees and operating engineers. Among carpenters in Ohio and North Carolina, nail gun injuries caused 3.9 % of workers' compensation claims. These injuries were concentrated in framework employees, and hands and fingers were the most often injured parts of body (Dement *et al.* 2003). Fredericks *et al.* (2005) conducted a survey of forty-eight roofing companies in Michigan, of which twenty-four completed the survey. The results showed that the most frequent injuries were hand and finger injuries due to cutting operations and back injuries due to manual material handling.

Lipscomb, Schoenfisch and Cameron (2013) examined 24,830 carpenters working in Washington State, of whom 21 % reported hand injuries. Carpenters aged forty years or older had more amputations, fractures, and multiple injuries but fewer contusions and cuts than younger ones.

In Spain, an analysis of 235,853 minor injuries in the Spanish construction industry in 2000 showed that the highest risk factors were projection of fragments and being struck by objects. These were the most specific mechanisms of injury in the subgroup of bricklayers and unskilled construction employees (Benavides *et al.* 2003). Pérez-Alonso and his co-workers (2012) found 180 injuries in the greenhouse-construction industry in Spain during the 1999–2007 period. Cuts, punctures and contact with hard material were the most typical injuries, and the eyes, thorax, and back were the most affected parts of the body.

Tüchsen and Hannerz (2004) compared living in building-site camps and daily commuting from home to sites at the Great Belt Bridge construction sites in Denmark. Living at camps was safer than daily commuting as staying at sites eliminated commuting injuries.

At Turkish construction sites, there were 168 fatal traffic accidents and 206 fatal construction equipment injuries. The leading reasons for construction equipment fatalities were equipment fall-over, runover by equipment, and being caught between equipment elements. Falls, contact with electricity, and falling objects were the main types of fatalities (Gürcanli, Müngen and Akad 2008).

In Taiwan, almost three out of four fatalities on the construction sites occurred on rainy days (Liao and Perng 2008).

Subcontracting is also one of the risk factors in the construction industry. Quinlan (1999) wrote that many studies showed a high injury rate among self-employed workers. Johnstone, Mayhew and Quinlan (2001) found that, in a review of twenty-nine studies, twenty-three studies showed negative occupational health and safety outcomes from outsourcing. In their review of twenty-five studies, Quinlan and Bohle (2008) found that 92 % of the studies showed poorer occupational health and safety outcomes. Eleven studies showed unanimously that subcontracting increased the risk of injury. Salminen *et al.* (1993) have shown that subcontractors' employees had a higher risk of injury than the employees of the main contractors. Mayhew and Gibson (1996) interviewed 500 self-employed builders in Queensland, Australia. They found a mismatch between the builders' perceptions of hazard exposures and their injury patterns. A poor understanding of occupational health and safety legislation was one of the risk factors for subcontractors. Mayhew, Quinlan and Ferris (1997) interviewed 255 subcontracting employees, of which thirty-one worked in the construction industry in Australia. As self-employed, they experienced more economic and time pressures, wherefore they took fewer days off after injury than salary employees. Further, the production planning and organisation of activities by the subcontracted companies were additional factors for falls on a Brazilian construction site (Jackson *et al.* 2012).

The research dealt with in this chapter demonstrates that falling from a height is the most frequent and most dangerous type of occupational accident for both injuries and fatalities. Struck by an object, hit by a falling object, and sprains and strains are also common types of accidents. Everywhere in the world, the most typical injuries at construction sites are fractures and wounds on the hands and back. Regular safety inspections can improve tidiness and order at construction sites, thus, reducing the risk of occupational injuries and fatalities.

CHAPTER THIRTEEN

TRANSPORT AND COMMUTING

Road traffic is a significant cause of work-related injuries and fatalities. One hour during commuting is on average more hazardous than one hour in the workplace (Salminen and Lähdeniemi 2001). Three Finnish data sets also indicate that traffic injuries during working hours are more serious than commuting injuries (Salminen 2003).

The first study on work-related road traffic fatalities was done in Australia from 1982 to 1984, indicating that 39 % of fatalities at work occurred on public roads (Harrison, Mandryk and Frommer 1993). Later, 1989–1992, the proportion dropped to 30 % (Mitchell, Driscoll and Healey 2004). In the late 1980s, work-related crashes caused 27 % of all occupational fatalities in the US (Miller 1995). In 2005, the proportion was 43 % (Pegula, Marsh and Jackson 2007). One half (50 %) of occupational fatalities in Finland were due to traffic crashes (Salminen 2000). In France, road accidents accounted for 40 % of work-related fatalities (Charbotel, Martin and Chiron 2010). In Spain, occupational transportation caused 38 % of work-related fatalities in 2002 (Peirò-Pèrez *et al.* 2006). In New Zealand, work-related traffic crashes accounted for 29 % of all work-related fatal injuries (McNoe, Langley and Feyer 2005). Further, a comparison of three countries showed that motor vehicle traffic deaths accounted for 16 % of deaths in New Zealand, 22 % in the United States, and 31 % in Australia (Driscoll *et al.* 2005). An analysis of data sets from thirty-four countries showed that occupational fatalities are strongly related to deaths on roads but not to personality characteristics (Lajunen 2001).

Risk Groups

Professional drivers had the highest injury incidence of work-related traffic in Sweden (Bylund, Björnstig and Larsson 1997). In Denmark, the rate of injury-related hospital contacts among male truck drivers was no higher than that of other drivers (Shibuya *et al.* 2008).

In Australia, transport employees and car drivers were the most frequent victims of work-related crashes (Boufous and Williamson 2006; 2009).

Larger heavy vehicle companies in Australia had poorer claim rates than smaller companies (Mooren *et al.* 2014).

In the US, transportation-related occupations and extraction occupations had the highest fatal motor vehicle rate among men (Loomis 1991). Moreover, truck drivers had the largest number of work-related fatalities between 1975 and 1999 (Lyman and Braver 2003) and between 2003 and 2008 (Chen, Amandus and Wu 2014). The death rate of truck drivers in Wisconsin was nine times higher than that of other drivers (Karlson and Baker 1978). The most dangerous companies in the US trucking industry were small companies (Moses and Savage 1996). Younger, inexperienced and male truck drivers were involved in crashes among truck drivers in Oregon (McCall and Horwitz 2005).

Emergency medical technicians in the US were involved in transportation-related injury five times more often than the national average (Maguire 2011). The risk of fatal occupational highway fatality increased among drivers over sixty-five between 1992 and 2000 (Janicak 2003).

British company car drivers were more likely to actively cause collisions than other drivers (Clarke *et al.* 2009).

French managers were at a lower risk of injury crash involvement than unskilled employees (Lenguerrand *et al.* 2008) and professional drivers had the highest risk of crashing in France (Fort *et al.* 2016).

Sawmill employees living in the countryside in British Columbia, Canada, were involved in motor car crashes more often than their colleagues living in urban areas (Ostry *et al.* 2009). Unskilled laborers suffered two out of three deaths that occurred on the roads in Turkey (Müngen and Gürcanli 2005).

Amorim *et al.* (2012) interviewed 267 professional mototaxi drivers in the city of Feira de Santana, Brazil. The risk factors for crashes included muscular fatigue in the lower limbs and musculoskeletal complaints. Da Silva *et al.* (2012) found that alternation of work shift and speeding increased the risk of motorcycle injuries in southern Brazil.

Mini-bus taxi-drivers in Addas Ababa, Ethiopia, reported one crash per year, on average (Mamo, Newnam and Tulu 2014). Employees in the transportation industry were naturally more often involved in work-related crashes than employees in other industries.

Fatigue and Sleepiness

A review of twenty-five epidemiological studies showed that fatigue and sleepiness were consistently related to an increased risk of work-related traffic injuries (Robb *et al.* 2008).

Among Australian truck drivers, solo drivers experienced more fatigue during several five-to-six-day roundtrips than drivers in two-up crews (Hartley *et al.* 1994). Occupational demands and imperturbability predicted the traffic injuries of Australian truck drivers (Hartley and El Hassani 1994). A telephone interview of 301 drivers in Sydney, Australia, showed that work was a common reason for sleep loss before fatigue-related accidents (Newnam *et al.* 2016) and this concerned crashes five times more often, especially among shift-workers (Fell and Black 1997). Also, in Australia, work-related crashes were less likely to involve alcohol, with drivers being fatigued or driving overspeed more often than in crashes by leisure-time drivers (Mitchell, Bambach and Friswell 2014). Tiredness, not using the seat belt and excessive speed were the risk factors of crashes among occupational light-vehicle drivers in New South Wales, Australia (Stuckey *et al.* 2010). Further, in New South Wales, work-related fatigue-involved crashes occurred around dawn, whereas non-fatigue crashes were concentrated in peak-hour traffic (Williamson and Boufous 2007).

Little sleep and a rush to get to work were the most important risk factors in traffic among basic healthcare professionals in Leon, Spain (Diez-Juárez, Naviero-Rilo and Pérez-La Orden 2013).

A questionnaire study of 1,121 Finnish drivers showed that male drivers fell asleep at the wheel 2.5 times more often than female drivers (Radun and Radun 2008). A questionnaire study of 683 Finnish professional drivers showed that the risk of fatigue was highest among those drivers who were not allowed to choose the time of their breaks (Perttula, Ojala and Kuosma 2011). When the job duty period exceeded twelve hours, the injury risk was doubled (Brown 1994).

An interview study of 160 truck drivers at the gates of Haifa and Ashdod ports indicated that poor sleep quality and frequent difficulties finding a parking space when tired were related to crashes (Sabbagh-Ehrlich, Friedman and Richter 2005). An analysis of fatal commercial motor vehicle collisions in Kentucky, US, showed that drivers who were fatigued or fell asleep were twenty-one times more likely to be involved in a fatal collision (Bunn *et al.* 2005).

Among drivers of the Gothenburg Public Transport Company, Sweden, those with obstructive sleep apnoea were involved in traffic injuries more often than those without sleep problems (Karimi *et al.* 2013).

Among study subjects in the GAZEL data set, it was found that sleepy driving and phone use during driving decreased soon after retirement (Bhatti *et al.* 2008).

Safety climate and occupational stress predicted fatigue-related near misses among Australian company drivers (Strahan, Watson and Lennon 2008).

Mobile Phone Use

Using a mobile phone while driving is a big issue in the area of traffic safety. It increases the risk of collision fourfold (Redelmeier and Tibshirani 1997), sixfold (Violanti and Marshall 1996) or even ninefold (Violanti 1998). It also increased the collision risk among trucks drivers (Fowles, Loeb and Clarke 2013). Mobile phone use and other types of in-vehicle distraction caused 2 % of road fatalities in England and Wales (Stevens and Minton 2001).

Brookhuis, de Vries and de Waard (1991) tested different ways to use mobile phones and found that handsfree phones give drivers better possibilities to control driving than handheld phones. On the other hand, using handsfree mobile phones had a negative effect on drivers' reaction time on a rather straight road (Alm and Nilsson 1994).

Reactions slowed down under mobile phone distractions especially among drivers over fifty (McKnight and McKnight 1993; Alm and Nilsson 1995). Overall, casual conversation did not disturb driving (Briem and Hedman 1995).

In Australia, in 1997, 12 % of mobile phone users reported road accidents (Chapman and Schofield 1998). In a Finnish study (Lamble *et al.* 1999), using a mobile phone while driving impaired brake reaction time by 0.5 s and time-to-collision by 1 s. Another Finnish study with 6,121 respondents showed that men, younger persons and respondents with mental symptoms had experienced more close calls and accidents than other drivers (Korpinen and Pääkkönen 2012).

With new technology, it has become possible to use a car as a mobile office (Eost and Flyte 1998), which is likely to cause further safety hazards.

Haigney and Westerman (2001) have presented a critical review of the application of experiments and conversational tasks when examining the effects of concurrent mobile phone use on driving performance. They point out that it is problematic to draw conclusions about real traffic situations in this way. However, my view is that the use of mobile phones increases the risk of accidents, whereas handsfree systems make is possible to better control traffic situations.

Other Risk Factors

Apart from fatigue and sleepiness and mobile phone use, work-related traffic injuries are also influenced by many other factors in the workplace.

Injuries at work were strongly related to the traffic injuries of medical staff members in Germany (Kirkcaldy, Trimpop and Cooper 1997). Occupational stress predicted occupational injuries among company car drivers in the United Kingdom (Cartwright, Cooper and Barron 1996). Also, absence from work predicted crashes of British bus drivers (af Wåhlberg and Dorn 2009).

Among 317 Finnish male truck drivers, 11 % were involved in a crash because of thinking about work while driving (Salminen 2008a). Risk factors for Australian heavy vehicle drivers included attending to cargo and working alone (Jones, Ibrahim and Ozanne-Smith 2011). Among Finnish sales and marketing and construction employees, driving fast and using mobile phones were risk factors in work-related traffic (Salminen and Lähdeniemi 2002).

In Norway, accident data showed that excessive speed, failure to use the seat belt, and insufficient information gathering were the most important risk factors of work-related driver fatalities (Naevestad, Phillips and Elvebakk 2015).

Based on the French GAZEL cohort, it was shown that uncomfortable positions at work were a risk factor for commuting injuries among women (Chiron *et al.* 2008). In the Rhône area, France, difficulties with superiors, imposed tasks and carrying heavy objects were risk factors for traffic injuries. Time pressure among French drivers was not related to injuries reported (Coeugnet *et al.* 2013).

The safety climate did not predict the number of crashes among Australian drivers (Wills, Watson and Biggs 2009). In American companies, a low level of safety climate was related truck drivers' crashes (Swedler, Pollack and Agnew 2015).

Improving Safety in Work-related Traffic

Various solutions have been figured out to improve safety in traffic. Roche Australia implemented a traffic safety programme with the following four steps (Murray, White and Ison 2012):

– driver risk assessment
– policy development
– process and outcomes, and

– continuous review of policies.

Newnam *et al.* (2011), in turn, introduced an occupational driver scale including four dimensions: speeding, violation, inattention, and driving while tired. The scale has been tested with Australian drivers and shown to be a reliable and valid measure. Later, Newnam and Oxley (2016) developed the Safety Management for the Occupational Driver programme, which is partly based on 360-degree feedback and leadership coaching at the top level of the company.

Naveh and Marcus (2007) examined forty American trucking companies applying the ISO 9002:1994 certification. Their drivers crashed less often than drivers from companies not using the certification.

In Norway, Njå, Bjelland and Braut (2015) applied internal control principles to work-related traffic, taking into consideration the ISO 39001:2012 "Road Traffic Safety Management Systems and Companies." A Delphi study with thirty-six managers showed that they needed to recognise their own need for managing traffic safety. Darby, Murray and Raeside (2009) concluded that British transportation companies should build a safety culture that includes the attitudes and behaviour of drivers.

In Australia, Murray and Watson (2010) identified a "work drive effect," where a driver can spread the traffic safety habits and attitudes from the workplace to homes and neighbourhoods. Similarly, we found in Finland that employees who learn traffic safety principles from professional safety experts can apply them to leisure-time driving (Salminen 2008b).

The aim of the discussion method is to improve road safety in companies. It was originally based on Lewin's (1947) classical social psychological experiment. Subsequently, Misumi (1989) conducted three experiments on group discussions at Japanese shipyards.

In road traffic, the discussion method has been used in a large Swedish telephone company with about 40,000 employees, of whom 15,000 drove company cars (Gregersen, Brehmer and Morén 1996). Of these drivers, 900 were divided into four test groups, whereby members in one group met three times to discuss problems in work-related traffic. The greatest decrease in the number of accidents was found in the driver training and in the discussion group. When injury costs were calculated, the group discussion method was ranked as the most effective of them all. The method requires no external consultants and is, thus, advantageous to the company.

In a Finnish study, 172 electricians participated in three discussion sessions. In the first round, they identified 183 problems in work-related traffic. In the second round, they made 594 suggestions to solve these problems. In the final round, they committed themselves to fifty-three changes in their own traffic behaviour. In the eight-year follow-up period, the number of work-related traffic injuries decreased by 72 % (Salminen 2008b).

The above examples demonstrate that it is possible to reduce work-related traffic injuries with "soft" methods.

All in all, the great number of studies conducted indicates that a large amount of interest has been shown in work-related traffic injuries and their prevention in different countries. However, more research is needed as the number of road fatalities is still at a high level.

CHAPTER FOURTEEN

MINES

Mining is responsible for nearly 8 % of occupational fatalities worldwide (Mainardi 2005), being one of the most hazardous work environments. For example, in Spain, mining had an incident ratio 5.5 times higher than that of the total economic sector (Sanmiquel *et al.* 2010). Based on an analysis of twelve industrial and developing economies, Mainardi (2005) showed that fatal injuries in mining have decreased with increasing levels of development and private investment rates.

In their review of literature, Bennett and Passmore (1984) concluded that younger miners had a much higher rate of disabling injuries than older ones. Experienced miners had a lower risk of fatal injuries than inexperienced colleagues. Small mines were more hazardous than large ones. Although this review is rather old, the observations still hold true.

Based on the data set of the Mine Safety and Health Administration, Kecojevic *et al.* (2007) found that the equipment used in American mines caused 37 % to 88 % of mining fatalities. The most common types of equipment involved were haul trucks, belt conveyors and front-end loaders. Inexperienced mine employees had the highest risk of injury.

In Australian mines, there were 162 fatalities between 1989 and 1992. Travelling for work purposes, obtaining minerals, and maintenance tasks were the most common activities at the moment of death. The most common mechanism of fatal injury was being hit by a falling object during a roof collapse (Mitchell *et al.* 1999). Shephard and Kahler (2004) identified 342 drill and blast injuries in the open-cut mines in Queensland and Western Australia. The most common types of accidents were falls of miners, falls of objects, and lifting. The most typical types of damaging energy were fires on drill rigs and collisions with vehicles.

In our study of ninety-nine severe injuries in Finland, one fatality had occurred at an underground construction site, when a roof collapsed on one of the workers (Salminen 1997).

In Turkey, the Zonguldak area holds 95 % of all the coal reserves of the country. Kucuker (2006) found 164 fatalities there between 1994 and 2003. Subsidence caused almost one half and railway injuries one fifth of the fatalities, while methane poisoning caused one out of ten fatalities. Onder (2013) analysed non-fatal injuries in Turkish coal mines. The typical victim was a maintenance employee in the thirty-five to forty-four age group working in a surface plant and being injured to the lower extremities by machinery.

Ghosh, Bhattacherjee and Chau (2004) undertook a case-control study of 202 coal miners with at least one injury and 202 controls (with no injuries). The results showed that injuries were associated with older age, poor perception of work conditions, poor work environment, and emotional instability. Later, the same research group (Bhattacherjee *et al.* 2007) conducted a survey of 516 French coal miners. There were strong relationships between injuries and the number of job tasks, face work, poor health, and psychotropic drug use. Kunar and Bhattacherjee (2006) also compared eighty-two Indian coal miners with at least one injury with eighty-two miners without injuries. Injuries were associated with diseases, alcohol consumption, overtime work, and no-formal-education. In addition, Kunar, Bhattacherjee and Chau (2008) interviewed 245 male underground coal miners with injuries and 330 controls (without injuries) in southern India. Handling materials, poor working conditions, and geological hazards were associated with injuries.

Stojadinovic and his co-workers (2012) conducted a follow-up study on coal mine injuries in Serbia from 2000 to 2009. They found 5,850 injuries, of which only sixteen were fatal. Morning-shift miners and the youngest miners had the highest injury rate.

Mining is a vital part of the economy and work life in many African countries. In Zambia, for example, mining is of great importance for foreign exchange earnings (Miller *et al.* 2006), about 15 % of formally employed employees work in metal mining (Michelo, Brätveit and Moen 2009). Copper in particular is a significant contributor to Zambia's economy. During a period of two years, 120 injuries and twenty fatalities were registered in four Zambian copper mines. The highest injury frequency was observed in underground departments, and falling rock caused most of the fatalities (Michelo, Båtveit and Moen 2009). Kunda, Frantz and Karachi (2013) conducted a survey of 202 underground mine employees in the Mopani mines in Kitwe. Four out of ten miners were injured with at least one injury, and electricians and mechanics reported the highest injury frequency.

In Zimbabwe, Chimamise and others (2013) compared 156 miners with injuries to 156 miners without injuries. Severe occupational injuries were associated with working underground, having targets per shift, inadequate personal protective equipment, and working more than eight hours per shift.

Elenge, Leveque and de Brouwer (2013) undertook a survey of 180 miners in the Lupoto mine in the Province of Katanga, the Democratic Republic of Congo. Three out of four miners were involved in injuries. Tools handling accounted for almost one half of injuries, followed by handling heavy loads, and falls.

Paul and Maiti (2008) compared 175 underground coal miners (with at least one injury) with 200 controls (without injury) in eastern India. The results showed that job dissatisfaction had a positive relationship to work injury and safe work behaviour had a negative relationship to work injury. Social support decreased the risk of injury.

In China, there were an average of 1,238 coal mine fatalities every year in the period from 2002 to 2011 (Yu and Chen 2013). Cui *et al.* (2015) interviewed 3,618 mine employees who suffered 137 injuries in the Shanxi province. The risk factors for mine injury were male gender, young and old age, heavy physical job, working in the underground frontline, short experience of shift work, and extroversion. Zhang and his co-workers (2016) analysed 320 coal mine injuries in the Shandong province. They found that unsafe conditions of rules and regulations affected almost all injuries. Unsafe behaviour of the operator was a significant contributing factor for injuries.

In the Swedish mining industry, subcontractor miners had 1.7 times more injuries than mining company employees in 1989. Injuries to subcontractors were also more serious. Moreover, injuries to subcontractor employees were not officially recorded at that time (Blank *et al.* 1995).

In the Spanish energetic mining industry, young miners under forty had a higher risk of injury, while older miners experienced serious injuries more often. Small mines with less than ten employees had the greatest risk of injury, and injuries in small mines were also more often serious (Sanmiquel, Freijo and Rossell 2012).

Despite the progress that has been achieved in reducing mining injuries and fatalities, mines are still among the most hazardous workplaces. A strong employee-related contributing factor for mine injuries is inexperience. On the other hand, older miners experience higher rates of fatal injuries. These findings are in line with findings in other fields. (Salminen 2004b).

It is obvious that underground mines are more hazardous than surface mining sites. The greatest hazards, however, are obviously found in unofficial mines, although no research data is available thereon.

CHAPTER FIFTEEN

FORESTRY

Forest work is among the most hazardous kinds of work. In the 1990s, the fatality rate of loggers in Australia was forty-nine times higher than that of all workers (Driscoll *et al.* 1995) and in New Zealand it was twenty-nine times higher than that of the whole workforce (Marshall *et al.* 1994a) and nineteen times higher than that of all silviculture workers (Marshall *et al.* 1994b). In the US, the fatality rate of forestry workers was twenty-two times higher than that of the entire employed population overall (Toscano and Windau 1994).

Efforts have been made to reduce the risks for loggers by training and the use of personal protectors. Several studies conducted in Finland, for instance, have proved the effectiveness of personal protectors. Nowadays, such protectors are widely used by professional forest workers.

Wood processing is an important industrial sector in many countries. The forest sector is also an important source of employment. In the 1980s, in Finland, the use of personal protectors was found to decrease the risk of injury by one half—compared with loggers using no protectors (Klen 1985). Later, however, a questionnaire of 1,200 forest workers revealed no reduction in injuries due to personal protectors (Klen 1997). A further questionnaire study of 1,194 loggers then confirmed the result of the first study, showing that safety boots prevented the greatest number of injuries compared to other protectors (Klen and Väyrynen 1984).

A questionnaire study of 228 Finnish loggers showed that the main causes of injuries were losing one's balance, a small flying object, and the chainsaw. The mechanisation of logging operations and the increased use of personal protectors decreased the injury rate of loggers by 54 % from 1986 to 1994 (Salminen, Klen and Ojanen 2001). Based on the same data set, Klen and Ojanen (1998) found considerable concordance between self-reported injuries and company records. Furthermore, Väyrynen and Könönen (1991) organised rehabilitation courses for Finnish loggers with lower back pain. Using the OWAS observation system, they presented new and better work techniques to the participants.

In Sweden, forestry has been studied from many different sides. Sundström-Frisk (1975) found that two out of three loggers used forbidden methods, because these methods were faster. Later, she (Sundström-Frisk 1984) showed that changing from piece-rate wages to time-based wages decreased the injury frequency by one third. Johansson, Rask and Stenberg (2010) made a review of thirty-one studies on piece-rate wages on safety. The vast majority of the studies showed that piece rate had a negative effect on health and safety. Larsson (1988b) found 687 severe occupational injuries among forestry workers in 1983. Fractures, lacerations and amputations were the most typical injuries. Between 1970 and 1990, the injury frequency for chainsaw operators dropped to one half and that for logging-machine operators to two thirds. In addition, vibration-induced white finger, caused by chainsaws, was reduced (Axelsson 1998). Neely and Wilhelmson (2006) conducted a survey of 156 self-employed forestry workers. About 40 % of them had been involved in injuries during the previous twenty-four months and half of them did not use full safety gear. Among those who made firewood for homes, men over fifty most often suffered injuries (Lindroos *et al.* 2008).

In British Columbia, Canada, loggers paid by piece did not have more injuries than their colleagues on salaries, but they had severe injuries more often (Mason 1976/1977). Later, Salisbury *et al.* (1991) found eighty-seven fatalities in British Columbia from 1981 to 1987. The risk factors for fatalities were lack of work experience and young age. Paques, Massé and Bèlanger (1989) examined 1,164 accidents of 1,342 employees in eight Quebec sawmills. One out of four injuries occurred while wood was blocked or jammed. These situations often led to padlocking. Laflamme and Cloutier (1988) showed that the injury risk at mechanised forest sites was only one third of that at conventional sites. Maintenance and repair work caused most of the injuries in mechanised sites. In British Columbia, there is a mandatory certification for tree-fallers. However, McLeod *et al.* (2015) found that this certification failed to reduce the risk of work injury among loggers.

New Zealand is one of the countries where a large number of studies has been done on injuries in the forest industry. Approximately 90 % of New Zealand's 1,239,000 ha of plantation forests has been planted in Pinus radiata (Kirk and Parker 1994). Gaskin, Smith and Wilson (1988) interviewed 299 loggers and found that felling, trimming and skid work were the most hazardous forest jobs. One out of four logging injuries occurred on skid sites (Bentley *et al.* 2002) and almost half of the injuries were chainsaw cuts to the leg (Sullman *et al.* 1999). Gaskin and Parker (1993) also conducted a questionnaire survey of 225 forest workers in New Zealand. The loggers considered that felling, trimming and landing work were the most hazardous logging tasks.

Further, in New Zealand, Bentley, Parker and Ashby (2005) analysed 351 lost-time injuries, among which one out of four occurred in felling. Inexperienced forest employees had the greatest numbers of injuries. The leading cause of death in forestry was contact with falling trees (Marshall *et al.* 1994b). One out of three injuries for both loggers and silviculture employees were caused by chainsaw (Kawachi *et al.* 1994). Later, Kawachi, Marshall and Cryer (1995) analysed 351 chainsaw injuries of loggers between 1979 and 1988. The most typical types of injury were injuries to hand, leg, feet and arm. Lilley *et al.* (2002) made a survey to 367 forest workers. Lost-time injuries were associated with the length of time at work, ethnicity, and near-miss injury events. A review written by Slappendel *et al.* (1999) showed that studies made in New Zealand focused on tasks involving chainsaws, such as felling and delimbing. Felling seems to be the most hazardous job in forest work in New Zealand.

The forestry and paper industries accounted for 2 % of Australia's GDP in the early 1990s. Almost one in a thousand loggers died in timber work from 1989 to 1992 (Mitchell *et al.* 2001). Crowe (1986) examined 452 hardwood injuries in southeastern and western Australia. While fallers accounted for one third of the loggers, they suffered two out three injuries. The researcher also found an association between a high level of productivity and a high level of injuries and regarded piece rate as a major obstacle to safety measures.

In the US forest industry, falling objects, motor vehicles, and machinery were the leading causes of fatalities (Myers and Fosbroke 1994). Two out of three victims of 780 logger fatalities were tree fallers (Scott 2004). In Wisconsin, occasional woodcutters had injuries three times more often than professional loggers (Fischer *et al.* 2005). Doyle and Conroy (1989) found sixty-two chainsaw injuries in Ireland in 1986. The main risk groups were farmers, self-employed loggers and domestic users.

In China, there were 4,499 nonfatal injuries and 105 fatalities among forest workers between 1980 and 1991. The highest number of injuries and fatalities occurred in the northeastern Jilin Province, where a stroke to the head caused most fatalities, whereas most nonfatal injuries were to the lower extremities (Wang, Bell and Grushecky 2003).

Enez, Topbas and Acar (2014) interviewed 378 Turkish loggers. The injury risk increased when handling chainsaws, using hookaroons and when smoking. It was also affected by the number of breaks and experience. Melemez (2015) interviewed fifty forest professionals (loggers, managers and professors) in the Western Black Sea region in Turkey. These professionals estimated that the main causes of forest fatalities were personal factors and organisational factors.

CHAPTER SIXTEEN

FISHING AND SEAFARING

In 2020, the number of people working in fishing worldwide amounted to around 37.88 million. Alongside forest, mining and construction work, fishing is one of the most dangerous occupations. In Finland, for instance, the risk of fatality in fishing was about 100 times higher than in all occupations. Foundering, fires and explosions, and wrecking caused the greatest number of fatalities. Falling overboard and going missing were the major causes of death (Wagner 2003).

In Iceland, there were 3,282 fishermen in 2005. Among them, fatalities decreased from twenty-three to one or two from 1980 to 2005. The most common causes of fatalities were foundering of the vessel, man overboard, and falling into the harbour (Petursdottir, Hjoervar and Snorrason 2007). Based on the Daysy database, for the years 1991–1996, Bull, Riise and Moen (2001) found 707 injuries among Norwegian fishers, eight of which happened to women. The highest injury rate was found in the twenty to twenty-nine age group. The most typical injuries were bruises and cuts, and the most frequent injury events were falls.

In France, one out of three injuries in fishery occurred when the vessel was in port. Loading and unloading from and to vessel were among the major tasks causing injuries, while maintenance and processing the catch caused most of the injuries. The major risks were falls and excessive efforts (Le Bouar and Chauvin 2006).

Perez-Labajos *et al.* (2006) analysed the distribution of injuries of the Spanish fishing fleet from 1994 to 2002. The highest injury rate was found among fishing boats operating from the Canary Islands and Catalonia.

Lawrie *et al.* (2003) sent a postal questionnaire to 2,170 Scottish fishermen, of whom 1,157, or 57 %, responded. One out of five fishermen had received medical treatment at sea and skippers and deckhands were most often mentioned. One third of injuries were blows to the back.

In Portugal, there were 476 non-fatal fishing injuries in 2002 to 2003. Antäo *et al.* (2008) interviewed seventy-three fishermen involved in injuries in the region of Lisbon and the Tagus River valley. "Macho attitude" or "risk-taking behaviour" contributed to their injuries.

Frantzeskou *et al.* (2012) conducted a questionnaire study with 100 Greek fishers, among whom there were seven females. One out of four fishers had been involved in injuries and one out of seven had experienced near-drowning. Four out of five fishers were overweight. Norrish and Cryer (1990) found seventy-nine fatalities in the New Zealand fishing industry, 1975–1984. The fatality rate was highest on the western coast, where many fishing ports are situated near river or harbour bars that are extremely hazardous to cross in rough weather.

Being situated between two oceans—the Pacific and Atlantic Oceans—commercial fisheries provide an important source of employment for North America. In Alaska, Schnitzer, Landen and Russell (1993) found 278 fatalities among 45,000 fishermen from 1980 to 1988. The fatality rate was highest in February and lowest during the summer months. Most of the victims were Caucasian men. Later, Lucas *et al.* (2014) found 712 work-related injuries during the twelve years from 2001 to 2012. The fatal injury rate in the freezer-trawlers was almost double that of freezer-longline vessels. Most of injuries in the trawlers occurred in factories and freezer holders, whereas the majority of injuries in longline vessels occurred on deck.

On the West Coast (California, Oregon and Washington), the fatality rate of commercial fishing was double that of the whole country. The Northwest Dungeness crab fishery had the highest fatality rate (Lincoln and Lucas 2008). Later, Lucas, Woodward and Lincoln (2013) found eight fatalities and twenty-seven work-related injuries in the southern shrimp fleet operating in the Gulf of Mexico and the Atlantic coast from Florida to North Carolina. Injuries involving a winch drum had a very much higher risk of fatality than injuries involving a winch cathead. Most of injuries were to the wrist and 13 % to the back.

Hasselback and Neutel (1990) found eighty-four fatalities among 31,415 fishermen on the Atlantic coast of Canada. Young fishers under thirty-five were at the highest risk of death. On the West coast of Canada, Brooks, Howard and Neifer (2005) examined 130 fishermen who died from immersion in British Columbia, 1976–2002. Underlying causes of drowning were cold shock, swimming failure, and hypothermia. The majority of drownings occurred in water below 15°C.

Neto, Cordeiro and Haddad (2005) interviewed ninety-two fishermen from the Medium Araguiaia River region, Brazil, of whom fifty-six reported a work-related injury. The biggest age group was between thirty-one and fifty years of age. Most of victims had over ten years of work experience

Driscoll *et al.* (1994) examined forty-seven fatalities among Australian fishermen from 1982 to 1984. Two thirds of decedents drowned, 13 % died from physical trauma, and sharks killed two fishermen. Bad weather, non-seaworthy vessels, inadequate use of personal rescue devices, and inexperience were associated with these fatalities.

Zytoon (2012) interviewed 686 fishermen in the El-Maaddiya fisher port in Egypt. Two out of three fishermen reported bruises caused by falling to the surface. Men working in trawlers had a higher rate of amputations than others.

Besides fishing, merchant seafaring also comprises many elements that could lead to occupational accidents, injuries and fatalities. Jensen *et al.* (2004a) carried out a questionnaire study to 6,461 seafarers from eleven countries. About 9 % of the subjects had been involved in injuries. Younger seafarers and non-officers in long tours had a higher risk of injury than others. Long working hours alone were not related to injuries. The same research group (Jensen *et al.* 2004b) showed, in a questionnaire study with 1,068 seafarers from Finland, Denmark, the Philippines, Croatia and Spain, that a work week longer than seventy hours increased the risk of injury.

In British merchant shipping, there were 835 traumatic fatalities for 1,136,427 seafarer-years. Over half of them were caused by injuries, fifty-five by suicide, and seventeen by homicide. The fatality rate among seafarers was sixteen times higher than in the general workforce (Roberts and Marlow 2005). A decade later, the fatality rate was twenty-one times higher than in the general British workforce. However, the highest fatality rate in merchant shipping was found among Swedish, Norwegian and German seafarers (Roberts *et al.* 2014).

Among Finnish seafarers, the injury frequency has been even lower than that of the whole wage-earning population. This may be due to the fact that there are many passenger ferries operating in Finland, which is also why women have been involved in about 40 % of the injuries. In the late 1980's, half of the injuries were directly connected to the working environment, such as a slippery deck (Saarni 1989). Saarni *et al.* (1996) analysed mortality among 942 Finnish sea pilots in the period from 1956 to 1985. Cardiovascular and ischaemic heart diseases were the most general causes of death, while violence, injuries and poisoning caused every tenth death. Halme (1992) examined the injury rate in six Finnish stevedoring companies and found it to be rather high (146/1,000 employees). Falling, sprains and squeezing of the leg were the most typical injuries among stevedores.

In Sweden, Larsson and Lindquist (1992) examined 223 deceased seafarers from 1984 to 1988. Traumatic fatalities accounted for one half of the deaths, while the rest were related to diseases. The most common causes of fatalities were drowned during work, disappearing at sea, and falling on board.

Jensen *et al.* (2005) conducted a questionnaire study to 6,896 seafarers from eleven countries and 6,461, or 93.7 %, responded. Almost half of their injuries (n = 467) were related to slips, trips and falls. The risk of STF injuries increased gradually with age, and the deck of the passenger ship was the place with the highest risk of STF injury.

Hansen *et al.* (2008) analysed 943 injuries of 11,786 seafarers on Danish ships. The results showed that the injury rate of East Asian seafarers (mainly from the Philippines) was one third of that of seafarers from the Western countries. There were 1,336 sea farers on Danish non-passenger merchant ships. Western European seafarers had a higher injury frequency than their colleagues from Eastern Europe, Southeast Asia and India. Western seafarers had back injuries more often (Àdàm *et al.* 2014).

As for injuries at sea outside of Europe, seafarers in Japan, for instance, were involved in injuries five times more often than employees in other industries. In 2000, there were 1,522 injuries at sea in Japan. Capsizing was the most frequent cause of injuries in both foreign- and domestic-trade vessels, whereas catch handling caused most of the injuries in fishing vessels (Hisamune *et al.* 2006).

Nielsen (1999) found 123 deaths on ships sailing under the flag of Hong Kong. The decedents were from thirteen countries, and the largest groups were from India, the People's Republic of China, and the Philippines. Maritime disasters caused over one half of deaths and illnesses caused one in six deaths, whereas one out of ten deaths were due to occupational injuries.

The factors affecting the injury and fatality risks of fishers and seafarers are slightly different. Vessel sinking and disappearance at sea are more frequent among fishers. Catch handling, on the other hand, causes minor injuries. "Macho attitude" or "risk taking behaviour" often contribute to injuries among fishermen.

Ship crews are often more multinational than fishing vessel crews. The highest injury rates are found among Western European seafarers and the lowest among Filipino seafarers. Long work weeks of over seventy hours increase the number of their injuries.

Even if safety at sea has improved considerably over the last decades, maritime disasters still happen, though this is rare. The sinking of the passenger ferry Estonia, in 1994, while crossing the Baltic Sea, was one of the worst maritime disasters of the twentieth century, with over 800 lives lost.

PART IV

MIGRATION AND CLIMATE CHANGE

CHAPTER SEVENTEEN

(IM)MIGRANT WORKERS' PLIGHT

Migration is a basic element of history. However, the more recent phenomenon of globalisation obviously explains the fact that concurrently with the decrease in the number of occupational fatalities in Europe and the US, the number of injuries increased from 1998 to 2001 in Asia and South America (Hämäläinen 2009). Similarly, occupational injuries have decreased in Western countries but increased in countries such as China and India as manufacturing industries have moved from industrialised countries to developing countries (Salminen and Seo 2015).

In 1995, the US National Safety Council reported that the highest work death rate was found in South Korea, followed by Guatemala and Zimbabwe. According to the OECD statistics between 1993 and 1998, the average annual incidence of fatal accidents was twelve times higher in South Korea (highest incidence) than in the UK (lowest incidence) (Nishikitani and Yano 2008). Although no longer part of the developing world, South Korea still has high rates of occupational injuries.

Nasrullah, Laflamme and Khan (2008) analysed the World Health Organization's (WHO) statistics for the two-year period 1996–1997. For men but not for women, the gross domestic product (GDP) was negatively correlated with accidental falls in the OECD countries. When rising standards of living led to safer technologies and better working conditions in industrialised countries, the more hazardous kinds of work were moved to developing countries. This is what has happened with ship-dismantling, for instance. At such work sites, there are often toxic chemicals and asbestos, while workers are breaking the ships with gas blowtorches and sledgehammers without proper protection.

This situation has, however, been changing further over the last few decades. With baby boomers reaching retirement age, Western countries need more immigrant and migrant workers in agriculture, food-processing, construction, manufacturing, healthcare, and low-wage services to ensure the productivity and the functioning of society. Many studies have suggested a higher occupational injury frequency among immigrant workers, which could considerably reduce their contribution to society.

The problem with comparisons between different countries is that occupational injuries and even fatalities are not only underreported but are also registered in different ways in different countries (Jacinto and Aspinwall 2004). In Finland, for instance, companies report injuries very extensively as they receive monetary compensation for the sick leaves of their injured employees. In Germany, the injury statistics are based on a sample of 10 % of all injuries.

The earliest study on immigrants and work-related injuries was carried out by Collins (1959). It was implemented at a naval shipyard in Singapore and revealed that non-citizens died from injuries three times more often than citizens. More recently, Carangan, Tham and Seow (2004) analysed a data set of 1,244 local and 1,936 foreign employees who had attended emergency departments. The results showed that foreign employees had one and a half times higher injury rate than native employees. However, most of the foreign employees in Singapore evaluated the safety training that they had received as sufficient (Ong, Habibah and Lee 2006).

The high occupational injury rate among immigrant workers is also a big issue in the European work life.

In Germany, Arndt *et al.* (2004) analysed mortality among 19,943 male construction employees between 1986 and 2000. They found that foreign-born employees were killed by falling objects significantly more often than German employees. Kyobutungi *et al.* (2006) analysed 34,393 ethnic German immigrants (*Aussiedler*) from the former Soviet Union moving back to North Rhine-Westphalia to determine their mortality from external causes. They found that male immigrants had a 39 % higher accident mortality than native Germans, while no difference was found among females.

In the Netherlands, the injury-related mortality was higher among males, but not females, in ethnic minorities compared to native employees (Stirbu *et al.* 2006).

In Helsinki, Finland, immigrant bus drivers had a lower rate of occupational injuries than native Finnish drivers (Salminen, Vartia and Giorgiani 2009). This suggests that immigrant workers can work as safely as native workers, when their working conditions and job contracts are at the same level as those of their native colleagues.

Salvatore *et al.* (2013) analysed the Italian Labour Force Survey, which comprised 148,221 interviews. They found that immigrant male employees had a higher injury rate than native Italian male employees, especially in the construction industry. Among women, there was no difference between immigrants and native Italians.

Guldenmund, Cleal and Mearns (2013) sent a questionnaire to 1,000 employees in a Danish logistics company and 327 of them responded. The results showed that immigrants had a higher injury rate than native Danes.

In the US, the first study in this field, conducted among immigrant farm employees in California, found that their injury rate was three times higher than among native American farmers (Fuentes 1974). More recently, Loh and Richardson (2004; Richardson 2005) analysed the data set of the Bureau of Labor Statistics and found that foreign-born employees had a 44 % higher fatality rate than native employees. Based on the National Health Interview Survey with 389,912 interviewed persons, Sinclair, Smith and Xiang (2006) showed that foreign-born employees were more likely to be injured than US-born employees. However, based on the same data set, 1997–2005, Zhang *et al.* (2009) found that foreign-born employees had a lower injury rate than US-born employees. The researchers gave no explanation for these contradictory results. Byler (2013) showed that the fatality rate among Hispanic/Latino employees was higher than among other employees and that foreign-born Hispanic employees had a higher fatality rate than their native-born colleagues. However, no difference was found in injury rates between Latino and non-Latino employees on horse farms (Swanberg *et al.* 2013).

In Canada, injuries to immigrants have been examined by Thurston and Verhoef (2003), who made a survey of 532 immigrant employees in Alberta. They found that immigrant employees were involved in occupational injuries 70 % more often than the workforce as a whole. Furthermore, immigrants who had arrived recently in Canada had a lower rate of both industrial injuries and fatalities. They had superior educational skills compared to the Canadian-born population (Tiagi 2015).

In some Asian countries, the proportion of foreign-born employees in the labour force is very high.

Al-Arrayed & Hamza (1995) found that, in Bahrain, the proportion of foreign-born employees in labour-intensive jobs was 60 % and foreign employees had a three times higher injury rate than native employees. In the city of Al-Khobar, Saudi Arabia, immigrant employees were injured four times more often than Saudi employees, who accounted for only 1.5 % of all injuries (Al-Dawood 2000). In the United Arab Emirates, 614 occupational injury hospitalisations were registered between March 2003 and April 2005 at the trauma hospital in the city of Al Ain. Foreign employees accounted for 96 % of injuries, whereas their proportion of the workforce was only 69 % (Barss *et al.* 2009). Moreover, immigrants from the Indian subcontinent suffered 73 % of injuries caused by falling objects (Grivna, Eid and Abu-Zidan 2015).

In Qatar, the injury rate of Nepalese, Indian and Filipino employees was many times higher than that of the Qatari employees (Al-Thani *et al.* 2015). In Kuwait, immigrants suffered 92 % of occupational injuries, whereas the proportion of Kuwaiti employees of these injuries was 8 % (Al-Kandary and Al-Waheeb 2015). However, in Lebanon, there was no significant difference between Lebanese and foreign-born employees in the severity of work injuries (Nuwayhid *et al.* 2003), nor was there any significant difference in the injury rate in Taiwan between Taiwanese employees and foreign employees (Wu *et al.* 1997).

In Malaysia, Indian immigrants had a three times higher injury rate than Malay employees (Abas *et al.* 2011). In South-Korea, immigrant employees were involved in occupational injuries two times more often than Korean employees (Cha and Cho 2014). According to a systematic review of nineteen articles, immigrants in China had a higher injury and fatality rate than Chinese employees. High-risk occupations for immigrant employees were found in the construction and manufacturing industries and in small mining companies (Fitzgerald *et al.* 2013).

In Australia, employees born overseas had a slightly higher fatality rate than the native population (Corvalan, Driscoll and Harrison 1994). On the other hand, based on the Multi-Purpose Household Survey, with 36,702 respondents, Reid and her co-workers (2014) showed that Australian-born employees had a higher injury rate than foreign-born employees. Precarious work, cultural factors and demands of production influenced the degree to which incidents were reported.

The first review of the injury rate of immigrants was published by Bollini and Siem (1995). They found four studies showing that immigrants had a two times higher injury rate than native employees. They explained this by the overrepresentation of immigrants in dangerous jobs. According to my review (Salminen 2011) of seventy-two studies on injuries of immigrant employees, the risk of occupational injury was two times higher for immigrant employees than for native employees. This conclusion was based on the results of thirty-one studies. In addition, a review of four American studies showed that foreign-born employees had more injuries than US-born employees (Argeseanu Cunningham, Ruben and Narayan 2008).

Apart from injuries, immigrants also suffer workplace violence. Sincavage (2005) found that the workplace homicide rate of foreign-born Asian employees was almost three times higher than that of native-born Asian employees. In Denmark, Hogh *et al.* (2011) conducted a survey of 3,109 healthcare employees; "non-Western" immigrants experienced bullying more often than Danes.

Moreover, interviews with safety experts in the Netherlands showed that immigrants had problems in communication and level of education, in addition to which they experienced difficulties with cultural differences, specific employment situations and cooperation with contractors (Schubert and Dijkstra 2009). According to an interview of 240 healthcare professionals, the main problems of immigrant employees in sixteen European countries were language barriers, social deprivation and traumatic experiences (Priebe *et al.* 2011).

In Canada, Premji, Messing and Lippel (2008) reported immigrants' problems in understanding their safety managers' advice, based on interviews with twenty-five immigrant employees in a garment factory in Montreal. According to another study, immigrants performed physically demanding work and worked in shifts more often than Canadian-born employees (Smith and Mustard 2010).

Machinery and hand tools were the most typical reasons for injury among Hispanic employees in the US (Forst *et al.* 2010). Fernández-Esquer *et al.* (2015) interviewed 327 Latino day labourers in the Houston area, Texas, and found that a higher education increased the risk of occupational injury.

Based on the 2010 Migrant Workers' Health and Safety Survey in Korea, Lee *et al.* (2015) analysed the results of 486 Korean Chinese migrant employees (*Chosŏnjok*). Poor health status, dissatisfaction with their job, physical and chemical hazards, and longer stay in Korea increased the risk of occupational injury.

In Taiwan, foreign employees had jobs with a high risk of occupational injuries more often than native employees (Cheng and Wu 2013).

To sum up, numerous studies conducted in different countries and continents show that immigrant and migrant employees have a higher injury rate than native employees. However, in some countries (including Finland), the injury rate of immigrant employees was found to be at the same level as among native employees. This suggests that if immigrants have the same working conditions as native employees, they are able to perform their work duties as safely as natives.

Another important finding is that, in contrast to men, there is no significant difference between immigrant and native employees among women. This may be due to the fact that when working in factories immigrant women often have lighter jobs than men, thus, having a lower injury risk. Another explanation could be that immigrant women often work as household servants or in other jobs with a low risk of injury. However, women may experience harassment the workplace.

One obvious reason for the higher injury rates of immigrant employees is the language barrier. Immigrants often fail to fully understand the guidance and warnings given by their boss. There are also cultural differences in the interpretation of warnings. In Finland, efforts have been made to overcome these difficulties by using a great deal of pictures when giving guidance to employees on work safety issues.

CHAPTER EIGHTEEN

UNDER THE CLIMATE THREAT

Climate change is increasing the average temperatures and leading to more frequent high-temperature extremes, such as heatwaves. This affects our health and also our safety at work. In several countries, many health problems and even deaths have been reported among outdoor workers. In addition, employees working in workplaces without air-conditioning suffer workplace-heat-related illnesses during the warmest season (Kjellstrom *et al.* 2017). High temperatures also weaken road traffic safety (Liang *et al.* 2022), which may be due to the fact that drivers are not able to keep up their concentration when it gets extremely hot.

On average, women have a 20 % smaller body mass but have greater body insulation than men. Under heat stress, women suffer higher skin temperature with greater body heat storage. On the other hand, women have a greater risk of cold injury (Burse 1979). A study with twenty-two healthy adults showed that both genders experienced thermal stress in laboratory conditions. However, women felt worse and were more stressed compared to men (Schoesch *et al.* 2021). Exposure to temperature extremes is one of the conditions for sudden-onset injuries, which means a momentary exchange between an agent and host (Keyserling and Smith 2007).

According to a meta-analysis of twenty-two original studies, both hot (over 32°C) and cold (below 10°C) temperatures have a negative impact on performance (Pilcher, Nadler and Busch 2002). Another meta-analysis of thirty-eight field studies with 2,409 outdoor workers indicated that the warming of climate considerably affects physical work capacity, which applies especially to manual work (Ioannou *et al.* 2022).

According to a systematic review of literature, with twenty-eight selected studies, increased temperature is positively correlated with trauma admissions, distal radius fractures being more sensitive to weather conditions than hip fractures (Ali and Willett 2015). In Finland, the risk of children´s forearm shaft fractures was 50 % higher on dry summer days than on rainy days. Temperature had no effect on these fractures (Sinikumpu *et al.* 2013).

Choi *et al.* (2022) analysed compensation claims in South Korea in 2017–2018 and found that high temperatures increased the risk of injury among construction employees. Non-permanent employees in particular suffered at the temperature of 33°C or higher in outdoor jobs.

In Uppsala, Sweden, high temperatures and rain cause no increases in the risk of accidents for low-speed buses. However, temperatures higher than those generally occurring in Sweden may have an influence on bus accidents (af Wåhlberg 2008).

Xianglong *et al.* (2018) examined 680 bus drivers from the Harbin public transport company in China. Young and novice drivers and drivers who drove long periods without breaks had more negative moods during high temperatures. High temperature is also one of the main causes of hazardous chemical accidents in China. Most of these injuries are caused by human errors during the hot season, aggravated by climate change (Wang, Li and Wu 2020).

In Melbourne, Australia, a significant positive association was found between temperature and occupational injuries. Male and young employees and employees engaged in heavy physical work were at increased risk of injury on hot days (McInnes *et al.* 2017). In Adelaide, southern Australia, a 1°C increase in the maximum temperature range was associated with a 0.2 % increase in daily injury claims. Temperature influenced the injury rate in agriculture, construction, finance, electrical and outdoor employees (Xiang *et al.* 2014; Xiang *et al.* 2015). Based on data from workers' compensation claims (224,631), the researchers found that the risk of work-related injuries increased when the outside temperature rose over 25°C. Extreme high temperatures were associated with a 30 % increase in claims.

Jay and Brotherhood (2016) analysed twenty-nine reports from different parts of Australia. The worst heat stress was experienced in military-related activities when marching with heavy loads was required in temperatures often exceeding 39.5°C. Heat stress was also experienced in sheep shearing, deep underground mining, and bushfire fighting.

In Sydney and Perth, Australia, heat exposure is expected to considerably increase respiratory disease hospitalisation costs between the 2010s and the 2050s, which also affects work life (Tong *et al.* 2022). Busch (2011) found three organisational capabilities necessary to adapt to climate change in Australian and Swiss electric utilities: climate knowledge absorption; climate-related operational flexibility; and strategic climate integration.

Moreover, climate change is expected to increase exposure to pesticides and disease vectors in facility management jobs as well as exposure to bioaerosols, soil-borne pathogens, UV radiation, and disinfectants (Lan *et al.* 2022).

The Trade Unions have recently required the European Commission to set a limit for maximum outside temperatures for working outside (Helsingin Sanomat 2022).

In addition to hot temperatures, cold weather has its effects on injuries. Hassi *et al.* (2000) analysed 72,716 mining injuries in seven US states. When temperature decreased, injury rates increased, especially for slip and fall injuries. In Japan, Inaba *et al.* (2005) compared forty-six female cold-storage employees to 115 other employees in the same company. About 70 %–80 % of cold-storage employees suffered cold sensations in different body regions, whereas other employees experienced cold sensations only in their feet. Haman and his co-workers (2022) showed that hypothermia is a risk in cold weather and that body mass plays a key role in mitigating the risks of hypothermia.

In conclusion, hot weather is clearly a risk factor in occupational injuries, especially for outdoor workers. However, there are no exact threshold temperatures at which hot weather becomes a health hazard. Any hazards are also influenced by other factors, such as air humidity. In addition, there are obviously individual differences in reactions to hot weather.

If temperatures keep rising in the future, risks in the world of work will increase. Although it might be possible to avoid extreme heat exposure for outdoor workers by working at night, this might increase risks of injury due to darkness and tiredness.

Concluding Remarks

In my own studies and in the studies I have presented in this book, the traditional approach to safety at work has mostly been applied, including accident and injury reporting, analyses of causes and risk factors, and tools for safety improvement. As a reaction to the persistently high rates of occupational accidents and injuries, there have also been new more proactive research approaches in the last two decades. These approaches seek to understand the ability of employees to adapt to problems and pressures as an alternative way to improve the level of safety in the workplace. This has been seen as necessary as the performance and productivity demands have increased and production systems have become more complex and, thus, more difficult to manage.

Traditionally, the aim has been to identify causes for accidents and injuries by searching for failures in work environments and procedures, employee behaviour and qualities, and the ways in which work has been organised. The objective of safety management has been to react to accidents that have happened and try to find ways to avoid or eliminate the risks behind them. The new way to examine safety problems is to look at how safety is achieved in everyday workplace actions when people adjust to varying workplace conditions in different ways. The starting point, here, is that adjustable and resilient employees make things go right.

In this context, the concept of resilience has been useful. On an individual level, it refers to the ability of an individual to bounce back from adversity, uncertainty, and risk of failure, and to adapt to changing and stressful life demands (Newman *et al.* 2014; Salminen 2018). Resilience engineering primarily looks at safety in the workplace. Its idea is that safety depends on how employees act in order to avoid injuries (Carayon *et al.* 2015). Furthermore, it focuses on how individual employees cope with complexity under pressure to achieve successful results (Wehbe, Al Hattab and Hamzeh 2016).

It seems worthwhile to combine these two ways of approaching safety at work. Both of them are needed as accidents still can and do happen. The keys to occupational safety are held by all those who apply the available safety information and methods to improve the safety of employees.

Bibliography

Abas, Adinegara Bin Lutfi; Said, Abdul Razzak Bin Mohd; Mohammed, Mohammed Azman Bin Aziz; Sathiakumar, Nalini. "Non-fatal occupational injuries among non-governmental employees in Malaysia". *International Journal of Occupational and Environmental Health* 17 (2011): 38–48.

Abbe, Omosefe O.; Harvey, Craig M.; Ikuma, Laura H.; Aghazadeh, Fereydoun. "Modeling the relationship between occupational stressors, psychosocial/physical symptoms and injuries in the construction industry". *International Journal of Industrial Ergonomics* 41 (2011): 106–117.

Ádám, Balázs; Rasmussen, Hanna Barbara; Pedersen, Randi Nørgaard Fløe; Jepsen, Jørgen Riis. "Occupational accidents in the Danish merchant fleet modelling". *Toxicology* 9 (2014): 35.

af Wåhlberg, Anders E. "If you can't take the heat: Influences of temperature on bus accident rates". *Safety Science* 46 (2008): 66–71.

af Wåhlberg, Anders E.; Dorn, Lisa. "Absence behavior as traffic crash predictor in bus drivers". *Journal of Safety Research* 40 (2009): 197–201.

Aggazzotti, Gabriella; Righi, Elena; Patorno, Elisabetta; Fantuzzi, Guglielmina; Fabiani, Leila; Giuliani, Anna Rita; Grappasonni, Iolanda; Petrelli, Fabio; Ricciardi, Walter; La Torre, Giuseppe; Sciacca, Salvatore; Angelillo, Italo; Bianco, Aida; Nobile, Carmelo; Gregorio, Pasquale; Lupi, Silvia; Perlangeli, Vincenza; Bonazzi, Chiara; Laviola, Francesco; Triassi, Maria; Iorfida, Evelina; Montegrosso, Sara; Rivosecchi, Paola; Serra, Maria Cristina; Adorisio, Eugenio; Gramiccia, Alessandra; Mura, Ida; Castiglia, Paolo; Romano, Gabriele; Poli, Albino; Tardivo, Stefano. "Work-related injuries in young workers: an Italian multicentric epidemiological survey". *Annali dell Instituto Superiore di Sanita* 42 (2006): 69–75.

Al-Arrayed, A.; Hamza, A. "Occupational injuries in Bahrain". *Occupational Medicine* 45 (1995): 231–233.

Al-Dawood, Kasim. "Non-fatal occupational injuries requiring admission to hospitals in Al-Khobar City, Saudi Arabia: Prospective cohort study". *Croatian Medical Journal* 41 (2000): 323–326.

Ali, A.M.; Willett, K. "What is the effect of the weather on trauma workload? A systematic review of the literature". *Injury* 46 (2015): 945–953.

Al-Kandary, Nadia; Al-Waheeb, Salah. "Patterns of accidental deaths in Kuwait: a retrospective descriptive study from 2003–2009". *BMC Public Health* 15 (2015): 302.

Allen, Harris M.; Slavin, Thomas; Bunn, William B. "Do long workhours impact health, safety, and productivity at a heavy manufacturer?". *Journal of Occupational and Environmental Medicine* 49 (2007): 148–171.

Alleyne, B. C.; Stuart, P.; Copes, R. "Alcohol and other drug use in occupational fatalities". *Journal of Occupational Medicine* 33 (1991): 496–500.

Alm, Håkan; Nilsson, Lena. "Changes in driver behaviour as a function of handsfree mobile phones – a simulator study". *Accident Analysis & Prevention* 26 (1994): 441–451.

Alm, Håkan; Nilsson, Lena. "The effects of a mobile telephone task on driver behaviour in a car following situation". *Accident Analysis & Prevention* 27 (1995): 707–715.

Al-Sari, M.I.; Al-Khatib, I.A. "Workers' safety in the construction industry in the southern West Bank of Palestine". *Eastern Mediterranean Health Journal* 18 (2012): 1028–1033.

Al-Thani, Hassan; El-Menyar, Ayman; Consunji, Rafael; Mekkodathil, Ahammed; Peralta, Ruben; Allen, Katharine A.; Hydar, Adrin A. "Epidemiology of occupational injuries by nationality in Qatar: Evidence for focused occupational safety programmes". *Injury, International Journal of the Care of the Injured* 46 (2015): 1806–1813.

Amorim, Camila Rego; de Araújo, Edna Maria; de Araújo, Tania Maria; de Oliveira, Nelson Fernandes. "Acidentes de trabalho com mototaxistas". *Revista Brasileira de Epidemiologica* 15 (2012): 25–37.

Amra, Babak; Dorali, Reza; Mortazavi, Salehe; Golshan, Mohammad; Farajzadegan, Ziba; Fietze, Ingo; Penzel, Thomas. "Sleep apnea symptoms and accident risk factors in Persian commercial vehicle drivers". *Sleep and Breathing* 16 (2012): 187–191.

Antão, P.; Almeida, T.; Jacinto, C.; Guedes Soares, C. "Causes of occupational accidents in the fishing sector in Portugal". *Safety Science* 46 (2008): 885–899.

Arch, Elizabeth C. "Risk-taking: A motivational basis for sex differences". *Psychological Reports* 73 (1993): 3–11.

Argeseanu Cunningham, Solveig; Ruben, Julia D; Narayan, Venkat K.M. “Health of foreign-born people in the United States: A review”. *Health & Place* 14 (2008): 623–635.

Arlinghaus, Anna; Lombardi, David A.; Willetts, Joanna L.; Folkard, Simon; Christiani, David C. “A structural equation modeling approach to fatigue-related risk factors for occupational injury”. *American Journal of Epidemiology* 176 (2012): 597–607. (a)

Arlinghaus, Anna; Lombardi, David A.; Courtney, Theodore K.; Christiani, David C.; Folkard, Simon; Perry, Melissa J. “The effect of rest breaks on time to injury – a study on work-related ladder-fall injuries in the United States”. *Scandinavian Journal of Work, Environment & Health* 38 (2012): 560–567. (b)

Arndt, V.; Rothenbacher, D.; Daniel, U.; Zschenderlein, B.; Schubert, S.; Brenner, H. “All-cause and cause specific mortality in a cohort of 20 000 construction workers; results from a 10-year follow up”. *Occupational and Environmental Medicine* 61 (2004): 419–425.

Arquillos, Antonio Lopez; Romero, Juan Carlos Rubio; Gibb, Alistair. “Analysis of construction accidents in Spain, 2003–2008”. *Journal of Safety Research* 43 (2012): 381–388.

Auld, M. Christopher; Emery, J.C. Herbert; Gordon, Daniel V.; McClintock, Douglas. “The efficacy of construction site safety inspections”. *Journal of Labor Economics* 19 (2001): 900–921.

Austin, John; Kessler, Maria Lynn; Riccobono, John E.; Bailey, Jon S. “Using feedback and reinforcement to improve the performance and safety of a roofing crew”. *Journal of Organizational Behavior Management* 16 (1996): 49–75.

Axelsson, Sven-Åke. “The mechanization of logging operations in Sweden and its effect on occupational safety and health”. *Journal of Forest Engineering* 9 (1998): 25–31.

BaHammam, Ahmad S.; Alkhunizan, Muath A.; Lesloum, Rabea H.; Alshanqiti, Amer M.; Aldakhil, Abdulrahman M.; Pandi-Perumal, Seithikurippu R.; Sharif, Munir M. “Prevalence of sleep-related accidents among drivers in Saudi Arabia”. *Journal of Thoracic Medicine* 9 (2014): 236–241.

Baidwan N.K.; Gerberich S.G.; Kim H.; Ryan A.D.; Church T.R.; Capistrant B. “A longitudinal study of work-related injuries: comparisons of health and work-related consequences between injured and uninjured aging United States adults”. *Injury Epidemiology* 5 (2018): 35.Bamberger, Peter A. “Work-based critical incidents and problem drinking”. *Work and Occupation* 32 (2005): 257–289.

Barnes, Christopher M.; Wagner, David T. "Changing to daylight saving time cuts into sleep and increases workplace injuries". *Journal of Applied Psychology* 94 (2009): 1305–1317.

Barss, Peter; Addley, Ken; Grivna, Michal; Stanculescu, Cristina; Abu-Zidan, Fikri. "Occupational injury in the United Arab Emirates: epidemiology and prevention". *Occupational Medicine* 59 (2009): 493–498.

Bauerle, Timothy J.; McGonagle, Alyssa K.; Magley, Vicki J. "Mere overrepresentation? Using cross-occupational injury and job analysis data to explain men's risk for workplace fatalities". *Safety Science* 83 (2016): 102–113.

Bauza, Alain M.; Emami, Parisa; Son, Jung H.; Langer, Paul; Zarbin, Marco; Bhagat, Neelakshi. "Work-related open-globe injuries: demographics and clinical characteristics". *European Journal of Ophthalmology* 23 (2013): 242–248.

Bellamy, Linda J.; Aneziris, Olga N. "Comparison of occupational accident risks and underlying causes between temporary and non-temporary workers". *Safety Science Monitor* 19 (2015): 2–3.

Belville, Renate; Pollack, Susan H.; Godbold, James H.; Landrigan, Philip J. "Occupational injuries among working adolescents in New York State". *Journal of American Medical Association (JAMA)* 269 (1993): 2754–2759.

Bena, Antonella; Giraudo, Massimiliano; Leombruni, Roberto; Costa, Giuseppe. "Job tenure and work injuries: a multivariate analysis of the relation with previous experience and differences by age". *BMC Public Health* 13 (2013): 869.

Benavides, Fernando G.; Giraldez, M.T.; Castejon, E.; Catot, N.; Zapiana, M.; Delclos, J.; Benachi, J.; Gimeno, D. "Análisis de los mecanismos de producción de las lesiones leves por accidents de trabajo en la construccion en España". *Gaceta Sanitaria* 17 (2003): 353–359.

Benavides, Fernando G.; Benach, J.; Muntaner, C.; Delclos, G.L.; Catot, N.; Amable, M. "Associations between temporary employment and occupational injury: what are the mechanisms?". *Occupational and Environmental Medicine* 63 (2006): 416–421.

Bendak, Salaheddine. "12–h workdays: current knowledge and future directions". *Work & Stress* 17 (2003): 321–336.

Bennett, J.D.; Passmore, D.L. "Correlates of coal mine accidents and injuries: A literature review". *Accident Analysis & Prevention* 16 (1984): 37–45.

Bentley, Tim A.; Parker, Richard J.; Ashby, Liz. "Understanding felling safety in the New Zealand forest industry". *Applied Ergonomics* 36 (2005): 165–175.

Berecki-Gisolf, Janneke; Clay, Fiona J.; Collie, Alex; McClure, Roderick J. "Predictors of sustained return to work after work-related injury or disease: Insights from workers' compensation claims records". *Journal of Occupational Rehabilitation* 22 (2012): 283–291.

Berecki-Gisolf, Janneke; Smith, Peter M.; Collie, Alex; McClure, Roderick J. "Gender differences in occupational injury incidence". *American Journal of Industrial Medicine* 58 (2015): 299–307.

Bhattacherjee, A.; Chau, N.; Sierra, C.O.; Legras, B.; Benamghar, L.; Michaely, J.-P.; Ghosh, A.K.; Guillemin, F.; Ravaud, J.-F.; Mur, J.-M.; Lorhandicap Group. "Relationships of job and some individual characteristics to occupational injuries in employed people: a community-based study". *Journal of Occupational Health* 45 (2003): 382–391.

Bhattacherjee, Ashis; Bertrand, Jean-Pierre; Meyer, Jean-Pierre; Benamghar, Lahoucine; Otero Sierra, Carmen; Michaely, Jean-Pierre; Ghosh, Apurna Kumar; d'Houtaud, Alphonse; Mur, Jean-Marie; Chau, Nearkasen; Lorhandicap Group. "Relationships of physical job tasks and living conditions with occupational injuries in coal mines". *Industrial Health* 45 (2007): 352–358.

Bhatti, Junaid A.; Constant, Aymery; Salmi, L-Rachid; Chiron, Mireille; Lafont, Sylviane; Zins, Marie; Lagarde, Emmanuel. "Impact of retirement on risky driving behavior and attitudes towards road safety among a large cohort of French drivers (the GAZEL cohort)". *Scandinavian Journal of Work, Environment and Health* 34 (2008): 307–315.

Biron, Michal; Bamberger, Peter A.; Noyman, Tamir. "Work-related risk factors and employee substance use: Insights from a sample of Israeli blue-collar workers". *Journal of Occupational Health Psychology* 16 (2011): 247–263.

Blackburn, Justin; Levitan, Emily B.; MacLellan, Paul A.; Owsley, Cynthia; McGwin, Gerald. "A case-crossover study of risk factors for occupational eye injuries". *Journal of Occupational and Environmental Medicine* 54 (2012): 42–47.

Blanch, Angel; Torrelles, Blai; Aluja, Anton; Salinas, José Antonio. "Age and lost working days as a result of an occupational accident: A study in a shiftwork rotation system". *Safety Science* 47 (2009): 1359–1363.

Blank, Vera L.G.; Andersson, Ragnar; Lindén, Arvid; Nilsson, Britt-Christine. "Hidden accident rates and patterns in the Swedish mining industry due to involvement of contractor workers". *Safety Science* 21 (1995): 23–35.

Boden, Leslie I.; Galizzi, Monica. "Income losses of women and men injured at work". *Journal of Human Resources* 38 (2003): 722–757.

Bollini, Paola; Siem, Harald. "No real progress towards equity: health of migrants and ethnic minorities on the eve of the year 2000". *Social Science and Medicine* 41 (1995): 819–828.

Boufous, Soufiane; Williamson, Ann. "Work-related traffic crashes: A record linkage study". *Accident Analysis & Prevention* 38 (2006): 14–21.

Boufous, Soufiane; Williamson, Ann. "Factors affecting the severity of work related traffic crashes in drivers receiving a worker's compensation claim". *Accident Analysis & Prevention* 41 (2009): 467–473.

Bourgkard, Eve; Wild, Pascal; Massin, Nicole; Meyer, Jean-Pierre; Otero Sierra, Carmen; Fontana, Jean-Marc; Benamghar, Lahoucine; Mur, Jean-Marie; Ravaud, Jean-François; Guillemin, Francis; Chau, Nearkasen; Lorhandicap Group. "Association of physical job demands, smoking and alcohol abuse with subsequent premature mortality: A 9–year follow-up population-based study". *Journal of Occupational Health* 50 (2008): 31–40.

Brede, Emily; Mayer, Tom G.; Gatchel, Robert J. "Prediction of failure to retain work 1 year after interdisciplinary functional restoration in occupational injuries". *Archives of Physical Medicine and Rehabilitation* 93 (2012): 268–274.

Breslin, F. Curtis; Tompa, Emile; Zhao, Ryan; Pole, Jason D.; Amick, Benjamin C. III; Smith, Peter M.; Hogg-Johnson, Sheilah. "The relationship between job tenure and work disability absence among adults: A prospective study". *Accident Analysis & Prevention* 40 (2008): 368–375.

Briem, Valdimar; Hedman, Leif R. "Behavioural effects of mobile telephone use during simulated driving". *Ergonomics* 38 (1995): 2536–2562.

Brookhuis, Karel A.; de Vries, Gerbrand; de Waard, Dick. "The effects of mobile telephoning on driving performance". *Accident Analysis & Prevention* 23 (1991): 309–316.

Brooks, Chris J.; Howard, K.A.; Neifer, S.K. "How much did cold shock and swimming failure contribute to drowning deaths in the fishing industry in British Columbia 1976–2002?". *Occupational Medicine* 55 (2005): 459–462.

Brorsson, Bengt. "Age and injury severity". *Scandinavian Journal of Social Medicine* 17 (1989): 287–290.

Brown, Ivan D. "Driver fatigue". *Human Factors* 36 (1994): 298–314.

Brown, Samantha; Brooks, Raina D.; Xiuwen, Dong Sue. "Injury inequalities among U.S. construction workers". *Journal of Occupational and Environmental Hygiene* 18 (2021): 159–168.

Bryan, Leslie A. "Drug testing in the workplace". *Professional Safety* 43 (1998): (10) 28–32.

Bull, N.; Riise, T.; Moen, B.E. "Occupational injuries to fisheries workers in Norway reported to insurance companies from 1991 to 1996". *Occupational Medicine* 51 (2001): 299–304.

Bunn, T.L.; Slavova, S.; Struttmann, T.W.; Browning, S.R. "Sleepiness/fatigue and distraction/inattention as factors for fatal versus nonfatal commercial motor vehicle driver injuries". *Accident Analysis & Prevention* 37 (2005): 862–869.

Bunn, William B.; Baver, Robin S.; Ehni, Thomas K.; Stowers, Allan D.; Taylor, David D.; Holloway, Anita M.; Duong, Duyen; Pikelny, Dan B.; Sotolongo, David. "Impact of a musculoskeletal disability management program on medical costs and productivity in a large manufacturing company". *American Journal of Managed Care* 12 (2006):SP27–SP32.

Burse, Richard L. "Sex differences in human thermoregulatory response to heat and cold stress". *Human Factors* 21 (1979): 687–699.

Burstyn, I.; Boffetta, P.; Järvholm, B.; Partanen, T.; Svane, O.; Langård, S.; Kauppinen, T.; Stücker, I.; Shaham, J.; Heederik, D.; Ahrens, W.; Bergdahl, I.; Cenée, S.; Hooiveld, M.; Randem, B.G.; Johansen, C.; Ferro, G.; Kromhout, H. "Risk of fatal industrial accidents and death from external causes among asphalt workers". *Occupational and Environmental Medicine* 61 (2004): 86–88.

Burt, Christopher D.B. 2015. "New employee safety: Risk factors and management strategies". Heidelberg: Springer.

Busch, Timo. "Organizational adaptation to disruptions in the natural environment: The case of climate change". *Scandinavian Journal of Management* 27 (2011): 389–404.

Byler, Christen G. "Hispanic/Latino fatal occupational injury rates". *Monthly Labor Review* 136 (2013): 14–23.

Bylund, Per-Olof; Björnstig, Ulf; Larsson, Tore J. "Occupational road trauma and permanent medical impairment". *Safety Science* 26 (1997): 187–200.

Byrnes, James P.; Miller, David C.; Schafer, William D. "Gender differences in risk taking: A meta-analysis". *Psychological Bulletin* 125 (1999): 367–383.

Cai, Mingming; Zhang, Jie. "Epidemiological characteristics of work-related ocular trauma in Southwest region of China". *International Journal of Environmental Research and Public Health* 12 (2015): 9864–9875.

Cakmak, S.S.; Unlu, M.K.; Olmez, G.; Caca, I., Sakalar, Y.B.; Acemoglu, H. "Penetrating eye injuries from southeastern Anatolia region of Turkey". *Public Health* 118 (2004): 570–575.

Calle Yuste, P.; Ladrón de Guevara, M. "Influencia del fumar en los accidentes laborales. Encuesta estadística". *Medicina Y Seguridad del Trabajo* 21 (1973): 38–46.

Camino Lopez, Miguel A.; Ritzel, Dale O.; Fontaneda, Ignacio; Gonzalez Alcantara, Oscar J. "Construction industry accidents in Spain". *Journal of Safety Research* 39 (2008): 497–507.

Campos-Serna, Javier; Ronda- Pérez, Elena; Artazcoz, Lucía; Benavides, Fernando G. "Desigualdades de género en salud laboral en España". *Gaceta Sanitaria* 26 (2012): 343–351.

Carangan, M.; Tham, K.Y.; Seow, E. "Work-related injury sustained by foreign workers in Singapore". *Annals of the Academy of Medicine*, Singapore 33 (2004): 209–213.

Carayon, Pascale; Hancock, Peter; Leveson, Nancy; Noy, Ian; Sznelwar, Laerte; van Hootegem, Geert "Advancing a sociotechnical systems approach to workplace safety – developing the conceptual framework". *Ergonomics* 4 (2015): 548–564.

Carter, Ned; Ulfberg, Jan; Nyström, Birgitta; Edling, Christer. "Sleep debt, sleepiness and accidents among males in the general population and male professional drivers". *Accident Analysis & Prevention* 35 (2003): 613–617.

Cartwright, Sue; Cooper, Cary L.; Barron, Andrea. "The company car driver, occupational stress as a predictor of motor vehicle accident involvement". *Human Relations* 49 (1996): 195–208.

Casey, Tristan W.; Riseborough, Karli M.; Krauss, Autumn D. "Do you see what I see? Effects of national culture on employees' safety-related perceptions and behaviour". *Accident Analysis & Prevention* 78 (2015): 173–184.

Catarino, Rosa; Spratley, Jorge; Catarino, Isabel; Lunet, Nuno; Pais-Clemente, Manuel. "Sleepiness and sleep-disordered breathing in truck drivers". *Sleep and Breathing* 18 (2014): 59–68.

Cellier, Jean-Marie; Eyrolle, Hèlène; Bertrand, Annick. "Effects of age and level of work experience on occurrence of accidents". *Perceptual and Motor Skills* 80 (1995): 931–940.

Cha, Seungman; Cho, Youngtae. "Fatal and non-fatal occupational injuries and diseases among migrant and native workers in South Korea". *American Journal of Industrial Medicine* 57 (2014): 1043–1052.

Chapman, Simon; Schofield, W.N. "Lifesavers and Samaritans: emergency use of cellular (mobile) phones in Australia". *Accident Analysis & Prevention* 30 (1998): 815–819.

Charbotel, Barbara; Martin, Jean Louis; Chiron, Mireille. "Work-related versus non-work-related road accidents, developments in the last decade in France". *Accident Analysis & Prevention* 42 (2010): 604–611.

Chau, Nearkasen; Gauchard, Gérome C.; Siegfried, Christian; Benamghar, Lahoucine; Dangelzer, Jean-Louis; Francais, Martine; Jacquin, Régis; Sourdot, Alain; Perrin, Philippe P.; Mur, Jean-Marie. "Relationships of job, age, and life conditions with the causes and severity of occupational injuries in construction workers". *International Archives of Occupational and Environmental Health* 77 (2004): 60–66. (a)

Chau, N.; Lemogne, C.; Legleye, S.; Choquet, M.; Falissard, B.; Fossati, P.; Lorhandicap Group. "Are occupational factors and mental difficulty associated with occupational injury?". *Journal of Occupational and Environmental Medicine* 53 (2011): 1452–1459.

Chau, Nearkasen; Mur, Jean-Marie; Benamghar, Lahoucine; Siegfried, Christian; Dangelzer, Jean-Louis; Francais, Martine; Jacquin, Régis; Sourdot, Alain. "Relationships between certain individual characteristics and occupational injuries for various jobs in the construction industry: A case-control study". *American Journal of Industrial Medicine* 45 (2004): 84–92. (b)

Chau, Nearkasen; Mur, Jean-Marie; Touron, Christian; Benamghar, Lahoucine; Dehaene, Dominique. "Correlates of occupational injuries for various jobs in railway workers: A case-control study". *Journal of Occupational Health* 46 (2004): 272–280 (c)

Chau, Nearkasen; Bourgkard, Eve; Bhattacherjee, A.; Ravaud, J.F.; Choquet, Marie; Mur, Jean-Marie; Lorhandicap Group. "Associations of job, living conditions, and lifestyle with occupational injury in working population: a population-based study". *International Archives of Occupational and Environmental Health* 81 (2008): 379–389.

Chau, Nearkasen; Dehaene, Dominique; Benamghar, Lacoucine; Bourgkard, Eve; Mur, Jean-Marie; Touron, Christian; Wild, Pascal. "Roles of age, length of service and job in work-related injury: A prospective study of 63,620 person-years in female workers". *American Journal of Industrial Medicine* 57 (2014): 172–183.

Chen, Guang-X.; Amandus, Harlan E.; Wu, Nan. "Occupational fatalities among driver/sales workers and truck drivers in the United States, 2003–

2008". *American Journal of Industrial Medicine* 57 (2014): 800–809.Chen, Guang-Xiang; Fosbroke, David E. "Work-related fatal-injury risk of construction workers by occupation and cause of death". *Human and Ecological Risk Assessment* 4 (1998): 1371–1390.

Chen, Li-Hui; Baker, Susan P.; Li, Guohua. "Drinking history and risk of fatal injury: comparison among specific injury cases". *Accident Analysis & Prevention* 37 (2005): 245–251.

Chen, Y.-H.; Lin, H.-T.; Lin, Y.-T.; Chao, Y.-H.; Lin, C.-H.; Wei, F.-C.; Lien, S.-H. "Self-perceived health and return to work following work-related hand injury". *Occupational Medicine* 62 (2012): 295–297.

Chen, Y.-Y.; Wu, K. C-C. "Sleep habits and excessive daytime sleepiness correlate with injury risks in the general population in Taiwan". *Injury Prevention* 16 (2010): 172–177.Cheng, C.-W.; Leu, S.-S.; Lin, C.-C.; Fan, C. "Characteristic analysis of occupational accidents at small construction enterprises". *Safety Science* 48 (2010): 698–707.

Cheng, Ching-Wu; Leu, Sou-Sen; Wu, Tsung-Chih; Lin, Chen-Chung. "Applying data mining techniques to explore factors contributing to occupational injuries in Taiwan's construction industry". *Accident Analysis & Prevention* 48 (2012): 214–222.

Cheng, Ching-Wu; Wu, Tsung-Chih. "An investigation and analysis of major accidents involving foreign workers in Taiwan´s manufacture and construction industries". *Safety Science* 57 (2013): 223–235.

Cheng, Melissa; Sauer, Brian; Johnson, Erin; Porucznik, Christina; Hegmann, Kurt. "Comparison of opioid-related deaths by work-related injury". *American Journal of Industrial Medicine* 56 (2013): 308–316.

Cherpitel, Cheryl J. "Alcohol and injuries: a review of international emergency rooms studies". *Addiction* 88 (1993): 923–937. (a)

Cherpitel, Cheryl J. "Alcohol, injury, and risk-taking behaviour: Data from a national sample". *Alcoholism: Clinical and Experimental Research* 17 (1993): 762–766. (b)

Cherpitel, Cheryl J.; Ye, Yu; Bond, Jason. "Attributable risk of injury collaborative alcohol analysis project". *American Journal of Public Health* 95 (2005): 266–272.

Cherry, Nicola; Burstyn, I.; Beach, J. "Mental ill-health and second claims for work-related injury". *Occupational Medicine* 62 (2012): 462–465.

Chimamise, C.; Gombe, N.T.; Tshimanga, M.; Chadambuka, A.; Shambira, G.; Chimusoro, A. "Factors associated with severe occupational injuries at mining company in Zimbabwe, 2010: a cross-sectional study". *Pan African Medical Journal* 14 (2013): https://doi.org/10.11604/pamj.2013.14.5.1148.

Chiron, Mireille; Bernard, Marléne; Lafont, Sylviane; Lagarde, Emmanuel. "Tiring job and work related injury road crashes in the GAZEL cohort". *Accident Analysis & Prevention* 40 (2008): 1096–1104.

Chiu, Hsiao-Yean; Tsai, Pei-Shan. "The impact of various work schedules on sleep complaints and minor accidents during work or leisure time". *Journal of Occupational and Environmental Medicine* 55 (2013): 325–330.

Chiu, Hsiao-Yean; Wang, Mei-Yeh; Chang, Cheng-Kuei; Chen, Ching-Min; Chou, Kuei-Ru; Tsai, Jen-Chen; Tsai, Pei-Shan. "Early morning awakening and nonrestorative sleep are associated with increased minor non-fatal accidents during work and leisure time". *Accident Analysis & Prevention* 71 (2014): 10–14.

Choi, Bokyoung; Choi, Hayon Michelle; Choi, Youngeun; Kim, Inah; Hwang, Seung-sik. "High temperature and its association with work-related injuries by employment status in South Korea, 2017–2018". *Journal of Occupational and Environmental Medicine* 64 (2022): 690–694.

Choi, Seong-Woo; Peek-Asa, Corinne; Sprince, Nancy L.; Rautiainen, Risto H.; Flamme, Gregory A.; Whitten, Paul S.; Zwerling, Craig. "Sleep quantity and quality as a predictor of injuries in a rural population". *American Journal of Emergency Medicine* 24 (2006): 189–196.

Choudhry, Rafiq M. "Behavior-based safety on construction sites: A case study". *Accident Analysis & Prevention* 70 (2014): 14–23.

Ciarapica, F.E.; Giacchetta, G. "Classification and prediction of occupational injury risk using soft computing techniques: An Italian study". *Safety Science* 47 (2009): 36–49.

Clarke, David D.; Ward, Patrick; Bartle, Craig; Truman, Wendy. "Work-related road traffic collisions in the UK". *Accident Analysis & Prevention* 41 (2009): 345–351.

Clarke, Sharon. "The effect of challenge and hindrance stressors on safety behavior and safety outcomes: A meta-analysis". *Journal of Occupational Health* Psychology 17 (2012): 387–397.

Clarke, Sharon, and Cooper, Cary. 2004. *Managing the risk of workplace stress: Health and safety hazards*. London: Routledge.

Coeugnet, Stephanie; Naveteur, Janick; Antoine, Pascal; Anceaux, Françoise. "Time pressure and driving: Work, emotions and risks". *Transportation Research* Part F 20 (2013): 39–51.

Colak, Basar; Etiler, Nilay; Bicer, Umit. "Fatal occupational injuries in the construction sector in Kocaeli, Turkey, 1990–2001". *Industrial Health* 42 (2004): 424–430.

Colantonio, A.; Mroczek, D.; Patel, J.; Lewko, J.; Fergenbaum, J.; Brisdon, R. "Examining occupational traumatic brain injury in Ontario". *Canadian Journal of Public Health* 101 (2010): Supplement 1, S58–S62.

Cole, Donald C.; Ibrahim, Selahadin; Shannon, Harry S. "Predictors of work-related repetitive strain injuries in a population cohort". *American Journal of Public Health* 95 (2005): 1233–1237.

Collins, C.P. "Accidents in a naval dockyard". *British Journal of Industrial Medicine* 16 (1959): 208–215.

Collins, James W.; Landen, D.D.; Kisner, S.M.; Johnston, J.J.; Chin, S.F.; Kennedy, R.D. "Fatal occupational injuries associated with forklifts, United States, 1980–1994". *American Journal of Industrial Medicine* 36 (1999): 504–512. (a)

Collins, James W.; Smith, Gordon S.; Baker, Susan P.: Landsittel, Douglas P.; Warner, Margaret. "A case-control study of forklift and other powered industrial vehicle incidents". *American Journal of Industrial Medicine* 36 (1999): 522–531. (b)

Collins, James W.; Smith, Gordon S.; Baker, Susan P.; Warner, Margaret. "Injuries related to forklifts and other powered industrial vehicles in automobile manufacturing". *American Journal of Industrial Medicine* 36 (1999): 513–521. (c)

Concalves, Cláudia Giglio de Oliveira; Dias, Adriano. "Trés anos acidentes do trabalho em uma metalúrgica: caminhos para seu entendimento". *Ciencia & Saúde Coletiva* 16 (2011): 635–646.

Cooper, M.D.; Phillips, R.A.; Robertson, I.T.; Duff, A.R. "Improving safety on construction sites by psychologically based techniques: Alternative approaches to the measurement of safety behaviour". *Revue européenne de Psychologie Appliquée* 43 (1993): 33–37.

Copeland, Arthur R. "Fatal occupational accidents – The five-year Metro Dade County experience, 1979–1983". *Journal of Forensic Sciences* 30 (1985): 494–503.

Cordeiro, Ricardo; Dias, Adriano. "Stressful life events and occupational accidents". *Scandinavian Journal of Work, Environment and Health* 31 (2005): 336–342.

Corvalan, Carlos F; Driscoll, Timothy R; Harrison, James E. "Role of migrant factors in work-related fatalities in Australia". *Scandinavian Journal of Work, Environment and Health* 20 (1994): 364–370.

Courtney, Theodore K.; Matz, Simon; Webster, Barbara S. "Disabling occupational injury in the US construction industry, 1996". *Journal of Occupational and Environmental Medicine* 44 (2002): 1161–1168.

Craig, Brian N.; Congleton, Jerome J.; Kerk, Carter J.; Amendola, Alfred A.; Gaines, William G. "Personal and non-occupational risk factors and occupational injury/illness". *American Journal of Industrial Medicine* 49 (2006): 249–260.

Crawford, J.O.; Graveling, R.A.; Cowie, H.A.; Dixon, K. "The health safety and health promotion needs of older workers". *Occupational Medicine* 60 (2010): 184–192.

Crowe, M.P. "Hardwood logging accidents and counter-measures for their reduction". *Australian Forestry* 49 (1986): 44–55.

Cui, Yan; Tian, Shuang-Shuang; Qiao, Nan; Wang, Cong; Wang, Tong; Huang, Jian-Jun; Sun, Chen-Ming; Liang, Jie; Liu, Xiao-Meng. "Associations of individual-related and job-related risk factors with nonfatal occupational injury in the coal workers of Shanxi province: A cross-sectional study". *PLoS ONE 10 (*2015): https://doi.org/10.1371/journal.pone.0134367.

Culver, Charles; Marshall, Michael; Connolly, Constance. "Analysis of construction accidents". *Professional Safety* 38 (1993): 22–27.

Dagan, Yaron; Doljansky, Julia T.; Green, Amit; Weiner, Ada. "Body mass index (BMI) as a first-line screening criterion for detection of excessive daytime sleepiness among professional drivers". *Traffic Injury Prevention* 7 (2006): 44–48.

Daley, M.; Morin, C.M.; LeBlanc, M.; Grégoire, J.P.; Savard, J.; Baillargeon, L. "Insomnia and its relationship to health-care utilization, work absenteeism, productivity and accidents". Sleep Medicine 10 (2009): 427–438.

Dalton, K. "Menstruation and accidents". *British Medical Journal*, November 12 (1960): 1425–1426.

Darby, Phil; Murray, Will; Raeside, Robert. "Applying online fleet driver assessment to help identify, target and reduce occupational road safety risks". *Safety Science* 47 (2009): 436–442.

da Silva, Daniela Wosiack; de Andrade, Selma Maffei; de Paula Soares, Doroteia Fatima Pelissari; de Freitas Mathias, Thais Aidar; Matsuo, Tiemi; de Souza, Regina Kazue Tanno. "Factors associated with road accidents among Brazilian motorcycle couriers". *Scientific World Journal* (2012): https://doi.org/10.1100/2012/605480.

Davies, J.C.; Kemp, G.J.; Stevens, G.; Frostick, S.P.; Manning, D.P. "Bifocal/varifocal spectacles, lightning and missed-step accidents". *Safety Science* 38 (2001): 211–226.

Daun, Åke; Mattlar, Carl-Erik; Alanen, Erkki. "Personality traits characteristic for Finns and Swedes". *Ethnologia Scandinavica* 19 (1989): 30–50.

Dawson, D.A. "Heavy drinking and the risk of occupational injury". *Accident Analysis & Prevention* 26 (1994): 655–665.

DeArmond, S.; Chen, P.Y. "Occupational safety: The role of workplace sleepiness". *Accident Analysis & Prevention* 41 (2009): 976–984.

Dell, Terry; Berkhout, Jan. "Injuries at a metal foundry as a function of job classification, length of employment and drug screening". *Journal of Safety Research* 29 (1998): 9–14.

Dembe, Allard E.; Erickson, J. Bianca; Delbos, Rachel G.; Banks, Steven. "Nonstandard shift schedules and the risk of job-related injuries". *Scandinavian Journal of Work, Environment and Health* 32 (2006): 232–240.

Dembe, Allard E; Delbos, Rachel; Erickson, J. Bianca. "Estimates of injury risks for healthcare personnel working night shifts and long hours". *Quality & Safety in Health Care* 18 (2009): 336–340.

Dement, John M.; Lipscomb, Hester; Li, Leiming; Epling, Carol; Desai, Tejas. "Nail gun injuries among construction workers". *Applied Occupational and Environmental Hygiene* 18 (2003): 374–383.

De Pinho, Rachel S.N.; da Silva-Júnior, Francisco P.; Bastos, João Paulo C.; Maia, Werllen S.; de Mello, Marco Túlio; de Bruin, Veralice M.S.; de Bruin, Pedro Felipe C. "Hypersomnolence and accidents in truck drivers: A cross-sectional study". *Chronobiology International* 23 (2006): 963–971.

de Vasconcelos, Roberto Borges A.; Santos, J.C.V.; Araujo, R.F.; de Souza, L.; Dantas, R.A.A.; Gurgel, R.Q. "Occupational injuries in children and adolescents in emergency services of Aracaju, Brazil". *Child: care, health and development* 36 (2010): 369–374.

Dias, Adriano; Cordeiro, Ricardo; Gonçalves, Cláudia Giglio de Oliveira. "Occupational noise exposure and work accidents". *Cadernos de Saúde Pública* 22 (2006): 2125–2130.

Dicke, Wolfgang. "Accidents with fork-lift trucks. Main cause of accidents in transport with fork-lift trucks: Driving errors". *Janus* 25 (1997): 13–15.

Diez-Juárez, M.D.; Naviero-Rilo, J.C.; Pérez-La Orden, A.M. "La seguridad vial en los desplazamientos al trabajo de los profesionales de atención primaria". *Semergen* 39 (2013): 130–138.

Dionne, Georges; Desjardins, Denise; Laberge-Nadeau, Claire; Maag, Urs. "Medical conditions, risk exposure, and truck drivers' accidents: An analysis with count data regression models". *Accident Analysis & Prevention* 27 (1995): 295–305.

Doi, Yuriko; Minowa, Masumi. "Gender differences in excessive daytime sleepiness among Japanese workers". *Social Science & Medicine* 56 (2003): 883–894.

Dong, Xiuwen. "Long workhours, work scheduling and work-related injuries among construction workers in the United States". *Scandinavian Journal of Work, Environment & Health* 31 (2005): 329–335.

Dorn, L.; af Wåhlberg, A. "Work-related road safety: An analysis based on U.K. bus driver performance". *Risk Analysis* 28(2008): 25–35.

Dorrian, Jillian; Lamond, Nicole; van den Heuvel, Cameron; Pincombe, Jan; Rogers, Ann E.; Dawson, Drew. "A pilot study of the safety implications of Australian nurses' sleep and work hours". *Chronobiology International* 23 (2006): 1149–1163.

Doyle, Y.G.; Conroy, R.M. "Prevention of timber felling and chainsaw-related accidents in the Republic of Ireland". *Accident Analysis & Prevention* 21 (1989): 529–534.

Driscoll, Timothy R.; Ansari, Guncha; Harrison, James E.; Frommer, Michael S.; Ruck, Elizabeth A. "Traumatic work related fatalities in commercial fishermen in Australia". *Occupational and Environmental Medicine* 51 (1994): 612–616.

Driscoll, Timothy R.; Ansari, Guncha; Harrison, James E.; Frommer, Michael S.; Ruck, Elizabeth A. "Traumatic work-related fatalities in forestry and sawmill workers in Australia". *Journal of Safety Research* 26 (1995): 221–233.

Driscoll, T.; Marsh, S.; McNoe, B.; Langley, J.; Stout, N.; Feyer, A-M; Williamson, A. "Comparison of fatalities from work related motor vehicle traffic incidents in Australia, New Zealand, and the United States". *Injury Prevention* 11 (2005): 294–299.

Dunn, Kathleen A.; Runyan, Carol W. "Deaths at work among children and adolescents". *American Journal of Disease Control* 147 (1993): 1044–1047.

Dunning, Kari; LeMasters, Grace; Levin, Linda; Bhattacharya, Amit; Alterman, Toni; Lordo, Kathy. "Falls in workers during pregnancy: risk factors, job hazards, and high risk occupations". *American Journal of Industrial Medicine* 44(2003): 664–672.

Dunning, K.K.; Davis, K.G.; Kotowski, S.E.; Elliott, T.; Jewell, G.; Lockey, J. "Can a Transitional Work Grant Program in a workers' compensation system reduce cost and facilitate return to work?". *Journal of Occupational and Environmental Hygiene* 5 (2008): 547–555.Egea Santaolalla, Carlos Javier; del Campo Matias, Felix. "Work-related accidents, absenteeism and productivity in patients with sleep apnea. A future consideration in occupational health assessments?". *Archivos de Bronconeumologia* 51 (2015): 209–210.

Eggensperger, N.M.; Danz, J.; Zimmermann, H.; Iizuka, T. "Occupational maxillofacial fractures: A 3–year survey in Central Switzerland". *Journal of Oral and Maxillofacial Surgery* 64 (2006): 270–276.

Ehsani, Johnathon P.; McNeilly, B.; Ibrahim, J.E.; Ozanne-Smith, J. "Work-related fatal injury among young persons in Australia, July 2000–June 2007". *Safety Science* 57 (2013): 14–18.

Elenge, Myriam; Leveque, Alain; de Brouwer, Christophe. "Occupational accidents in artisanal mining in Katanga, D.R.C". *International Journal of Occupational Medicine and Environmental Health* 26 (2013): 265–274.

Elliott, Karen; Shelley, Kyna. "Effects of drugs and alcohol on behaviour, job performance, and workplace safety". *Journal of Employment Counseling* 43 (2006): 130–134.

Emery, Mary. "Alcohol and safety in industry". *Journal of the Society of Occupational Medicine* 36 (1986): 18–23.

Enez, Korhan; Topbas, Murat; Acar, Hafiz Hulusi. "An evaluation of the occupational accidents among logging workers within the boundaries of Trabzon Forestry Directorate, Turkey". *International Journal of Industrial Ergonomics* 44 (2014): 621–628.

Eost, C.; Flyte, M.G. "An investigation into the use of the car as a mobile office". *Applied Ergonomics* 29 (1998): 383–388.

Essien, S.K.; Trask, C.; Feng, C. "Higher unemployment and higher work-related traumatic fatality: trends and associations from the Canadian province of Saskatchewan, 2007–2018". *Scandinavian Journal of Work, Environment & Health* 48 (2022): 273–282.

Fabiano, Bruno; Curró, Fabio; Reverberi, Andrea P.; Pastorino, Renato. "A statistical study on temporary Work and Occupational accidents: Specific risk factors and risk management strategies". *Safety Science* 46 (2008): 535–544.

Feinauer, Dale M. "The relationship between workplace accident rates and drug and alcohol abuse: The unproven hypothesis". *Labor Studies Journal* 15 (1990): 3–15.

Feinauer, Dale M.; Havlovic, Stephen J. "Drug testing as a strategy to reduce occupational accidents: A longitudinal analysis". *Journal of Safety Research* 24 (1993): 1–7.

Fell, Dallas L.; Black, Barbara. "Driver fatigue in the city". *Accident Analysis & Prevention* 29 (1997): 463–469.

Fernández-Esquer, Maria Eugenia; Fernández-Espada, Natalie; Atkinson, John A; Montano, Cecilia F. "The influence of demographics and working conditions on self-reported injuries among Latino day laborers". *International Journal of Occupational and Environmental Health* 21 (2015): 5–13.

Fidan, Fatma; Ünlü. Mehmet; Sezer, Murat; Kara, Ziya. "Kamyon sürücülerinde trafik kazasi ve uyku apne sendromu semptomlan arasindaki ilişki". *Tüberküloz ve Toraks Dergisi* 55 (2007): 278–284.

Fischer, Virginia; Young, Nancy; Mueller, Cathy; Stueland, Dean T. "Three times the injuries among occasional wood cutters compared to professional loggers: sample of emergency rooms in central and northern Wisconsin". *American Journal of Industrial Medicine* 47 (2005): 246–253.

Fitzgerald, S.; Chen, X.; Qu, H.; Sheff, M.G. "Occupational injury among migrant workers in China: a systematic review". *Injury Prevention* 19 (2013): 348–354.

Folkard, Simon. "Shift work, safety, and aging". *Chronobiology International* 25 (2008): 183–198.

Folkard, Simon; Tucker, Philip. "Shift work, safety and productivity". *Occupational Medicine* 53 (2003): 95–101.

Forrest, Kimberly Y.Z.; Call, Joseph M. "Epidemiology of lifetime work-related eye injuries in the U.S. population associated with one or more lost days of work". *Ophthalmic Epidemiology* 16 (2009): 156–162.

Forrester, B.G.; Weaver, M.T.; Brown, K.C.; Phillips, J.A.; Hilyer, J.C. "Personal health-risk predictors of occupational injury among 3415 municipal employees". *Journal of Occupational and Environmental Medicine* 38 (1996): 515–521.

Forst, Linda; Avila, Susan; Anozie, Stella; Rubin, Rachel. "Traumatic occupational injuries in Hispanic and foreign born workers". *American Journal of Industrial Medicine* 53 (2010): 344–351.

Fort, Emmanuel; Ndagire, Sheba; Gadegbeku, Blandine; Hours, Martine; Charbotel, Barbara. "Working conditions and occupational risk exposure in employees driving for work". *Accident Analysis & Prevention* 89 (2016): 118–127.

Fossum, Ingrid Nesdal; Bjorvatn, Björn; Waage, Siri; Pallesen, Stale. "Effects of shift and night work in the offshore petroleum industry: A systematic review". *Industrial Health* 51 (2013): 530–544.

Fowles, Richard; Loeb, Peter D.; Clarke, Wm. "The cell phone effect on truck accidents: A specification error approach". *Transportation Research* Part E 50 (2013): 18–28.

Franceschini, Marco; Pagliacci, M.C.; Russo, T.; Felzani, G.; Aito, S.; Marini, C. "Occurrence and predictors of employment after traumatic spinal cord injury: the GISEM study". *Spinal Cord* 50 (2011): 238–242.

Fransen, M.; Wilsmore, B.; Winstanley, J.; Woodward, M.; Grunstein, R.; Ameratunga, S.; Norton, R. "Shift work and work injury in the New Zealand Blood Donors' Health Study". *Occupational and Environmental Medicine* 63 (2006): 352–358.

Frantzeskou, Elpida; Kastania, Anastasia N.; Rize, Elena; Jensen, Olaf C.; Linos, Athena. "Risk factors for fishermen's health and safety in Greece". *International Maritime Health* 63 (2012): 155–161.Fredericks, Tycho K.; Abudayyeh, Osama; Choi, Sang O.; Wiersma, Mike; Charles, Marcia. "Occupational injuries and fatalities in the roofing contracting industry". *Journal of Construction Engineering and Management* 131 (2005): 1233–1240.

Fredin, Hans; Gerdman, Peter; Thorson, Jan. "Industrial accidents in the construction industry". *Scandinavian Journal of Social Medicine* 2 (1974): 67–77.

Frickmann, Frank; Wurm, Benjamin; Jeger, Victor; Lehmann, Beat; Zimmermann, Heinz; Exadaktylos, Aristomenis K. "782 consecutive construction accidents: who is at risk?". *Swiss Medical Weekly* 142 (2012): https://doi.org/10.4414/smw.2012.13674.

Frone, Michael R. 2004. "Alcohol, drugs, and workplace safety outcomes: a view from a general model of employee substance use and productivity". In *The psychology of workplace safety*, edited by Julian Barling, and Michael R. Frone, 127–146. Washington, DC: American Psychological.

Froom, P.; Melamed, S.; Kristal-Boneh, E.; Gofer, D.; Ribak, J. "Industrial accidents are related to relative body weight: the Israeli CORDIS study". *Occupational and Environmental Medicine* 53 (1996): 832–835.

Fuentes, José Angel. "The need for effective and comprehensive planning for migrant workers". *American Journal of Public Health* 64 (1974): 2–10.

Gander, Philippa; Signal, Leigh. "Who is too old for shift work? Developing better criteria". *Chronobiology International* 25 (2008): 199–213.

Garbarino, Sergio; Mascialino, Barbara; Penco, Maria Antonietta; Squarcia, Sandro; de Carli, Fabrizio; Nobili, Lino; Beelke, Manolo; Cuomo, Gianni; Ferrillo, Franco. "Professional shift-work drivers who adopt prophylactic naps can reduce the risk of car accidents during night work". *Sleep* 27 (2004): 1295–1302.

García, S.C.; Medina-Mora, M.E.; Vélez, N.M.; García, F.J.; Pérez, L.V. "Caracteristicas organizacionales, estrés y consumo de alcohol en trabajadores de una empresa textil Mexicana". *Salud Mental* 29 (2006): 63–70.

Gaskin, J.E.; Parker, R.J. "Accidents in forestry and logging operations in New Zealand". *Unasylva* 44 (1993): 19–24.

Gaskin, John; Smith, Barry; Wilson, Peter. "Accidents, safety and occupational injuries within the logging industry (an analysis of data collected in the 1986/87 logging workforce survey)". *Logging Industry Research Association Report* 13 (1988): 1–6.

Gebretsadik, Mulu; Kumie, Abera; Gebremichael, Gebrekiros. "Magnitude of occupational injury and associated factors among factory workers in Ethiopia: The case of Mugher cement factory". *Journal of Public Health and Epidemiology* 9 (2017): 318–331.

Gerber, Jonathan K.; Yacoubian, George S. "An assessment of drug testing within the construction industry". *Journal of Drug Education* 32 (2002): 53–68.

Ghosh, Apurna Kumar; Bhattacherjee, Ashis; Chau, Nearkasen. "Relationships of working conditions and individual characteristics to occupational injuries: A case-control study in coal miners". *Journal of Occupational Health* 46 (2004): 470–478.

Glasscock, David J.; Rasmussen, Kurt; Carstensen, Ole; Hansen, Ole N. "Psychosocial factors and safety behaviour as predictors of accidental work injuries in farming". *Work & Stress* 20 (2006): 173–189.

Glazner, Linda K. "Factors related to injury of shiftworking fire fighters in the Northeastern United States". *Safety Science* 21 (1996): 255–263.

Glendon, A. Ian; Hale, Andrew R., 1986. "Accidents to young people on the UK youth opportunities programme". In *The psychology of work and organization. Current trends and issues*, edited by G. Debus and H.-W. Schroiff, 329–336. North-Holland, Amsterdam: Elsevier Science Ltd.

Gold, Diane R.; Rogacz, Suzanne; Bock, Naomi; Tosteson, Tor D.; Baum,Timothy M.; Speizer, Frank E.; Czeisler, Charles A. "Rotating shift work, sleep, and accidents related to sleepiness in hospital nurses". *American Journal of Public Health* 82 (1992): 1011–1014.

Gonzalez-Delgado, Mery; Gómez-Dantés, Héctor; Fernández-Niño, Julián Alfredo; Borja, Víctor H.; Robles, Eduardo; Aguilar, Miriam. "Factors associated with fatal occupational accidents among Mexican workers: a national analysis". *PLoS ONE* 10 (2015): https://doi.org/10.1371/journal.pone.0121490.

Graves, Janessa M.; Miller, Mary E. "Reduced sleep duration and history of work-related injuries among Washington State adolescents with a history of working". *American Journal of Industrial Medicine* 58 (2015): 464–471.

Gregersen, Nils Peter; Brehmer, Berndt; Morén, Bertil. "Road safety improvement in large companies. An experimental comparison of different measures". *Accident Analysis & Prevention* 28 (1996): 297–306.

Grill, Martin; Grytnes, Regine; Törner, Marianne. "Approaching safety in the Swedish and Danish construction industry: Professionals' perceptions of safety culture differences". *Safety Science Monitor* 19 (2015): Issue 2, article 6, 1–17.

Grivna, Michal; Eid, Hani O.; Abu-Zidan, Fikri M. "Injuries from falling objects in the United Arab Emirates". *International Journal of Injury Control and Safety Promotion* 22 (2015): 68–74.

Grön, Sisse; Knudsen, Fabienne. "Why do Filipinos have fewer reported work accidents than other nationals? Findings from literature". *International Maritime Health* 63 (2012): 96–101.

Guadalupe, Maria. "The hidden costs of fixed term contracts: the impact on work accidents". *Labour Economics* 10 (2003): 339–357.

Guldenmund, Frank; Cleal, Bryan; Mearns, Kathryn. "An exploratory study of migrant workers and safety in three European countries". *Safety Science* 52 (2013): 92–99.

Gürcanli, G. Emre; Müngen, Ugur; Akad, Murat. "Construction equipment and motor vehicle related injuries on construction sites in Turkey". *Industrial Health* 46 (2008): 375–388.

Gutiérrez-Fisac, Juan; Regidor, Enrique; Ronda, Elena. "Occupational accidents and alcohol consumption in Spain". *International Journal of Epidemiology* 21 (1992): 1114–1120.

Gyekye, Seth Ayim; Salminen, Simo. "Age and workers' perceptions of workplace safety: A comparative study". *International Journal of Aging & Human Development* 68 (2009): 171–184.

Gyekye, Seth Ayim; Salminen, Simo. "Organizational safety climate: Impact of gender on perception of workplace safety". *International Journal of Psychological Research* 6 (2011): 461–478.

Haigney, D.; Westerman, S.J. "Mobile (cellular) phone use and driving: a critical review of research methodology". *Ergonomics* 44 (2001): 132–143.

Halme, Harri. 1992. "Accident prevention in stevedoring – a new approach". In *Advances in industrial ergonomics and safety IV*, edited by Shrawan Kumar, 147–152. London: Taylor & Francis.

Halvani, Gholam Hossein; Zare, Mohsen; Mirmohammadi, Seyed Jalil. "The relation between shift work, sleepiness, fatigue and accidents in Iranian industrial mining group workers". *Industrial Health* 47 (2009): 134–138.

Haman, François; Souza, Sara C.S.; Castellani, John W.; Dupuis, Maria-P.; Friedl Karl E.; Sullivan-Kwantes, Wendy; Kingma, Boris R.M. "Human vulnerability and variability in the cold: Establishing individual risks for cold weather injuries". *Temperature* 9 (2022): 158–195.

Hansen, H.L.; Laursen, L.H.; Frydberg, M.; Kristensen, S. "Major differences in rates of occupational accidents between different nationalities of seafarers". *International Maritime Health* 59 (2008): 7–18.

Harrison, James E.; Mandryk, John A.; Frommer, Michael S. "Work-related road fatalities in Australia, 1982–1984". *Accident Analysis & Prevention* 25 (1993): 443–451.

Hartley, L.R.; Arnold, P.K.; Smythe, G.; Hansen, J. "Indicators of fatigue in truck drivers". *Applied Ergonomics* 25 (1994): 143–156.

Hartley, L.R.; El Hassani, J. "Stress, violations and accidents". *Applied Ergonomics* 25 (1994): 221–230.

Hasselback, Paul; Neutel, C. Ineke. "Risk for commercial fishing deaths in Canadian Atlantic provinces". *British Journal of Industrial Medicine* 47 (1990): 498–501.

Hassi, Juhani; Gardner, Lytt; Hendricks, Scott; Bell, Jennifer. "Occupational injuries in the mining industry and their association with statewide cold ambient temperatures in the USA". *American Journal of Industrial Medicine* 38 (2000): 49–58.

Heaton, Karen; Azuero, Andres; Reed, Deborah. "Obstructive sleep apnea indicators and injury in older farmers". *Journal of Agromedicine* 15 (2010): 148–156.

Helsingin Sanomat. "EU: lta vaaditaan lämpötilarajaa ulkotyöläisille (The EU is required to set a limit for high temperatures for outdoor workers)". July 26, 2022.

Henry, Doug; McClellen, Dana; Rosenthal, Leon; Dedrick, David; Gosdin, Melissa. "Is sleep really for sissies? Understanding the role of work in insomnia in the US". *Social Science & Medicine* 66 (2008): 715–726.

Hepp, Urs; Moergeli, Hanspeter; Buchi, Stefan; Bruchhaus-Steinert, Helke; Sensky, Tom; Schnyder, Ulrich. "The long-term prediction of return to work following serious accidental injuries: A follow up study". *BMC Psychiatry* 11 (2011): 53.

Hillman, David R.; Murphy, Anita Scott; Antic, Ral; Pezzullo, Lynne. "The economic cost of sleep disorders". *Sleep* 29 (2006): 299–305.

Hilton, Michael F.; Whiteford, Harvey A. "Associations between psychological distress, workplace accidents, workplace failures and workplace successes". *International Archives of Occupational and Environmental Health* 83 (2010): 923–933.

Hingson, Ralph W.; Lederman, Ruth I.; Chapman Walsh, Diana. "Employee drinking patterns and accidental injury: A study of four New England states". *Journal of Studies on Alcohol* 46 (1985): 298–303.

Hinze, Jimmie; Russell, Debra Bosma. "Analysis of fatalities recorded by OSHA". *Journal of Construction Engineering and Management* 121 (1995): 209–214.

Hinze, Jimmie; Huang, Xinyu; Terry, Lani. "The nature of struck-by accidents". *Journal of Construction Engineering and Management* 131 (2005): 262–268.

Hinze, Jimmie W.; Teizer, Jochen. "Visibility-related fatalities related to construction equipment". *Safety Science* 49 (2011): 709–718.

Hintikka, Noora. "Accidents at work during temporary agency work in Finland—Comparisons between certain major industries and other industries". *Safety Science* 49 (2011): 473–483.

Hisamune, S.; Amagai, K.; Kimura, N.; Kishida, K. "A study of factors relating to work accidents among seamen". *Industrial Health* 44 (2006): 144–149.

Ho, C.-K.; Yen, Y.-L.; Chang, C.-H.; Chiang, H.-C.; Shen, Y.-Y.; Chang, P.-Y. "Epidemiologic study on work-related eye injuries in Kaohsiung, Taiwan". *Kaohsiung Journal of Medical Sciences* 23 (2007): 463–469.

Ho, C.-K.; Yen, Y.-L.; Chang, C.-H.; Chiang, H.-C.; Shen, Y.-Y.; Chang, P.-Y. "Case-control study on the prevention of occupational eye injuries". *Kaohsiung Journal of Medical Sciences* 24 (2008): 10–15.

Hogh, Annie; Carneiro, Isabella Gomes; Giver, Hanne; Rugulies, Reiner. "Are immigrants in the nursing industry at increased risk of bullying at work? A one-year follow-up study". *Scandinavian Journal of Psychology* 52 (2011): 49–56.

Holcom, Melvin L.; Lehman, Wayne E.K.; Simpson, D. Dwayne. "Employee accidents: influences of personal characteristics, job characteristics, and substance use in jobs differing in accident potential". *Journal of Safety Research* 24 (1993): 205–221.

Hollo, Claire D.; Leigh, James; Nurminen, Markku. "The role of alcohol in work-related fatal accidents in Australia 1982–1984". *Occupational Medicine* 43 (1993): 13–17.

Honkanen, Risto; Ottelin, J. "Blood alcohol levels in injury victims at the emergency station of a rural central hospital". *Annales Chirurgiae et Gynaecologiae* 65 (1976): 282–286.

Honkanen, Risto; Visuri, T. "Blood alcohol levels in a series of injured patients with special reference to accident and type of injury". *Annales Chirurgiae et Gynaecologiae* 65 (1976): 287–294

Honkasalo, Antero. “Vaarat ja riskinotto sosioteknisessä järjestelmässä (On dangers and risk-taking in socio-technical systems)”. *Hallinnon tutkimus* 7 (1988): 264–272. (in Finnish with an English summary)

Honkasalo, Antero. ”Työntekijöiden käsitykset riskeistä MIG-hitsauksessa. (The views of welders on risks in MIG-welding)”. *Hitsaustekniikka* 40 (1990): 39–41. In Finnish.

Honkasalo, Antero. “Finnish divers’ view of occupational risks and risk taking”. *Applied Ergonomics* 23 (1991): 202–206.

Hopcia, Karen; Dennerlein, Jack Tigh; Hashimoto, Dean; Orechia, Terry; Sorensen, Glorian. “Occupational injuries for consecutive and cumulative shift among hospital registered nurses and patient care associates. A case-control study”. *Workplace Health & Safety* 60 (2012): 437–444.

Horberry, T.; Larsson, T.J.; Johnston, I.; Lambert, J. “Forklift safety, traffic engineering and intelligent transport systems: a case study”. *Applied Ergonomics* 35 (2004): 575–581.

Howard, Mark E.; Desai, Anup V.; Grunstein, Ronald R.; Hukins, Craig; Armstrong, John G.; Joffe, David; Swann, Philip; Campbell, Donald A.; Pierce, Robert J. “Sleepiness, sleep-disordered breathing, and accident risk factors in commercial vehicle drivers”. *American Journal of Respiratory and Critical Care Medicine* 170 (2004): 1014–1021.

Hu, G.; Baker, S.P. “Recent increases in fatal and non-fatal injury among people aged 65 years and over in the USA”. *Injury Prevention* 16 (2010): 26–30. Huang, Arthur; Levinson, David. “The effects of daylight saving time on vehicle crashes in Minnesota”. *Journal of Safety Research* 41 (2010): 513–520.

Hunting, Katherine L.; Welch, Laura S.; Nessel-Stephens, Lisa; Anderson, Judith; Mawudeku, Abla. “Surveillance of construction worker injuries: The utility of trade-specific analysis”. *Applied Occupational and Environmental Hygiene* 14 (1999): 458–469.

Håvold, Jon Ivar. “National cultures and safety orientation: A study of seafarers working for Norwegian shipping companies”. *Work & Stress* 21 (2007): 173–195.

Hyttinen, Marita; Immonen, Stina. “Organisaatiokulttuuri ja johtamistapa eri toimintaympäristöissä (Organizational culture and supervisory behaviour in different environments)”. *Hallinnon Tutkimus* 1 (1994): 12–21.

Hyytiäinen, Kristiina; Saarela, Kaija Leena. “Comparison of methods to identify risk factors for low back injuries at work”. *Journal of Occupational Accidents* 11 (1990): 157–170.

Hägg, Shadi Amid; Torén, Kjell; Lindberg, Eva. "Role of sleep disturbances in occupational accidents among women". *Scandinavian Journal of Work, Environment & Health* 41 (2015): 377–383.

Häkkinen, Kari. "Crane accidents and their prevention". *Journal of Occupational Accidents* 1 (1978): 353–361.

Häkkinen, Kari. "The progress of technology and safety in the materials handling". *Journal of Occupational Accidents* 4 (1982): 157–163.

Häkkinen, Kari. "Crane accidents and their prevention revisited". *Safety Science* 16 (1993): 267–277.

Hämäläinen, Päivi. "The effect of globalization on occupational accidents". *Safety Science* 47 (2009): 733–742.

Hämäläinen, Päivi; Saarela, Kaija Leena; Takala, Jukka. "Global trend according to estimated number of occupational accidents and fatal work-related diseases at region and country level". *Journal of Safety Research* 40 (2009): 125–139.

Hämäläinen, Päivi; Takala, Jukka; Saarela, Kaija Leena. "Global estimates of occupational accidents". *Safety Science* 44 (2006): 137–156.

Hänecke, Kerstin; Tiedemann, Silke; Hachreiner, Friedhelm; Grzech-Sukalo, Hiltraud. "Accident risk as a function of hour at work and time of day as determined from accident data and exposure models for the German working population". *Scandinavian Journal of Work, Environment & Health* 24 (1998): suppl. 3, 43–48.

Im, Hyoung-June; Oh, Dae-gyu; Ju, Young-Su; Kwon, Young-Jun; Jang, Tae-Won; Yim, Jun. "The association between nonstandard Work and Occupational injury in Korea". *American Journal of Industrial Medicine* 55 (2012): 876–883.

Inaba, Ryoichi; Mirbod, Seyed Mohammad; Kurokawa, Junichi; Inoue, Masato; Iwata, Hirotoshi. "Subjective symptoms among female workers and winter working conditions in a consumer cooperative". *Journal of Occupational Health* 47 (2005): 454–465.

Ioannou, Leonidas G.; Foster, Josh; Morris, Nathan B.; Piil, Jacob F.; Havenith, George; Mekjavic, Igor B.; Kelly, Glen P.; Nybo, Lars; Flouris, Andreas D. "Occupational heat strain in outdoor workers: A comprehensive review and meta-analysis". *Temperature* 9 (2022): 67–102.

Irumba, Richard. "Spatial analysis of construction accidents in Kampala, Uganda". *Safety Science* 64 (2014): 109–120.

Jacinto, Celeste; Aspinwall, Elaine. "A survey on occupational accidents' reporting and registration systems in the European Union". *Safety Science* 42 (2004): 933–960.

Jackson Filho, José M.; Fonseca, E.D.; Lima, F.P.A.; Duarte, F.J.C.M. "Organizational factors related to occupational accidents in construction". *Work* 41 (2012): 4130–4136.

James, David V.; Fineberg, Naomi A.; Shah, Ajit K.; Priest, Robert G. "An increase in violence on an acute psychiatric ward: A study of associated factors". *British Journal of Psychiatry* 156 (1990): 846–852.

Janicak, Christopher A. "Differences in relative risks for fatal occupational highway transportation accidents". *Journal of Safety Research* 34 (2003): 539–545.

Jay, Ollie; Brotherhood, John R. "Occupational heat stress in Australian workplaces". *Temperature* 3 (2016): 394–411.

Jensen, Olaf C.; Sörensen, J.F.L.; Canals, M.L.; Hu, Yunping P.; Nikolic, N.; Thomas, M. "Incidence of self-reported occupational injuries in seafaring – an international study". *Occupational Medicine* 54 (2004): 548–555. (a)

Jensen, Olaf C.; Sörensen, Jens F.L.; Kaerlev, Linda; Canals, M. Luisa.; Nikolic, Nebojsa; Saarni, Heikki. "Self-reported injuries among seafarers – Questionnaire validity and results from an international study". *Accident Analysis & Prevention* 36 (2004): 405–413. (b)

Jensen, Olaf C.; Sörensen, Jens .F.L.; Canals, M.L.; Hu, Yunping; Nikolic, N.; Mozer, A.A. "Non-fatal occupational injuries related to slips, trips and falls in seafaring". *American Journal of Industrial Medicine* 47 (2005): 161–171.

Jensen, Sune Qvotrup; Kyed, Morten; Christensen, Anne-Dorte; Bloksgaard, Lotte; Hansen, Claus D; Nielsen, Kent Jacob. "A gender analysis, perspective on work-related accidents". *Safety Science* 64 (2014): 190–198.

Jeong, Byung Yong. "Occupational deaths and injuries in the construction industry". *Applied Ergonomics* 29 (1998): 355–360.

Jing, Hung-Sying; Lu, C. Joseph; Peng, Shang-Jee. "Culture, authoritarianism and commercial aircraft accidents". *Human Factors and Aerospace Safety* 1 (2001): 341–359.

Johansson, Antero; Salminen, Simo. "A minority with few occupational accidents: The case of Swedish-speaking Finns". *American Journal of Industrial Medicine* Suppl. 1 (1999): 37–38.

Johansson, Bo; Rask, Kjell; Stenberg, Magnus. "Piece rates and their effects on health and safety – A literature review". *Applied Ergonomics* 41 (2010): 607–614.

Johnson, Kevin D.; Patel, Sanjay R.; Baur, Dorothee M.; Edens, Edward; Sherry, Patrick; Malhotra, Atul; Kales, Stefanos N. "Association of sleep habits with accidents and near misses in United States transportation operators". *Journal of Occupational and Environmental Medicine* 56 (2014): 510–515.

Johnson, Mark D.; Sharit, Joseph. "Impact of a change from an 8-h to a 12-h shift schedule on workers and occupational injury rates". *International Journal of Industrial Ergonomics* 27 (2001): 303–319.

Johnston, Janet J. "Occupational injury and stress". *Journal of Occupational and Environmental Medicine* 37 (1995): 1199–1203.

Johnstone, Richard; Mayhew, Claire; Quinlan, Michael. "Outsourcing risk? The regulation of occupational health and safety where subcontractors are employed". *Comparative Labor Law & Policy Journal* 22 (2001): 351–393.

Jones, Christopher B.; Ibrahim, Joseph E.; Ozanne-Smith, Joan. "Work-related non-crash heavy vehicle driver fatalities in Australia, 2000–9". *Injury Prevention* 17 (2011): 271–274.

Jones, D.; Switzer-McIntyre, S. "Falls from trucks: A descriptive study based on a workers' compensation database". *Work* 20 (2003): 179–184.

Julià, Mireia; Catalina-Romero, Carlos; Calvo-Bonacho, Eva; Benavides, Fernando G. "The impact of job stress due to the lack of organisational support on occupational injury". *Occupational and Environmental Medicine* 70 (2013): 623–629.

Kaestner, R.; Grossman, M. "The effect of drug use on workplace accidents". *Labour Economics* 5 (1998): 267–294.

Kantermann, Thomas; Haubruge, Damien; Skene, Debra J. "The shift-work accident rate is more related to the shift type than to shift rotation". *Human and Ecological Risk Assessment* 19 (2013): 1586–1594.

Karimi, Mahssa; Eder, Derek N.; Eskandari, Davoud; Zou, Ding; Hedner, Jan A.; Grote, Ludger. "Impaired vigilance and increased accident rate in public transport operators is associated with sleep disorders". *Accident Analysis & Prevention* 51 (2013): 208–214.

Karlson, Trudy A., and Baker, Susan P. 1978. "Fatal occupational injuries associated with motor vehicles". In *Proceedings of the 22nd Conference of the American Association for Automotive Medicine*, Vol 1, 229–241. Arlington Heights, IL: American Association of Automotive Medicine.

Karsh, Ben-Tzion; Moro, Francisco, B.P.; Smith, Michael J.; Booske, Bridget; Sainfort, François. "A case-control study of medication use and acute occupational injury". *Proceedings of the Human Factors and Ergonomics Society Annual Meeting* 44 (2000): 316–319.

Kartam, Nabil A.; Bouz, Rami G. "Fatalities and injuries in the Kuwaiti construction industry". *Accident Analysis & Prevention* 30 (1998): 805–814.

Kauppinen-Toropainen, Kaisa; Kandolin, Irja; Haavio-Mannila, Elina. "Sex segregation of work in Finland and the quality of women's work". *Journal of Organizational Behavior* 9 (1988): 15–27.

Kawachi, Ichiro; Marshall, Stephen W.; Cryer, P. Colin; Wright, Diana; Slappendel, Carol; Laird, Ian. "Work-related injury among forestry workers in New Zealand". *Journal of Occupational Health and Safety – Australia and New Zealand* 10 (1994): 213–223.

Kawachi, Ichiro; Marshall, Stephen W.; Cryer, P. Colin "Trends in work-related chainsaw injury among forestry workers in New Zealand, 1979–1988". *Journal of Occupational Health and Safety – Australia and New Zealand* 11 (1995): 145–152.

Kecojevic, Vladislav; Komljenovic, Dragan; Groves, William; Radomsky, Mark. "An analysis of equipment-related fatal accidents in U.S. mining and risk operations: 1995–2005". *Safety Science* 45 (2007): 864–874.

Kelsh, Michael A.; Sahl, Jack D. "Sex differences in work-related injury rates among electric utility workers". *American Journal of Epidemiology* 143 (1996): 1050–1058.

Kessler, Ronald C.; Berglund, Patricia A.; Coulouvrat, Catherine; Fitzgerald, Timothy; Hajak, Goeran; Roth, Thomas; Shahly, Victoria; Shillington, Alicia C.; Stephenson, Judith J.; Walsh, James K. "Insomnia, comorbidity, and risk of injury among insured Americans: Results from the America Insomnia Survey". *Sleep* 35 (2012): 825–834.

Kessler, Ronald C.; Lane, M.; Stang, P.E.; van Brunt, D.L. "The prevalence and workplace costs of adult attention deficit hyperactivity disorder in a large manufacturing firm". *Psychological Medicine* 39 (2009): 137–147.

Keyserling, W. Monroe; Smith, Gordon S. "Using process control concepts to model conditions required for sudden-onset occupational injuries". *Journal of Occupational and Environmental Hygiene* 4 (2007): 467–475.

Khlat, M.; Ravaud, J.F.; Brouard, N.; Chau, N.; Lorhandicap Group. "Occupational disparities in accidents and roles of lifestyle factors and disabilities: a population-based study in north-eastern France". *Public Health* 122 (2008): 771–783.Khosravi, Yahya; Asilian-Mahabadi, Hassan; Hajizadeh, Ebrahim; Hassanzadeh-Rangi, Narmin; Bastani, Hamid; Behzadan, Amir H. "Factors influencing unsafe behaviors and accidents on construction sites: A review". *International Journal of Occupational Safety and Ergonomics* 20 (2014): 3–17.

Kiani, Fariba; Samavatyan, H.; Pourabdian, S.; Jafari, E. "Predictive power of incidents reporting rate and its dimensions by job stress among workers' Isfahan Steel Company". *Iranian Journal of Public Health* 40 (2011): 105–112.

Kica, Joanna; Rosenman, Kenneth D. "Surveillance for work-related skull fractures in Michigan". *Journal of Safety Research* 51 (2014): 49–56.

Kifle, Manay; Engdaw, Dagnew; Alemu, Kassahun; Sharma, Hardeep Rai; Amsalu, Senafikish; Feleke, Amsalu; Worku, Walelegn. "Work related injuries and associated risk factors among iron and steel industries workers in Addis Ababa, Ethiopia". *Safety Science* 63 (2014): 211–216.

Kim, Hwan-Cheol; Lamichhane, Dirga Kumar; Jung, Dal-Young; Kim, Hyoung-Ryoul; Choi, Eun-Hee; Oh, Sung-Soo; Kang, Hee-Tae; Rhee, Kyung-Yong; Chang, Sei-Jin. "Association of active and passive smoking with occupational injury in manual workers: a cross-sectional study of the 2011 Korean working conditions survey". *Industrial Health* 53 (2015): 445–453.

Kim, Hwan-Cheol; Min, Jin-Young; Min, Kyoung-Bok; Park, Shin-Goo. "Job strain and the risk for occupational injury in small- to medium-sized manufacturing enterprises: A prospective study of 1,209 Korean employees". *American Journal of Industrial Medicine* 52 (2009): 322–330.

Kim S.K.; Son J.M.; So J.Y.; Kim H.; Lee K.; Oh S.S.; Ko S.B. "The Relationship between Waist Circumference and Work-related Injury in Reference to the Fourth Korea National Health and Nutrition Examination Survey". *Annals of Occupational and Environmental Medicine* 25 (2013): 29. https://doi.org/10.1186/2052-4374-25-29.Kines, Pete; Spangenberg, Sören; Dyreborg, Johnny. "Prioritizing occupational injury prevention in the construction industry: Injury severity or absence?". *Journal of Safety Research* 38 (2007): 53–58.

Kirk, Patrick; Parker, Richard. "The effect of spiked boots on logger safety, productivity and workload". *Applied Ergonomics* 25 (1994): 106–110.

Kirkcaldy, Bruce D; Trimpop, Rüdiger; Cooper, Cary L. "Working hours, job stress, work satisfaction, and accident rates among medical practitioners and allied personnel". *International Journal of Stress Management* 4 (1997): 79–87.

Kisner, S.M.; Pratt, S.G. "Occupational injury fatalities among older workers in the United States, 1980-1994". *American Journal of Industrial Medicine*, Supplement 1 (1999): 24–25.Kivimäki, Mika; Vahtera, Jussi; Virtanen, Marianna; Elovainio, Marko; Pentti, Jaana; Ferrie, Jane E. "Temporary employment and risk of overall and cause-specific mortality". *American Journal of Epidemiology* 158 (2003): 663–668.

Kjellstrom, Tord; Wegman, David; Nybo, Lars; Fluoris, Andreas; Kajfez-Bogata, Lucka. "Climate change impacts on occupational health via workplace heat". *Occupational and Environmental Medicine* 74 (2017): suppl. 1, A130.

Klen, Tapio. 1985. "Incidence of accidental injuries caused by chain saw among users and non-users of personal protectors in logging – preliminary results". In *Fjärde nordiska olycksfallforskningsseminariet*, edited by J. Suokas, 173–180. Espoo: Valtion teknillinen tutkimuskeskus.

Klen, Tapio. "Personal protectors and working behaviour of loggers". *Safety Science* 25 (1997): 89–103.

Klen, Tapio; Ojanen, Kari. "The correspondence of self-reported accidents with company records". *Safety Science* 28 (1998): 45–48.

Klen, Tapio; Väyrynen, Seppo. "The role of personal protection in the prevention of accidental injuries in logging work". *Journal of Occupational Accidents* 6 (1984): 263–275.

Kling, Rakel N.; McLeod, Christopher B.; Koehoorn, Mieke. "Sleep problems and workplace injuries in Canada". *Sleep* 33 (2010): 611–618.

Kling, Rakel N.; Demers, Paul A.; Alamgir, Hasanat; Davies, Hugh W. "Noise exposure and serious injury to active sawmill workers in British Columbia". *Occupational and Environmental Medicine* 62 (2012): 211–216.

Knauth, Peter. "Designing better shift systems". *Applied Ergonomics* 27 (1996): 39–44.

Knauth, Peter. "Extended work periods". *Industrial Health* 45 (2007): 125–136.

Knowles, Eric S.; Cutter, Henry S.G.; Walsh, David H.; Casey, Nancy A. "Risk-taking as a personality trait". *Social Behavior and Personality* 1(1973): 123–136.

Knudsen, H.K.; Ducharme, L.J.; Roman, P.M. "Job stress and poor sleep quality: Data from an American sample of full-time workers". *Social Science & Medicine* 64 (2007): 1997–2007.

Koepp G.A.; Snedden B.J.; Levine J.A. "Workplace slip, trip and fall injuries and obesity". *Ergonomics 5 (*2015): 674–679.Konda, Srinivas; Reichard, Audrey; Tiesman, Hope M.; Hendricks, Scott. "Non-fatal work-related traumatic brain injuries treated in US hospital emergency departments, 1998–2007". *Injury Prevention* 21 (2015): 115–120.

Kouvonen, Anne; Kivimäki, Mika; Oksanen, Tuula; Pentti, Jaana; De Vogli, Roberto; Virtanen, Marianna; Vahtera, Jussi. "Obesity and occupational injury: A prospective cohort study of 69,515 public sector employees". *PLoS ONE* 8 (2013): https://doi.org/10.1371/journal.pone.0077178.

Koranyi, Isa; Jonsson, Johanna; Rönnblad, Torkel; Stockfelt, Leo; Bodin, Theo. "Precarious employment and occupational accidents and injuries – a systematic review". *Scandinavian Journal of Work, Environment & Health* 44 (2018): 341–350.

Korpinen, Leena; Pääkkönen, Rauno. "Accidents and close call situations connected to the use of mobile phones". *Accident Analysis & Prevention* 45 (2012): 75–82.

Kristensen, Gert; Christiansen, Jesper. "Alkohol og arbejdsulykker". *Ugeskrift for Laeger* 142 (1980): 3147–3148.

Kronholm, Erkki; Partonen, Timo; Laatikainen, Tiina; Peltonen, Markku; Härmä, Mikko; Hublin, Christer; Kaprio, Jaakko; Aro, Arja R.; Partinen, Markku; Fogelholm, Mikael; Valve, Raisa; Vahtera, Jussi; Oksanen, Tuula; Kivimäki, Mika; Koskenvuo, Markku; Sutela, Hanna. "Trends in self-reported sleep duration and insomnia-related symptoms in Finland from 1972 to 2005: a comparative review and re-analysis of Finnish population samples". *Journal of Sleep Research* 17 (2008): 54–62.

Kucuker, Hudaverdi. "Occupational fatalities among coal mine workers in Zonguldak, Turkey, 1994–2003". *Occupational Medicine* 56 (2006): 144–146.

Kumar, Shrawan. "Injury profile of the construction injury in Alberta in Canadian context: A case study of the impact of a non-monetary motivational factor in a multicenter Albertan company". *International Journal of Industrial Ergonomics* 8 (1991): 197–204.

Kumar, S. Ganesh; Rathnakar, U.P.; Kumar, H.N. Harsha. "Epidemiology of accidents in tile factories of Mangalore City in Karnataka". *Indian Journal of Community Medicine* 35 (2010): 78–81.

Kunar, Bijay Mihir; Bhattacherjee, Ashis. "Study of some occupational and individual factors in coal miners injuries". *Journal of Mines, Metals & Fuels* 54 (2006): 356–361.

Kunar, Bijay Mihir; Bhattacherjee, Ashis; Chau, Nearkasen. "Relationships of job hazards, lack of knowledge, alcohol use, health status and risk taking behavior to work injury of coal miners: A case-control study in India". *Journal of Occupational Health* 50 (2008): 236–244.

Kunda, Richard; Frantz, José; Karachi, Farhana. "Prevalence and ergonomic risk factors of work-related musculoskeletal injuries amongst underground mine workers in Zambia". *Journal of Occupational Health* 55 (2013): 211–217.

Kurtaran, A.; Akbal, A.; Ersöz, M.; Selcuk, B.; Yalcin, E.; Akyüz, M. "Occupation in spinal cord injury patients in Turkey". *Spinal Cord* (2009): 1–4.

Kurzthaler, Ilsemarie; Wambacher, Markus; Golser, Karl; Sperner, Gernot; Sperner-Unterweger, Barbara; Heidekker, Alexander; Pavlic, Marion; Kemmler, Georg; Fleischhacker, W. Wolfgang. "Alkohol- und/oder benzodiazepinkonsum bei arbeitsunfällen im vergleich zu unfallen anderer genese". *Wiener Medizinische Wochenschrift* 154 (2004): 482–488.

Kyobutungi, Catherine; Ronellenfitsch, Ulrich; Razum, Oliver; Becher, Heiko. "Mortality from external causes among ethnic German immigrants from former Soviet Union countries, in Germany". *European Journal of Public Health* 16 (2006): 376–382.

Laberge-Nadeau, C.; Dionne, G.; Maag, U.; Desjardins, D.; Vanasse, C.; Ékoé, J.-M. "Medical conditions and the severity of commercial motor vehicle drivers' road accidents". *Accident Analysis & Prevention* 28 (1996): 43–51.

Laflamme, Lucie; Cloutier, Esther. "Mechanization and risk of occupational accidents in the logging industry". *Journal of Occupational Accidents* 10 (1988): 191–198.

Laflamme, Lucie; Menckel, Ewa. "Aging and occupational accidents: A review of the literature of the last three decades". *Safety Science* 21 (1995): 145–161.

Lahelma, Eero. 1974. "Työturvallisuus ja alkoholi (Occupational safety and alcohol)". *Alkoholipoliittisen tutkimuslaitoksen tutkimusseloste* N.o 71. Helsinki: Oy Alko Ab.

Lahti, Tuuli; Sysi-Aho, Janne; Haukka, Jari; Partonen, Timo. "Work-related accidents and daylight saving time in Finland". *Occupational Medicine* 61 (2011): 26–28.

Laitinen, Heikki; Hannula, Mika; Lankinen, Taru; Monni, Tiina-Mari; Rasa, Pirkko-Liisa; Räsänen, Tuula; and Visuri, Marko. 1999. "The quality of the work environment and labor productivity in metal manufacturing companies". In *Productivity & Quality Management Frontiers – VIII*, edited by William Jr. Werther; Josu Takala, David J. Sumanth, 449–459. Bradford, West Yorkshire: MCB University Press.

Laitinen, Heikki; Marjamäki, Markku; Päivärinta, Keijo. "The validity of the TR safety observation method in building construction". *Accident Analysis & Prevention* 31(1999): 463–472.

Laitinen, Heikki; Päivärinta, Keijo. "A new-generation safety contest in the construction industry – A long-term evaluation of a real-life intervention". *Safety Science* 48 (2010): 680–686.

Laitinen, Heikki; Rasa, Pirkko-Liisa; Räsänen, Tuula; Lankinen, Taru; Nykyri, Erkki. "ELMERI observation method for predicting the accident rate and the absence due to sick leaves". *American Journal of Industrial Medicine* Suppl. 1 (1999): 86–88.

Laitinen, Heikki; Rasa, Pirkko-Liisa; Räsänen, Tuula; Nykyri, Erkki. "An observation method as a tool for workplace risk assessment". *Technology, Law and Insurance* 3 (1998): 57–61.

Laitinen, Heikki; Ruohomäki, Ismo. "The effects of feedback and goal setting on safety performance at two construction sites". *Safety Science* 24 (1996): 61–73.

Laitinen, Heikki; Saari, Jorma; Kivistö, Marketta; Rasa, Pirkko-Liisa. "Improving physical and psychosocial working conditions through a participatory ergonomic process: A before-after study at an engineering workshop". *International Journal of Industrial Ergonomics* 21 (1998): 35–45.

Laitinen, Heikki; Saari, Jorma; Kuusela, Jukka. "Initiating an innovative change process for improved working conditions and ergonomics with participation and performance feedback: A case study in an engineering workshop". *International Journal of Industrial Ergonomics* 19 (1997): 299–305.

Laitinen, Heikki; Vuorinen, Marko; Simola, Antti; Yrjänheikki, Erkki. "Observation-based proactive OHS outcome indicators – Validity of the Elmeri+ method". *Safety Science* 54 (2013): 69–79.

Lajunen, Timo. "Personality and accident liability: are extraversion, neuroticism and psychoticism related to traffic and occupational fatalities?". *Personality and Individual Differences* 31 (2001): 1365–1373.

Lalic, H. "Occupational Medicine in taking over work injuries from family practice – A one-year follow-up". *Collegium Antropologium* 33 (2009): 939–943.

Lam, L.T. "Uncorrected or untreated vision problems and occupational injuries among the adolescent and adult population in Australia". *Injury Prevention* 14 (2008): 396–400.

Lamble, Dave; Kauranen, Tatu; Laakso, Matti; Summala, Heikki. "Cognitive load and detection thresholds in car following situations: safety implications for using mobile (cellular) telephones while driving". *Accident Analysis & Prevention* 31 (1999): 617–623.

Lan, Tianxiang; Goh, Yang Miang; Jensen, Olivia; Asmone, Ashan Senel. "The impact of climate change on workplace safety and health hazard in facilities management: An in-depth review". *Safety Science* 151 (2022): https://doi.org/10.1016/j.ssci.2022.105745.

Larsen, Ann D.; Hannerz, Harald; Möller, Simone V.; Dyreborg, Johnny; Bonde, Jens Peter; Hansen, Johnni; Kolstad, Henrik A.; Hansen, Åse

Marie; Garde, Anne Helene. "Night work, long work weeks and risk of accidental injuries. A register-based study". *Scandinavian Journal of Work, Environment & Health* 43 (2017): 578–586.

Larsson, Tore. "Risk and the inexperienced worker: attitudes of a social anthropologist". *Journal of Occupational Health and Safety – Australia and New Zealand* 4 (1988): 35–40. (a)

Larsson, Tore. "Severe occupational injuries and disabilities among Swedish woodworkers: accident epidemiology and no-fault liability insurance". *Journal of Occupational Health and Safety – Australia and New Zealand* 4 (1988): 325–334. (b)

Larsson, Tore J. "Permanent occupational disabilities among Swedish metal workers in 1986". *Journal of Occupational Accidents* 12 (1990): 283–293.

Larsson, Tore J.; Björnstig, Ulf. "The epidemiology of occupational accidents: three ways to measure the problem in a Swedish municipality". *Journal of Occupational Health and Safety – Australia and New Zealand* 6 (1990): 39–52.

Larsson, Tore J.; Field, Brian. "The distribution of occupational injury risks in the Victorian construction industry". *Safety Science* 40 (2002): 439–456.

Larsson, Tore J.; Lindquist, Christian. "Traumatic fatalities among Swedish seafarers 1984–1988". *Safety Science* 15 (1992): 173–182.

Larsson, Tore J.; Rechnitzer, G. "Forklift trucks – analysis of severe and fatal occupational injuries, critical incidents and priorities for prevention". *Safety Science* 17 (1994): 275–289.

Laundry, Brian R.; Lees, Ronald E.M. "Industrial accident experience of one company on 8- and 12-hour shift systems". *Journal of Occupational Medicine* 33 (1991): 903–906.

Lauridsen, Övind; Tonnesen, Tor. "Injuries related to the aspects of shift working – a comparison of different offshore shift arrangements". *Journal of Occupational Accidents* 12 (1990): 167–176.

Lavie, P: Kremerman, S.; Wiel, M. "Sleep disorders and safety at work in industrial workers". *Accident Analysis & Prevention* 14 (1982): 311–314.

Lawrie, Thane; Matheson, Catriona; Murphy, Elizabeth; Ritchie, Lewis; Bond, Christine. "Medical emergencies at sea and injuries among Scottish fishermen". *Occupational Medicine* 53 (2003): 159–164.

Layne, Larry A.; Landen, Deborah D. "A descriptive analysis of nonfatal occupational injuries to older workers, using a national probability sample of hospital emergency departments". *Journal of Occupational and Environmental Medicine* 39 (1997): 855–865.

Layne, Larry A.; Pollack, K.M. "Nonfatal occupational injuries from slips, trips, and falls among older workers treated in hospital emergency departments, United States 1998". *American Journal of Industrial Medicine* 46 (2004): 32–41.

Le Bouar, Gilbert; Chauvin, Christine. "An analysis of the risk in the French sea fishing industry. An example of the dockside accident risk". *International Maritime Health* 57 (2006): 103–113.

Lee, Hyeonkyeong; Chae, Duckhee; Yi, Kwan Hyung; Im, Soe; Cho, Sung Hye. "Multiple risk factors for work-related injuries and illnesses in Korean-Chinese migrant workers". *Workplace Health & Safety* 63 (2015): 18–26.

Lee, S.; Chen, P.P.; Lee, A.; Ma, M.; Wong, C.M.; Gin, T. "A prospective evaluation of health-related quality of life in Hong Kong Chinese patients with chronic non-cancer pain". *Hong Kong Medical Journal* 11 (2005): 174–180.

Lee, Woncheol; Ha, Jaehyeok. "The association between nonstandard employment and suicidal ideation: Data from the First–Fourth Korea National Health and Nutrition Examination Surveys". *Korean Journal of Occupational and Environmental Medicine* 23 (2011): 89–97.

Leechawengwongs, Manoon; Leechawengwongs, Evelyn; Sukying, Chakrit; Udomsubpayakul, Umaporn. "Role of drowsy driving in traffic accidents: A questionnaire survey of Thai commercial bus/truck drivers". *Journal of the Medical Association of Thailand* 89 (2006): 1845–1850.

Léger, Damien; Bayon, Virginie; Ohayon, Maurice M.; Philip, Pierre; Ement, Philippe; Metlaine, Arnaud; Chennaoui, Mounir; Faraut, Brice. "Insomnia and accidents: a cross-sectional study (EQUINOX) on sleep-related home, work and car accidents in 5293 subjects with insomnia from 10 countries". *Journal of Sleep Research* 23 (2014): 143–152.

Legood, Rosa; Scuffham, P.; Cryer, C. "Are we blind to injuries in the visually impaired? A review of the literature". *Injury Prevention* 8 (2002): 155–160.

Lehtola, Marika M.; van der Molen, Henk F.; Lappalainen, Jorma; Hoonakker, Peter L.T.; Hsiao, Hongwei; Haslam, Roger A.; Hale, Andrew R.; Verbeek, Jos H. "The effectiveness of interventions for preventing injuries in the construction industry: A systematic review". *American Journal of Preventive Medicine* 35 (2008): 77–85.

Leigh, J. Paul. "Alcohol abuse and job hazards". *Journal of Safety Research* 27 (1996): 17–32.

Leistikow, Bruce N.; Martin, Daniel C.; Jacobs, Jeffrey; Rocke, David M.; Noderer, K. "Smoking as a risk factor for accident death: a meta-analysis of cohort studies". *Accident Analysis & Prevention* 32 (2000): 397–405.

Lenguerrand, E.; Martin, J.-L.; Chiron, M.; Lagarde, E.; Laumon, B. "Road crash involvement and professional status: A prospective study using the French Gazel cohort". *Accident Analysis & Prevention* 40 (2008): 126–136.

Lesuffleur, Thomas; Chastang, Jean-François; Sandret, Nicolas; Niedhammer, Isabelle. "Psychosocial factors at work and occupational injury. Results from the French National SUMER Survey". *Journal of Occupational and Environmental Medicine* 57 (2015): 262–269.

Levin, Lester; Oler, Jacqueline; Whiteside, Jeffrey R. "Injury incidence rates in a paint company on rotating production shifts". *Accident Analysis & Prevention* 17 (1985): 67–73.

Lewin, Kurt. "Frontiers in group dynamics". *Human Relations* 1 (1947): 5–38.

Lewis, Robert J.; Cooper, Sharon P. "Alcohol, other drugs, and fatal work-related injuries". *Journal of Occupational Medicine* 31 (1989): 23–28.

Lewko, John H.; Runyan, Carol W.; Tremblay, Cindy-Lynne S.; Staley, John A.; Volpe, Richard. "Workplace experiences of young workers in Ontario". *Canadian Journal of Public Health* 101 (2010): 380–384.

Li, Guohua; Baker, Susan P.; Lamb, Margaret W.; Qiang, Yandong; McCarthy, Melissa L. "Characteristics of alcohol-related fatal general aviation crashes". *Accident Analysis & Prevention* 37 (2005): 143–148.

Li, Leah; Roberts, Ian; Power, Chris. "Physical and psychological effects of injury". *European Journal of Public Health* 11 (2001): 81–83.

Liang, Mingming; Min, Min; Guo, Xianwei; Song, Qiuxia; Wang, Hao; Li, Ning; Su, Wanying; Liang, Qiwei; Ding, Xiuxiu; Ye, Pengpeng; Duan, Leilei; Sun, Yehuan. "The relationship between ambient temperatures and road traffic injuries: a systematic review and meta-analysis". *Environmental Science and Pollution Research* 29 (2022): 50647–50660.

Liao, Chia-Wen; Perng, Yeng-Horng. "Data mining for occupational injuries in the Taiwan construction industry". *Safety Science* 46 (2008): 1091–1102.

Lilley, Rebbecca; Feyer, Anne-Marie; Kirk, Patrick; Gander, Philippa. "A survey of forest workers in New Zealand: Do hours of work, rest, and recovery play a role in accidents and injury?". *Journal of Safety Research* 33 (2002): 53–71.

Lilley, Rebbecca; Davie, Gabrielle; Ameratunga, Shanthi; Derrett, Sarah. "Factors predicting work status 3 months after injury: results from the prospective outcomes of injury study". *BMJ Open* 2 (2012): https://doi.org/10.1136/bmjopen-2011-000400.

Lin, Sheng-Hsuan; Lee, Hsin-Yi; Chang, Yu-Yin; Jang, Yuh; Chen, Pau-Chung; Wang, Jung-Der. "Increased mortality risk for workers with a compensated, permanent occupational disability of the upper or lower extremities: A 21-year follow-up study". *American Journal of Epidemiology* 171 (2010): 917–923.

Lin, Tin-chi; Verma, Santosh K.; Courtney, Theodore K. "Does obesity contribute to non-fatal occupational injury? Evidence from the National Longitudinal Survey of Youth". *Scandinavian Journal of Work, Environment & Health* 39 (2013): 268–275.

Lin, Yen-Hui; Chen, Chih-Yong; Luo, Jin-Lan. "Gender and age distribution of occupational fatalities in Taiwan". *Accident Analysis & Prevention* 40 (2008): 1604–1610.

Lincoln, J.; Lucas, D. "Commercial fishing fatalities – California, Oregon, and Washington, 2000–2006". *Morbidity and Mortality Weekly Report* 57 (2008): 425–429.

Lindberg, Eva; Carter, Ned; Gislason, Thorarinn; Janson, Christer. "Role of snoring and daytime sleepiness in occupational accidents". *American Journal of Respiratory and Critical Care Medicine* 164 (2001): 2031–2035.

Lindqvist, K.; Schelp, L.; Timpka, T. "Gender aspects of work-related injuries in a Swedish municipality". *Safety Science* 31 (1999): 183–196.

Lindroos, Ola; Wilhelmson Aspman, Emma; Lidestav, Gun; Neeley, Gregory. "Accidents in family forestry's firewood production". *Accident Analysis & Prevention* 40 (2008): 877–886.

Ling, Florence Yean Yng; Liu, Min; Woo, Yue Chiau. "Construction fatalities in Singapore". *International Journal of Project Management* 27 (2009): 717–726. Lings, S.; Jensen, J.; Christensen, S.; Möller, J.T. "Occupational accidents and alcohol". *International Archives of Occupational and Environmental Health* 53 (1984): 321–329.

Lipscomb, Hester J.; Schoenfisch, Ashley; Cameron, Wilfrid. "Work-related injuries involving a hand or fingers among union carpenters in Washington State, 1989 to 2008". *Journal of Occupational and Environmental Medicine* 55 (2013): 832–838.

Liu, Margaret; Wei, Wenli; Fergenbaum, Jennifer; Comper, Paul; Colantonio, Angela. "Work-related mild-moderate traumatic brain injury and the construction industry". *Work* 39 (2011): 283–290.

Loh, Katherine; Richardson, Scott. "Foreign-born workers: trends in fatal occupational injuries, 1996–2001". *Monthly Labor Review* 127 (2004): 42–53.

Lombardi, David A.; Jin, Kezhi; Courtney, Theodore K.; Arlinghaus, Anna; Folkard, Simon; Liang, Youxin; Perry, Melissa J. "The effects of rest breaks, work shift start time, and sleep on the onset of severe injury among workers in the People's Republic of China". *Scandinavian Journal of Work, Environment & Health* 40 (2014): 146–155.

Lombardi, David A.; Pannala, R.; Sorock, G.S.; Wellman, H.; Courtney, T.K.; Verma, S.; Smith, G.S. "Welding related occupational eye injuries: a narrative analysis". *Injury Prevention* 11 (2005): 174–179.

Lombardi, David A.; Wirtz, Anna; Willetts, Joanna L.; Folkard, Simon. "Independent effects of sleep duration and body mass index on the risk of a work-related injury; Evidence from the US National Health Interview Survey (2004–2010)". *Chronobiology International* 29 (2012): 556–564.

Loomis, Dana P. "Occupation, industry, and fatal motor vehicle crashes in 20 states, 1986–1987". *American Journal of Public Health* 81 (1991): 733–735.

Loudoun, Rebecca; Allan, Cameron. "The effect of time of day on injury amongst adolescents in Australia". *Applied Ergonomics* 39 (2008): 663–670.

Low, J.M.; Griffith, G.R.; Alston, C.L. "Australian farm work injuries: Incidence, diversity and personal risk factors". *Australian Journal of Rural Health* 4 (1996): 179–189.

Lu, Chin-Shan; Lai, Kee-hung; Lun, Y.H. Venus; Cheng, T.C.E. "Effects of national culture on human failures in container shipping: The moderating role of Confucian dynamism". *Accident Analysis & Prevention* 49 (2012): 457–469.

Lucas, Devin L.; Kincl, Laurel D.; Bovbjerg, Viktor E.; Lincoln, Jennifer M.; Branscum, Adam J. "Work-related traumatic injuries onboard freezer-trawlers and freezer-longliners operating in Alaskan waters during 2001–2012". *American Journal of Industrial Medicine* 57 (2014): 826–836.

Lucas, Devin; Woodward, Chelsea; Lincoln, Jennifer. "Fatal and nonfatal injuries involving fishing vessel winches – Southern shrimp fleet, United States, 2000–2011" *Morbidity and Mortality Weekly Report* 62 (2013): 157–160.

Lunardi, Mariana dos Santos; Soliman, Lucas Alexandre Pedrollo; Pauli, Carla; Lin, Katia. "Epilepsy and occupational accidents in Brazil". *Arquivos de Neuro-Psiquiatria* 69 (2011): 332–335.

Lyman, Stephen; Braver, Elisa R. "Occupant deaths in large truck crashes in the United States: 25 years of experience". *Accident Analysis & Prevention* 35 (2003): 731–739.

Lyng, Stephen. "Edgework: A social psychological analysis of voluntary risk taking". *American Journal of Sociology* 95 (1990): 851–886.

Lysaght, Rosemary; Sparring, Cynthia; Ouellette-Kuntz, Héléne; Marshall, Carrie Anne. "Injury incidence and patterns in workers with intellectual disability: A comparative study". *Journal of Intellectual & Developmental Disability* 36 (2011): 284–288.

Maag, Urs; Vanasse, Charles; Dionne, Georges; Laberge-Nadeau, Claire. "Taxi drivers' accidents: how binocular vision problems are related to their rate and severity in terms of the number of victims". *Accident Analysis & Prevention* 29 (1997): 217–224.

Macdonald, Scott. "The role of drugs in workplace injuries: Is drug testing appropriate?". *Journal of Drug Issues* 25 (1995): 703–722.

Macdonald, Scott; Wells, Samantha; Lothian, Shelley. "Comparison of lifestyle and substance use factors related to accidental injuries at work, home and recreational events". *Accident Analysis & Prevention* 30 (1998): 21–27.

Mackiewicz, Jerzy; Machowicz-Matejko, Eulalia; Salaga-Pylak, Monika; Piecyk-Sidor, Marta; Zagórski, Zbigniew. "Work-related, penetrating eye injuries in rural environments". *Annals of Agricultural and Environmental Medicine* 12 (2005): 27–29.

Maguire, Brian J. "Transportation-related injuries and fatalities among emergency medical technicians and paramedics". *Prehospital and Disaster Medicine* 26 (2011): 346–352.

Mahmud, Norashikin; Schonstein, Eva; Schaafsma, Frederieke; Lehtola, Marika M.; Fassier, Jean-Baptiste; Reneman, Michiel F.; Verbeek, Jos H. "Pre-employment examinations for preventing occupational injury and disease in workers". *Cochrane Database of Systematic Reviews* 12 (2010): https://doi.org/10.1002/14651858.CD008881.

Mainardi, Stefano. "Earnings and work accident risk: a panel data analysis on mining". *Resources Policy* 30 (2005): 156–167.

Mamo, Wondwesen Girma; Newman, Sharon; Tulu, Getu Segni. "Investigating the individual and organisational predictors of work-related driving crash involvement in Ethiopia". *Transportation Research* Part F 23 (2014): 156–164.

Mandryk, John; Harrison, James; Driscoll, Tim; Ruck, Elizabeth. "Forklift-related fatalities in Australia, 1982–84". *Journal of Occupational Health and Safety – Australia and New Zealand* 12 (1996): 219–227.

Mansouri, M.R.; Hosseini, M.; Mohebi, M.; Alipuor, F.; Mehrdad, R. "Work-related eye injury: the main cause of ocular trauma in Iran". *European Journal of Ophthalmology* 20(2010): 770–775.

Marques, Paulo H.; Jesus, Vasco; Olea, Serafin A.; Vairinhos, Valter; Jacinto, Celeste. "The effect of alcohol and drug testing at the workplace on individual's occupational accident risk". *Safety Science* 68 (2014): 108–120.

Marshall, Stephen W.; Kawachi, Ichiro; Cryer, P. Colin; Wright, Diana; Slappendel, Carol; Laird, Ian. "The epidemiology of forestry work-related injuries in New Zealand, 1975–88: fatalities and hospitalisations". *New Zealand Medical Journal* 107 (1994): 434–437. (a)

Marshall, Stephen W; Kawachi, Ichiro; Cryer, P. Colin; Wright, Diana; Slappendel, Carol; Laird, Ian. "Long-term secular trends in the rate of work-related injury among forestry workers in New Zealand". *Journal of Occupational Health and Safety – Australia and New Zealand* 10 (1994): 225–232. (b)

Marucci-Wellman, Helen R.; Willetts, Joanna L.; Lin, Tin-Chi; Brennan, Melanye J.; Verma; Santosh K. "Work in multiple jobs and the risk of injury in the US working population". *American Journal of Public Health* 104 (2014): 134–142.

Mason, Keith. "The effect of piecework on accident rates in the logging industry (incorporating a different approach to the exposure problem)". *Journal of Occupational Accidents* 1 (1976/1977): 281–294.

Matre, D.; Skogstad, M.; Sterud, T.; Nordby, K.-C.; Knardahl, S.; Christensen, J.O.; Lie, J.-A.S. "Safety incidents associated with extended working hours. A systematic review and meta-analysis". *Scandinavian Journal of Work, Environment & Health* 47 (2021): 415–424.

Mattila, Markku. "Improvement in the occupational health program in a Finnish construction company by means of systematic workplace investigation of job load and hazard analysis". *American Journal of Industrial Medicine* 15 (1989): 61–72.

Mattila, Markku. 1990. "Improving working practices and workplace safety through behaviour analysis in the veneer industry". In *Advances in Industrial Ergonomics and Safety II*, edited by Biman Das, 957–961. London: Taylor & Francis.

Mattila, Markku; Hyttinen, Marita; Rantanen, Eeva. "Effective supervisory behaviour and safety at building site". *International Journal of Industrial Ergonomics* 13 (1994): 85–93.

Mattila, Markku; Hyödynmaa, Marjo. "Promoting job safety in building: An experiment on the Behaviour Analysis Approach". *Journal of Occupational Accidents* 9 (1988): 255–267.

Mattila, Markku; Kivi, Pertti. "Hazard screening and proposals for prevention by occupational health service: An experiment with job load and hazard analysis at a Finnish construction company". *Journal of the Society of Occupational Medicine* 41 (1991): 17–22.

Mattila, Markku; Rantanen, Eeva; Hyttinen, Marita. "The quality of work environment, supervision and safety in building construction". *Safety Science* 17 (1994): 257–268.

Mayhew, Claire. "Occupational violence risk for precariously employed adolescents: multiple vulnerabilities to multiple risk factors". *Policy and Practice in Health and Safety* 2 (2004): 5–24.

Mayhew, Claire; Chappell, Duncan. "Workplace violence: An overview of patterns of risk and the emotional/stress consequences on targets". *International Journal of Law and Psychiatry* 30 (2007): 327–339.

Mayhew, Claire; Gibson, Graeme. "Self-employed builders: factors which influence the probability of work-related injury and illness". *Journal of Occupational Health and Safety – Australia and New Zealand* 12 (1996): 61–67.

Mayhew, Claire; Quinlan, Michael; Ferris, Rande. "The effects of subcontracting/outsourcing on occupational health and safety: Survey evidence from four Australian industries". *Safety Science* 25 (1997): 163–178.

Mayhew, Claire, and Quinlan, Michael. 2000. "The relationship between precarious employment and patterns of occupational violence". In *Health effects of the new labour market*, edited by Kerstin Isaksson, Christer Hogstedt, Charli Eriksson and Töres Theorell, 183–205. New York: Kluwer Academic/Plenum Publishers.

McCall, Brian P.; Horwitz, Irwin B. "Occupational vehicular accident claims: A workers' compensation analysis of Oregon truck drivers 1990–1997". *Accident Analysis & Prevention* 37 (2005): 767–774.

McCall, Brian P.; Horwitz, Irwin B.; Taylor, O.A. "Occupational eye injury and risk reduction: Kentucky workers' compensation claim analysis 1994–2003". *Injury Prevention* 15 (2009): 176–182.

McCann, Michael. "Deaths in construction related to personnel lifts, 1992–1999". *Journal of Safety Research* 34 (2003): 507–514.

McCann, Michael. "Heavy equipment and truck-related deaths on excavation work sites". *Journal of Safety Research* 37 (2006): 511–517.

McInnes, J.A.; Akram, M.; MacFarlane, E.M.; Keegel, T.; Sim, M.R.; Smith, P. "Association between high ambient temperature and acute work-related injury: a case-crossover analysis using workers' compensation claims data". *Scandinavian Journal of Work, Environment & Health* 43 (2017): 86–94.

McKnight, A. James; McKnight, A. Scott. "The effect of cellular phone use upon driver attention". *Accident Analysis & Prevention* 25 (1993): 259–265.

McLeod, Christopher; Sarkany, Daniel; Davies, Hugh; Lyons, Kevin; Koehoorn, Mieke. "Prevention in dangerous industries: does safety certification prevent tree-faller injuries?". *Scandinavian Journal of Work, Environment & Health* 41 (2015): 478–485.

McNeilly, Briohny; Ibrahim, Joseph Elias; Bugeja, Lyndal; Ozanne-Smith, Joan. "The prevalence of work-related deaths associated with alcohol and drugs in Victoria, Australia, 2001–6". *Injury Prevention* 16 (2010): 423–428.

McNoe, Bronwen; Langley, John; Feyer, Anne-Marie. "Work-related fatal traffic crashes in New Zealand: 1985–1998". *New Zealand Medical Journal* 118 (2005): 1–11.

Mearns, K.; Yule, S. "The role of national culture in determining safety performance: Challenges for the global oil and gas industry". *Safety Science* 47 (2009): 777–785.

Melamed, Samuel; Oksenberg, Arie. "Excessive daytime sleepiness and risk of occupational injuries in non-shift daytime workers". *Sleep* 25 (2002): 315–322.

Melemez, Kenan. "Risk factor analysis of fatal forest harvesting accidents: A case study in Turkey". *Safety Science* 79 (2015): 369–378.

Memarian, Babak; Mitropoulos, Panagiotis. "Accidents in masonry construction: The contribution of production activities to accidents, and the effect on different workers groups". *Safety Science* 59 (2013): 179–186.

Messing, Karen; Courville, Julie; Boucher, Micheline; Dumais, Lucie; Seifert, Ana Maria. "Can safety risks of blue-collar jobs be compared by gender?". *Safety Science* 18 (1994): 95–112.

Michelo, Prudence; Bråtveit, Magne; Moen, Bente E. "Occupational injuries and fatalities in copper mining in Zambia". *Occupational Medicine* 59 (2009): 191–194.

Mikkelsen, Kim L.; Spangenberg, S.; Kines, P. "Safety walkarounds predict injury risk and reduce injury rates in the construction industry". *American Journal of Industrial Medicine* 53 (2010): 601–607.

Miller, Hugh B.; Sinkala, Thomson; Renger, Ralph F.; Peacock, Erin M.; Tabor, Joseph A.; Burgess, Jefferey L. "Identifying antecedent conditions responsible for the high rate of mining injuries in Zambia". *International Journal of Occupational and Environmental Health* 12 (2006): 329–339.

Miller, Ted R. "Injuries to workers and their dependents". *Journal of Safety Research* 26 (1995): 75–86.

Miller, Ted R.; Lestina, Diane C.; Smith, Gordon S. "Injury risk among medically identified alcohol and drug abusers". *Alcoholism: Clinical and Experimental Research* 25 (2001): 54–59.

Miller, Ted R.; Waehrer, Geetha M. "Costs of occupational injuries to teenagers, United States". *Injury Prevention* 4 (1998): 211–217.

Misumi, J. "Research on leadership and group discussion in Japanese organisation". *Applied Psychology: An International Review* 38 (1989): 321–336.

Mitchell, Rebecca; Driscoll, Timothy; Hull, Brynley; Healey, Sandra; Mandryk, John, "Traumatic work-related fatalities involving mining in Australia, 1989 to 1992". *Safety Science Monitor* 3 (1999): Article 2.

Mitchell, Rebecca; Driscoll, Timothy; Healey, Sandra; Mandryk, John; Hendrie, L.; Hull, Brynley. "Fatal injuries in forestry and logging work in Australia, 1989 to 1992". *Journal of Occupational Health and Safety – Australia and New Zealand* 17 (2001): 567–577.

Mitchell, R.J.; Bambach, M.R.; Friswell, R. "Work and non-work-related vehicle crashes: The contribution of risky driving practices". *Safety Science* 68 (2014): 65–72.

Mitchell, Rebecca; Driscoll, Timothy; Healey, Sandra. "Work-related road fatalities in Australia". *Accident Analysis & Prevention* 36 (2004): 851–860.

Moll van Charante, A.W.; Snijders, C.J.; Mulder, P.G.H. "Posture control and the risk of industrial accident: a stabilographic investigation in a naval shipyard". *Annals of Occupational Hygiene* 35 (1991): 505–515.

Monk, Timothy H.; Wagner, Jon A. "Social factors can outweigh biological ones in determining night shift safety". *Human Factors* 31 (1989): 721–724.

Mooren, Lori; Grzebieta, Raphael; Williamson, Ann; Olivier, Jake; Friswell, Rena. "Safety management for heavy vehicle transport: A review of the literature". *Safety Science* 62 (2014): 79–89.

Moradinazar, Mehdi; Kurd, Nematullah; Farhadi, Rozita; Amee, Vahid; Najafi, Farid. "Epidemiology of work-related injuries among construction workers of Ilam (Western Iran) during 2006–2009". *Iranian Red Crescent Medical Journal* 15 (2013): https://doi.org/10.5812/ircmj.8011.

Morassaei, Sara; Breslin, F. Curtis; Shen, Min; Smith, Peter M. "Examining job tenure and lost-time claim rates in Ontario, Canada, over a 10-year period, 1999–2008". *Occupational and Environmental Medicine* 70 (2013): 171–178.

Morassaei, S.; Smith, P.M. "Switching to daylight saving time and work injuries in Ontario, Canada: 1993–2007". *Occupational and Environmental Medicine 12 (2010): 878–880.*

Moses, Leon N.; Savage, Ian. "Identifying dangerous trucking firms". *Risk Analysis* 16 (1996): 359–366.

Munnoch, K.; Bridger, R.S. "Smoking and injury in Royal Marines' training". *Occupational Medicine* 57 (2007): 214–216.

Müngen, Ugur; Gürcanli, G. Emre. "Fatal traffic accidents in the Turkish construction industry". *Safety Science* 43 (2005): 299–322.

Murata, K.; Kawakami, N.; Amari, N. "Does job stress affect injury due to labor accident in Japanese male and female blue-collar workers?". *Industrial Health* 38 (2000): 246–251.

Murray, Will; Watson, Barry. "Work-related road safety as a conduit for community road safety". *Journal of the Australasian College of Road Safety* 21 (2010): 2, 65–71.

Murray, Will; White, J.; Ison, S. "Work-related road safety: A case study of Roche Australia". *Safety Science* 50 (2012): 129–137.

Myers, John R.; Fosbroke, David E. "Logging fatalities in the United States by region, cause of death, and other factors – 1980 through 1988". *Journal of Safety Research* 25 (1994): 97–105.

Naevestad, Tor-Olav; Phillips, Ross Owen; Elvebakk, Beate. "Traffic accidents triggered by drivers at work – A survey and analysis of contributing factors". *Transportation Research* Part F 34 (2015): 94–107.

Nag, P.K.; Patel, V.G. "Work accidents among shiftworkers in industry". *International Journal of Industrial Ergonomics* 21 (1998): 275–281.

Nakata, Akinori; Ikeda, Tomoko; Takahashi, Masaya; Haratani, Takashi; Fujioka, Yosei; Fukui, Satoe; Swanson, Naomi G.; Hojou, Minora; Araki, Shunichi. "Sleep-related risk of occupational injuries in Japanese small and medium-scale enterprises". *Industrial Health* 43 (2005): 89–97.

Nakata, Akinori; Ikeda, Tomoko; Takahashi, Masaya; Haratani, Takashi; Hojou, Minora; Swanson, Naomi G.; Fujioka, Yosei; Araki, Shunichi. "The prevalence and correlates of occupational injuries in small-scale manufacturing enterprises". *Journal of Occupational Health* 48 (2006): 366–376.

Nasrullah, Muazzam; Laflamme, Lucie; Khan, Jahangir. "Does economic level similarly matter for injury mortality in the OECD and non-OECD countries?". *Safety Science* 46 (2008): 784–791.

National Safety Council. "International accident facts". Itasca, IL, 1995.

Naus, Antonin; Engler, V.; Hetychova, M.; Vavreckova, O. "Work injuries and smoking". *Industrial Medicine and Surgery* 35 (1966): 880–881.

Naveh, Eitan; Marcus, Alfred. "Financial performance, ISO 9000 standard and safe driving practices effects on accident rate in the U.S. motor carrier industry". *Accident Analysis & Prevention* 39 (2007): 331–342.

Neely, Gregory; Wilhelmson, Emma. "Self-reported incidents, accidents, and use of protective gear among small-scale forestry workers in Sweden". *Safety Science* 44 (2006): 723–732.

Nenonen, Sanna. "Fatal workplace accidents in outsourced operations in the manufacturing industry". *Safety Science* 49 (2011): 1394–1403.

Neto, Domingos Garrone; Cordeiro, Ricardo Carlos; Haddad, Vidal. "Acidentes do trabalho em pescadores artesanais de região do Mèdio Rio Araguaia, Tocantins, Brasil". *Cadernos de Saúde Pùblica* 21 (2005): 795–803.

Newman, Alexander; Ucbasaran, Deniz; Zhu, Fei; Hirst, Giles. "Psychological capital: A review and synthesis". *Journal of Organizational Behavior* (2014) 35: S120–S138.

Newnam, Sharon; Greenslade, Jaimi; Newton, Cameron; Watson, Barry. "Safety in occupational driving: Development of a driver behavior scale for the workplace context". *Applied Psychology* 60 (2011): 576–599.

Newnam, Sharon; Oxley, Jennie. "A program in safety management for the occupational driver: Conceptual development and implementation case study". *Safety Science* 84 (2016): 238–244.

Newnam, Sharon; Sheppard, Dianne M.; Griffin, Mark A.; McClure, Roderick J.; Heller, Gillian; Sim, Malcolm R.; Stevenson, Mark R. "Work-related road traffic injury: a multilevel systems protocol". *Injury Prevention* 22 (2016): A372–A385.

Ngo, Cheryl S.; Leo, S.W. "Industrial accident-related ocular emergencies in a tertiary hospital in Singapore". *Singapore Medical Journal* 49 (2008): 280–285.

Nielsen, D. "Deaths at sea – a study of fatalities on board Hong Kong-registered merchant ships (1986–95)". *Safety Science* 32 (1999): 121–141.

Nielsen, Kent Jacob; Hansen, Claus D., Bloksgaard, Lotte; Christensen, Ann-Dorte; Jensen, Sune Qvotrup; Kyed, Morten. "The impact of masculinity on safety oversights, safety priority and safety violations in two male-dominated occupations". *Safety Science* 76 (2015): 82–89.

Nielsen, Mette Lykke; Dyreborg, J.; Kines, P.; Nielsen, K.J.; Rasmussen, K. "Exploring and expanding the category of 'young workers' according to situated ways of doing risk and safety – a case study in retail industry". *Nordic Journal of Working Life Studies* 3 (2013): 219.

Nishikitani, M.; Yano, E. "Differences in the lethality of occupational accidents in OECD countries". *Safety Science* 46 (2008): 1078–1090.

Niskanen, Toivo. "Accidents and minor accidents of the musculoskeletal system in heavy (concrete reinforcement work) and light (painting) construction work". *Journal of Occupational Accidents* 7 (1985): 17–32.

Niskanen, Toivo; Lauttalammi, Jouni. "Accident risks during handling of materials at building construction sites". *Construction Management and Economics* 7 (1989): 283–301.

Niskanen, Toivo; Saarsalmi, Olli. "Accident analysis in the construction of buildings". *Journal of Occupational Accidents* 5 (1983): 89–98.

Njå, Ove, Bjelland, Henrik, and Braut, Geir Sverre. 2015. "Work related traffic safety – the potential of expanding enterprises' HES management to encompass traffic safety issues". In *Proceedings book of the WOS 8th international conference*, edited by Manuela Fernandes, 332–341. Lisbon: University of Minho.

Nolting, Hans-Dieter; Berger, J.; Schiffhorst, G.; Genz, H.O.; Kordt, M. "Psychischer Stress als Risikofaktor für Arbeitsunfälle bei Pflegekräften im Krankenhaus". *Gesundheitswesen* 64 (2002): 25–32.

Nordin, Maria; Knutsson, Anders; Sundbom, Elisabet; Stegmayr, Birgitta. "Psychosocial factors, gender, and sleep". *Journal of Occupational Health Psychology* 10 (2005): 54–63.

Normand, Jacques; Salyards, Stephen D.; Mahoney, John J. "An evaluation of preemployment drug testing". *Journal of Applied Psycho*logy 75 (1990): 629–639.

Norrish, Alan E.; Cryer, Colin P. "Work related injury in New Zealand commercial fishermen". *British Journal of Industrial Medicine* 47 (1990): 726–732.

Notkola, Veijo, and Vänskä, Jukka. 1999. "Määräaikaisten työntekijöiden työtapaturmat ja koetut työperäiset sairaudet (Occupational injuries of temporary employees and work-related diseases)". In *Työn vaarat*, edited by S. Paananen, 45–59. Helsinki: Statistics Finland.

Nuwayhid, Iman; Fayad, Rim; Tamim, Hala; Kassak, Kassem; Khogali, Mustafa. "Work-related injuries in Lebanon: Does nationality make a difference?". *American Journal of Industrial Medicine* 44 (2003): 172–181.

Nykänen, Mikko; Puro, Vuokko; Tiikkaja, Maria; Kannisto, Henriikka; Lantto, Eero; Simpura, Frans; Uusitalo, Jose; Lukander, Kristian; Räsänen, Tuula; Heikkilä, Tarja; Teperi, Anna-Maria. "Implementing and evaluating novel safety training methods for construction sector workers: Results for a randomized controlled trial". *Journal of Safety Research* 75 (2020): 205–221.

Okoye, O.I.; Umeh, R.E. "Eye health of industrial workers in Southeastern Nigeria". *Western African Journal of Medicine* 21 (2002): 132–137.

Onder, Seyhan "Evaluation of occupational injuries with lost days among opencast coal mine workers through regression models". *Safety Science* 59 (2013): 86–92.

Ong, C.N.; Phoon, W.O.; Iskandar, N.; Chia, K.S. "Shiftwork and work injuries in an iron and steel mill". *Applied Ergonomics* 18 (1987): 51–56.

Ong, Victor Yeok Kein; Habibah, A.K.; Lee, F.C.Y. "Safety among foreign workers and impact on emergency medicine services in Singapore". *Singapore Medical Journal* 47 (2006): 121–128.

Oortwijn, W.; Nelissen, E.; Adamini, S.; van den Heuvel, S.; Geuskens, G.; Burdof, L. "Social determinants state of the art reviews – Health of people of working age – Full report". Luxembourg: European Commission, Directorate General for Health and Consumers, 2011.

Ordoñana, Juan R.; Caspi, Avshalom; Moffitt, Terrie E. "Unintentional injuries in a twin study of preschool children: Environmental, not genetic, risk factors". *Journal of Pediatric Psychology* 33 (2008): 185–194.

Ore, Timothy. "Trends and costs of injuries and disease in the New South Wales construction industry". *Safety Science* 15 (1992): 1–20.

Østerlund, Anna H.; Lander, Flemming; Nielsen, Kent; Kines, Pete; Möller, Jette; Lauritsen, Jens. "Transient risk factors of acute occupational injuries: a case-crossover study in two Danish emergency departments". *Scandinavian Journal of Work, Environment & Health* 43 (2017): 217–225.

Ostry, Aleck; Maggi, Stefania; Hershler, Ruth; Chen, Lisa; Louie, Amber; Hertzman, Clyde. "A case control study of differences in non-work injury and accidents among sawmill workers in rural compared to urban British Columbia, Canada". *BMC Public Health* 9 (2009): https://doi.org/10.1186/1471-2458-9-432.

Ott, M. Gerald; Oberlinner, Christoph; Lang, Stefan; Hoffmann, Gerhard; Nesterlack, Michael; Pluto, Rolf-Peter; Trauth, Bernd; Messerer, Peter; Zober, Andreas. "Health and safety protection for chemical industry employees in a rotating shift system: Program design and acute injury and illness experience at work". *Journal of Occupational and Environmental Medicine* 51 (2009): 221–231.

Ozminkowski, Ronald J.; Mark, Tami L.; Goetzel, Ron Z.; Blank, David; Walsh, J. Michael; Cangianelli, Leo. "Relationships between urinalysis testing for substance use, medical expenditures, and the occurrence of injuries at a large manufacturing firm". *American Journal of Drug and Alcohol Abuse* 29 (2003): 151–167.

Åkerstedt, Torbjörn. "Psychosocial stress and impaired sleep". *Scandinavian Journal of Work, Environment & Health* 32 (2006): 493–501.

Åkerstedt, T.; Fredlund, P.; Gillberg, M.; Jansson, B. "A prospective study of fatal occupational accidents – relationship to sleeping difficulties and occupational factors". *Journal of Sleep Research* 11 (2002): 69–71.

Palmer, Keith T.; Harris, Elizabeth Clare; Coggon, David. "Chronic health problems and risk of accidental injury in the workplace: A systematic literature review". *Occupational and Environmental Medicine* 65 (2008): 757–764.

Papalia, L.; Goldoni, M.; Spaggiari, M.C.; Roscelli, F.; Corradi, M.; Mutti, A. "Disturbi del sonno, rischio infortunistico e incidenti stradali in un gruppo di autisti di mezzi pubblici". *Giornale Italiano di Medicina del Lavoro ed Ergonomia* 34 (2012): 353–356.

Paques, Joseph-Jean; Massé, Serge; Bélanger, Raymond. "Accidents related to lockout in Quebec sawmills". *Professional Safety* 34 (1989): 17–20.

Park, Jae Bum; Nakata, Akinori; Swanson, Naomi G.; Chun, Heekyoung. "Organizational factors associated with work-related sleep problems in a nationally representative sample of Korean workers". *International Archives of Occupational and Environmental Health* 86 (2013): 211–222.

Park, Sungjin; Lee, June-Hee; Lee, Wanhyung. "The effects of workplace rest breaks on health problems related to long working hours and shift work among male apartment janitors in Korea". *Safety and Health at Work* 10 (2019): 512–517.

Park, Tae-Jun; Paek, Do-Myung; Joh, Kee-Ock; Park, Jung-Sun; Cho, Sung-il. "The relationship between shift work and work-related injuries among Korean workers". *Korean Journal of Occupational and Environmental Medicine* 24 (2012): 52–60.

Park, Yong-Seung; Butler, Richard J. "The safety costs of contingent work: Evidence from Minnesota". *Journal of Labor Research* 22 (2001): 831–849.

Parkes, Katharine R. "Shiftwork, job type and the work environment as joint predictors of health-related outcomes". *Journal of Occupational Health* Psychology 4 (1999): 256–268.

Parkes, Katharine R. "Shift schedules on North Sea oil/gas installations: A systematic review of their impact on performance, safety and health". *Safety Science* 50 (2012): 1636–1651.

Paul, P.S.; Maiti, J. "The synergic role of sociotechnical and personal characteristics on work injuries in mines". *Ergonomics* 51 (2008): 737–767.

Pegula, S.; Marsh, S.M.; Jackson, L.L. "Fatal occupational injuries – United States, 2005". *Morbidity and Mortality Weekly Report* 56 (2007): 13, 297–301.

Peirò-Pèrez, Rosana; Segui-Gòmez, Maria; Pèrez-Gonzàlez, Catherine; Miralles-Espi, Maite; Lòpez-Maside, Aurora; Benavides, Fernando G. "Lesiones por tráfico, de ocio y domèsticas y laborales. Descripción de la situaciòn en España". *Gacita Sanitaria* 20 (2006): 32–40.

Pekkarinen, Anneli; Anttonen, Hannu. "The comparison of accidents in a foreign construction project with construction in Finland". *Journal of Safety Research* 20 (1989): 187–195.

Pekkarinen, Anneli; Anttonen, Hannu. "Pohjois-Suomessa syntyneiden tapaturmat 30 ikävuoteen saakka (Injuries of people born in Northern Finland up to the age of 30)". *Työ ja ihminen* 14 (2000): 15–26.

Peng, Lu; Chan, A. "A meta-analysis of the relationship between ageing and occupational safety and health". *Safety Science* 112 (2019): 162–172.

Perez, Caroline Criado. 2020. "Näkymättömät naiset. Näin tilastot paljastavat miten maailma on suunniteltu miehille (Invisible women. Exposing data bias in a world designed for men)". Translated by Arto Schroderus. Helsinki: WSOY.

Pérez-Alonso, José; Carreño-Ortega, Ángel; Vázquez-Cabrera, Fernando J.; Callejòn-Ferre, Ángel Jesús. "Accidents in the greenhouse-construction industry of SE Spain". *Applied Ergonomics* 43 (2012): 69–80.

Pérez-Chada, Daniel; Videla, Alejandro J.; O'Flaherty, Martin E.; Palermo, Patricia; Meoni, Jorgelina; Sarchi, Maria I.; Khoury, Marina; Durán-Cantolla, Joaquin. "Sleep habits and accident risk among truck drivers: A cross-sectional study in Argentina". *Sleep* 28 (2005): 1103–1108.

Perez -Labajos, C.; Azofra, M.; Blanco, B.; Achutegui, J.; González, J. "Analysis of accident inequality of the Spanish fishing fleet". *Accident Analysis & Prevention* 38 (2006): 1168–1175.

Perttula, Pia; Merjama, Juha; Kiurula, Mari; Laitinen, Heikki. "Accidents in materials handling at construction sites". *Construction Management and Economics* 21(2003): 729–736.

Perttula, Pia; Ojala, Tarja; Kuosma, Eeva. "Factors in the fatigue of heavy vehicle drivers". *Psychological Reports* 108 (2011): 507–514.

Petursdottir, Gudrun; Hjoervar, Tryggvi; Snorrason, Hilmar. "Fatal accidents in the Icelandic fishing fleet 1980–2005". *International Maritime Health* 58 (2007): 47–58.

Philip, Pierre; Åkerstedt, Torbjörn. "Transport and industrial safety, how are they affected by sleepiness and sleep restriction?". *Sleep Medicine Reviews* 10 (2006): 347–356.

Picard, Michel; Girard, Serge André; Simard, Marc; Larocque, Richard; Leroux, Tony; Turcotte, Fernand. "Association of work-related accidents with noise exposure in the workplace and noise-induced hearing loss based on the experience of some 240,000 person-years of observation". *Accident Analysis & Prevention* 40 (2008): 1644–1652

Pidd, Ken; Roche, Ann M. "How effective is drug testing as a workplace safety strategy? A systematic review of the evidence". *Accident Analysis & Prevention* 71 (2014): 154–165.

Pilcher, June J.; Nadler, Eric; Busch, Caroline. "Effects of hot and cold temperature exposure on performance: a meta-analytic review". *Ergonomics* 45 (2002): 682–698.

Pines, Anatol; Halfon, S.-T.; Prior, R. "Occupational accidents in the construction industry of Israel". *Journal of Occupational Accidents* 9 (1987): 225–243.

Plurad, David; Talving, Peep; Tang, Andrew; Green, Donald; Lam, Lydia; Inaba, Kenji; Demetriades, Demetrios. "Alcohol ingestion is independently associated with complications after work place injuries: A national trauma data bank analysis of injury severity and outcomes". *Journal of Trauma: Injury, Infection and Critical Care* 71 (2011): 1035–1039.

Pokorny, M.L.I; Blom, D.H.J; van Leeuwen, P. "Shifts, duration of work and accident risk of bus drivers". *Ergonomics* 30 (1987): 61–88.

Pollack, Earl S.; Franklin, Gary M.; Fulton-Kehoe, Deborah; Chowdhury, Risana. "Risk of job-related injury among construction laborers with a diagnosis of substance abuse". *Journal of Occupational and Environmental Medicine* 40 (1998): 573–577.

Pollack, Keshia M.; Cheskin, Lawrence J. "Obesity and workplace traumatic injury: does the science support the link?". *Injury Prevention* 13 (2007): 297–302.

Pollack, Keshia M.; Sorock, Gary S.; Slade, Martin D.; Cantley, Linda; Sircar, Kanta; Taiwo, Oyebode; Cullen, Mark R. "Association between body mass index and acute traumatic workplace injury in hourly manufacturing employees". *American Journal of Epidemiology* 166 (2007): 204–211.

Poston, Walker S.C.; Jitnarin, Nattinee; Haddock, C. Keith; Jahnke, Sara. "Obesity and Injury-Related Absenteeism in a Population-Based Firefighter Cohort". *Obesity* 19 (2011): 2076–2081.

Pransky, Glenn S.; Benjamin, Katy L.; Savageau, Judith A.; Currivan, Douglas; Fletcher, Kenneth. "Outcomes in work-related injuries: A comparison of older and younger workers". *American Journal of Industrial Medicine* 47 (2005): 104–112.

Pratt, Stephanie G.; Rodriguez-Acosta, Rosa L. "Occupational highway transportation deaths among workers aged ≥ 55 years – United States, 2003–2010". *Morbidity and Mortality Weekly Report* 62 (2013): 653–657.

Premji, Stèphanie; Messing, Karen; Lippel, Katherine. "Broken English, broken bones? Mechanisms linking language proficiency and occupational health in a Montreal garment factory". *International Journal of Health Services* 38 (2008): 1–19.

Price, James; Shi, Junxin; Lu, Bo; Smith, Gary A.; Stallones, Lorann; Wheeler, Krista K.; Xiang, Huiyun. "Nonoccupational and occupational injuries to US workers with disabilities". *American Journal of Public Health* 102 (2012): e38–e46.

Priebe, Stefan; Sandhu, Sima; Dias, Sònia; Gaddini, Andrea; Greacen, Tim; Ioannidis, Elisabeth; Kluge, Ulrike; Krasnik, Allan; Lamkaddem, Majda; Lorant, Vincent; Riera, Rosa Puigpinósi; Sarvary, Attila; Soares, Joaquim J.F.; Stankunas, Mindaugas; Strassmayr, Christa; Wahlbeck, Kristian; Weibel, Marta; Bogic, Marija. "Good practice in health care for migrants: views and experiences for care professionals in 16 European countries". *BMC Public Health* 11 (2011): 187.

Probst, Tahira M.; Brubaker, Ty L. "The effects of job insecurity on employee safety outcomes: Cross-sectional and longitudinal explorations". *Journal of Occupational Health Psychology* 6 (2001): 139–159.

Probst, Tahira M.; Jiang, Lixin; Graso, Maja. "Leader–member exchange: Moderating health and safety outcomes of job insecurity". *Journal of Safety Research* 56 (2016): 47–56.

Pukkila, Pertti. "Ikääntyvien tapaturmariski lähes kolminkertainen nuoriin verrattuna (The injury risk of older employees nearly three times higher than that of younger ones)". *Tapaturmavakuutus* 68 (1995): 32–35.

Quinlan, Michael. "The implications of labour market restructuring in industrialized societies for occupational health and safety". *Economic and Industrial Democracy* 20 (1999): 427–460.

Quinlan, Michael; Mayhew, Claire; Bohle, Philip. "The global expansion of precarious employment, work disorganization, and consequences for occupational health: A review of recent research". *International Journal of Health Services* 31 (2001): 335–414.

Quinlan, Michael; Bohle, Philip. "Under pressure, out of control, or home alone? Reviewing research and policy debates on the occupational health and safety effects of outsourcing and home-based work". *International Journal of Health Services* 38 (2008): 489–523.

Radford, K.; Phillips, J.; Drummond, A.; Sach, T.; Walker, M.; Tyerman, A.; Haboubi, N.; Jones, T. "Return to work after traumatic brain injury: Cohort comparison and economic evaluation". *Brain Injury* 27 (2017): 507–520.Radun, Igor, and Radun, Jenni. 2008. *Väsyneenä ajaminen: Mikä on tilanne Suomessa?* (Fatigue and driving: the situation in Finland). Helsinki: Liikenneturva.

Ramdan, Iwan M.; Candra, Krishna Purnawan; Arlita, Dewi; Tura, Sakina. "Association of demographic characteristics of construction workers and work environments to workplace accident in high building (hotel)". *Indian Journal of Public Health Research and Development* 10 (2019): 1251–1256.

Rasmussen, Kurt; Hansen, Claus D.; Nielsen, Kent J.; Andersen, Johan H. "Incidence of work injuries amongst Danish adolescents and their association with work environment factors". *American Journal of Industrial Medicine* 54 (2011): 143–152.

Rautji, Ravi; Lalwani, S.; Dogra T.D. "Fatal occupational injuries in the South Delhi construction: A retrospective study". *Medicine, Science and the Law* 45 (2005): 169–173.

Ray, Paul S.; Frey, Austen. "Validation of the behavioral safety index". *Professional Safety* 44 (1999): 25–28.

Reber, Robert A.; Wallin, Jerry A. "Validation of a behavioral measure of occupational safety". *Journal of Organizational Behavior Management* 5 (1983): 69–77.

Redelmeier, Donald A.; Tibshirani, Robert J. "Association between cellular-telephone calls and motor vehicle collisions". *New England Journal of Medicine* 336 (1997): 453–458.

Reid, Alison; Lenguerrand, Erik; Santos, Iracema; Read, Ursula; LaMontagne, Anthony D.; Fritschi, Lin; Harding, Seeromanie. "Taking risks and survival jobs: Foreign-born workers and work-related injuries in Australia". *Safety Science* 70 (2014): 378–386.

Reniers, G.; Gidron, Y. "Do cultural dimensions predict prevalence of fatal work injuries in Europe?". *Safety Science* 58 (2013): 76–80.

Rey de Castro, A.B.; Fujishiro, K.; Rue, T.; Tagalog, E.A.; Samaco-Paquiz, L.P.G.; Gee, G.C. "Associations between work schedule characteristics and occupational injury and illness". *International Nursing Review* 57 (2010): 188–194.

Rey de Castro J.; Gallo J.; Loureiro H. "Tiredness and sleepiness in bus drivers and road accidents in Peru: a quantitative study". *Revista Panamericana de Salud Pública* 16 (2004): 11–18.Rhie, J.; Jeong, I.;

Won, J.U. "Return-to-work according to impairment type among occupationally injured workers in Korea". *Journal of Korean Medical Sciences* 28 (2013): 1581–1586.

Richardson, Scott. "Fatal work injuries among foreign-born Hispanic workers". *Monthly Labor Review* 128 (2005),10: 63–67.

Richter, E.D. & Jacobs, J. "Work injuries and exposures in children and young adults: review and recommendations for action". *American Journal of Industrial Medicine* 19 (1991): 747–769.

Robb, Gillian; Sultana, Shaheen; Ameratunga, Shanti; Jackson, Rod T. "A systematic review of epidemiological studies investigating risk factors for work-related road traffic crashes and injuries". *Injury Prevention* 14 (2008): 51–58.

Roberts, Stephen E.; Nielsen, D.; Kotlowski, A.; Jaremin, B. "Fatal accidents and injuries among merchant seafarers worldwide". *Occupational Medicine* 64 (2014): 259–266.

Roberts, Stephen E.; Marlow, P.B. "Traumatic work related mortality among seafarers employed in British merchant shipping, 1976–2002". *Occupational and Environmental Medicine* 62 (2005): 172–180.

Robinson, Andrew M.; Smallman, Clive. "The contemporary British workplace: a safer and healthier place?". *Work, employment and society* 20 (2006): 87–107.

Roccia, F., Boffano, P., Bianchi, F.A.; Gerbino, G. "Maxillofacial injuries due to work-related accidents in the North West of Italy". *Oral and Maxillofacial Surgery* 17 (2013): 181–186.

Rowe, Richard; Simonoff, Emily; Silberg, Judy L. "Psychopathology, temperament, and unintentional injury: cross-sectional and longitudinal relationships". *Journal of Child Psychology and Psychiatry* 48 (2007): 71–79.

Rundmo, Torbjörn. "Perceived risk, safety status, and job stress among injured and noninjured employees on offshore petroleum installations". *Journal of Safety Research* 26 (1995): 87–97.

Runyan, Carol W.; Gerken, Elizabeth A. "Epidemiology and prevention of adolescent injury: A review and research agenda". *Journal of American Medical Association (JAMA)* 16 (1989): 2273–2279.

Ryan, James; Zwerling, Craig; Orav, Endel John. "Occupational risks associated with cigarette smoking: a prospective study". *American Journal of Public Health* 82 (1992): 29–32.

Rygol, Krystian; Kabiesz-Neniczka, Stanislawa; Olszowy, Zofia. "Wypadkowosc w pracy w zwiazku z nietrzezwoscia (Accidents in the workplace caused by alcohol intoxication)". *Archiwum Medycyny Sadowej i Kryminologii* 54 (2004): 234–241.

Räsänen, Tuula; Laitinen, Heikki; Rasa, Pirkko-Liisa. "The effect of age on subjective assessment of hygienic work environment in the metal industry". *International Journal of Industrial Ergonomics* 25 (2009): 483–489.

Saari, Jorma. 1992. "Scientific housekeeping studies". In *Profits are in order*, edited by F.E. Bird Jr, 27–42. Atlanta: International Loss Control Institute.

Saarni, Heikki. "Industrial accidents among Finnish seafarers". *Travel Medicine International* 7 (1989): 64–68.

Saarni, Heikki; Niemi, Leena; Koskela, Riitta-Sisko; Pentti, Jaana; Kuusela, A. "Mortality among Finnish sea pilots 1956–85: a retrospective cohort study". *Occupational Medicine* 46 (1996): 281–284.

Sabbagh-Ehrlich, S.; Friedman, L.; Richter, E.D. "Working conditions and fatigue in professional truck drivers at Israeli ports". *Injury Prevention* 11 (2005): 110–114.

Sacks, Jeffrey J.; Nelson, David E. "Smoking and injuries: An overview". *Preventive Medicine* 23 (1994): 515–520.

Saha, Asim; Ramnath, Takiar; Chaudhuri, Ramendra Narayan; Saiyed, Habibullah Nasrullah. "An accident-risk assessment study of temporary piece rate workers". *Industrial Health* 42 (2004): 240–245.

Saha, Asim; Kulkarni, P.K.; Chaudhuri, Ramendra; Saiyed, Habibullah. "Occupational injuries: Is job security a factor?". *Indian Journal of Medical Sciences* 59 (2005): 375–381.

Salem, Ahmed M.O.; Jaumally, B.A.; Bayanzay, K.; Khoury, K.; Torkaman, A. "Traumatic brain injuries from work accidents: a retrospective study". *Occupational Medicine* 63 (2013): 358–360.

Salisbury, D.A.; Brubaker, R.; Hertzman, C.; Loeb, G.R. "Fatalities among British Columbia fallers and buckers 1981–7". *Canadian Journal of Public Health* 82 (1991): 32–37.

Salminen, Simo. "The specific accident factor of older employees". *Accident Analysis & Prevention* 25 (1993): 99–102.

Salminen, Simo. "Risk taking and serious occupational accidents". *Journal of Occupational Health and Safety – Australia and New Zealand* 10 (1994): 267–274.

Salminen, Simo. "Epidemiological analysis of serious occupational accidents in southern Finland". *Scandinavian Journal of Social Medicine* 22 (1994): 225–227.

Salminen, Simo. "Serious occupational accidents in the construction industry". *Construction Management and Economics* 13 (1995): 299–306.

Salminen, Simo. "Work-related accidents among young workers in Finland". *International Journal of Occupational Safety and Ergonomics* 2 (1996): 305–314.

Salminen, Simo. 1997. *Risk taking, attributions and serious occupational accidents*. Helsinki: Finnish Institute of Occupational Health.

Salminen, Simo. "Traffic accidents during work and work commuting". *International Journal of Industrial Ergonomics* 26 (2000): 75–85.

Salminen, Simo. "Seriousness of traffic accidents during work and commuting". *Perceptual and Motor Skills* 97 (2003): 147–150.

Salminen, Simo. "Have young workers more injuries than older ones? An international literature review". *Journal of Safety Research* 35 (2004): 513–521. (a)

Salminen, Simo. 2004. "Tapaturmavaarat (Accident risks)". In *Työ ja terveys Suomessa 2003*, edited by Timo Kauppinen and others, 47–51. Helsinki: Työterveyslaitos. (b)

Salminen, Simo. 2008. "Work-related traffic accidents: A review of literature". In *Transportation Accident Analysis & Prevention*, edited by Anton De Smet, 253–262. Hauppauge, NY: Nova Science Publishers. (a)

Salminen, Simo. "Two interventions for the prevention of work-related road accidents". *Safety Science* 46 (2008): 545–550. (b)

Salminen, Simo. "Shift work and extended working hours as risk factors for occupational injury". *Ergonomics Open Journal* 3 (2010): 14–18.

Salminen, Simo. "Are immigrants at increased risk of occupational injury? A literature review". *Ergonomics Open Journal* 4 (2011): 139–144.

Salminen. Simo. "Commuting accidents". Accessed March 3, 2019. http://oshwiki.eu/wiki/Commuting_accidents. 19.3.2013.

Salminen, Simo. "Occupational safety research in Finland". *Safety Science Monitor* 18 (2014): Issue 1, article 2.

Salminen, Simo. "Long working hours and shift work as risk factors for occupational injury". *Ergonomics Open Journal* 9 (2016): 15–26.

Salminen, Simo. 2018. *Concept of Resilience and Individual Differences.* Berlin: Lambert Academic Publishing.

Salminen, Simo; Heinonen, Aino; Sysi-Aho, Janne. "Retirement age and occupational injury". Helsinki: Finnish Workers' Compensation Center, 2016.

Salminen, Simo; Johansson, Antero. "Occupational accidents of Finnish- and Swedish-speaking workers in Finland: A mental model view". *International Journal of Occupational Safety and Ergonomics* 6 (2000): 293–306.

Salminen, Simo; Johansson, Antero; Hiltunen, Erkki; Strömnes, Frode J. "Suomen- ja ruotsinkielisten työntekijöiden tapaturmasuhteet (Accident frequency of Finnish- and Swedish-speaking workers in Finland)". *Työ ja ihminen* 10 (1996): 125–136.

Salminen, Simo; Kivimäki, Mika; Elovainio, Marko; Vahtera, Jussi. "Stress factors predicting injuries of hospital personnel". *American Journal of Industrial Medicine* 44 (2003): 32–36.

Salminen, Simo; Klen, Tapio. "Accident locus of control and risk taking among forestry and construction workers". *Perceptual and Motor Skills* 78(1994): 852–854.

Salminen, Simo; Klen, Tapio; Ojanen, Kari. "Epidemiology of occupational accidents of Finnish forestry workers". *Journal of Forest Science* 47 (2001): 42–44.

Salminen, Simo; Klen, Tapio; Ojanen, Kari. "Risk taking and accident frequency among Finnish forestry workers". *Safety Science* 33 (1999): 143–153.

Salminen, Simo; Kouvonen, Anne; Koskinen, Aki; Joensuu, Matti; Väänänen, Ari. "Is a single item stress measure independently associated with subsequent severe injury: a prospective cohort study of 16,385 forest industry employees". *BMC Public Health* 14: https://doi.org/10.1186/1471-2458-14-543.

Salminen, Simo; Lähdeniemi, Erkki. "Tapaturmataajuus kuvaa onnettomuusriskiä. (Injury frequency describes the risk of injury)". *Työ Terveys Turvallisuus* 31 (2001) 12: 27.

Salminen, Simo; Lähdeniemi, Erkki. "Risk factors in work-related traffic". *Transportation Research* F 5 (2002): 375–384.

Salminen, Simo; Oksanen, Tuula; Vahtera, Jussi; Sallinen, Mikael; Härmä, Mikko; Salo, Paula; Virtanen, Marianna; Kivimäki, Mika. "Sleep disturbances as a predictor of occupational injuries among public sector workers". *Journal of Sleep Research* 19 (2010): 207–213.

Salminen, Simo; Perttula, Pia; Ratilainen, Henriikka; Kuosma, Eeva. "The effect of demographic factors on occupational injuries". *International Journal of Occupational Safety and Ergonomics* 23(2017): 225–228.

Salminen, Simo; Saarela, Kaija Leena; Saari, Jorma; and Räsänen, Tuula. 1991. "Human factors in severe occupational accidents due to moving parts of machines". In *Contemporary ergonomics*, edited by E.J. Lovesey, 55–60. London: Taylor & Francis.

Salminen, Simo; Saari, Jorma; Saarela, Kaija Leena; Räsanen, Tuula. "Risk factors for women in serious occupational accidents". *Journal of Occupational Health and Safety – Australia and New Zealand* 8(1992): 341–347. (a)

Salminen, Simo; Saari, Jorma; Saarela, Kaija Leena; Räsänen, Tuula. "Työkokemus ja vakavat työtapaturmat (Work experience and serious occupational injuries)". *Työ ja ihminen* 6 (1992): 289–298. (in Finnish with an English summary) (b)

Salminen, Simo; Saari, Jorma; Saarela, Kaija Leena; Räsanen, Tuula. "Organizational factors influencing serious occupational accidents". *Scandinavian Journal of Work, Environment & Health* 19(1993): 352–357.

Salminen, Simo; Saloniemi, Antti. "Fixed-term work and violence at work". *International Journal of Occupational Safety and Ergonomics* 16 (2010): 323–328.

Salminen, Simo; Seo, D. "Future of occupational injuries". *International Journal of Asian Social Science* 5 (2015): 341–354.

Salminen, Simo; Seppälä, Anne. "Safety climate in Finnish- and Swedish-speaking companies". *International Journal of Occupational Safety and Ergonomics* (JOSE) 11 (2005): 389–397.

Salminen, Simo; Vartia, Maarit; Giorgiani, Terhi. "Occupational injuries of immigrant and Finnish bus drivers". *Journal of Safety Research* 40 (2009): 203–205.

Salminen, Simo; Vuoksimaa, Eero; Rose, Richard J.; Kaprio, Jaakko. "Age, sex, and genetic and environmental effects on unintentional injuries in young and adult twins". *Twin Research and Human Genetics* 21 (2018): 502–506.

Saloniemi, Antti; Salminen, Simo. "Do fixed-term workers have a higher injury rate?". *Safety Science* 48 (2010): 693–697.

Saloniemi, Antti; Virtanen, Pekka; Koivisto, Anna-Maija. "Is fixed-term employment a new risk for adverse physical working conditions?". *International Journal of Occupational Safety and Ergonomics* (JOSE) 10 (2004): 33–40.

Salvatore, Michele Antonio; Baglio, Giovanni; Cacciani, Laura; Spagnolo, Amedeo; Rosano, Aldo. "Work-related injuries among immigrant workers in Italy". *Journal of Immigrant and Minority Health* 15 (2013): 182–187.

Sanati, Kaveh A.; Yadegarfar, Ghasem; Naghavi, Hamidreza; Mansouri, Massoud; Sanati, Javad G.H. "Temporal trend of occupational injuries; first versus second half of a working shift". *International Journal of Occupational Safety and Ergonomics* 16 (2010): 49–54.

Sanmiquel, Lluís; Freijo, Modesto; Edo, Joaquín; Rossell, Josep M. "Analysis of work related accidents in the Spanish mining sector from 1982–2006". *Journal of Safety Research* 41 (2010): 1–7.

Sanmiquel, Lluís; Freijo, Modesto; Rossell, Josep M. "Exploratory analysis of Spanish energetic mining accidents". *International Journal of Occupational Safety and Ergonomics* (JOSE) 18 (2012): 209–219.

Sarmiento-Salinas, Rodrigo; López-Rojas, Pablo; Marín-Cotoñieto, Irma Araceli; Godínez-Rocha, Arturo; Haro-García, Luis; Salinas-Tovar, Santiago. "Factores de riesgo asociados a los accidents de trabajo en la industria de la construcción del Valle de Mèxico". *Gaceta médica de México* 140 (2004): 593–597.

Savery, Lawson K.; Wooden, Mark. "The relative influence of life events and hassles on work-related injuries: Some Australian evidence". *Human Relations* 47 (1994): 283–305.

Schnitzer, P.G.; Landen, D.D.; Russell, J.C. "Occupational injury deaths in Alaska´s fishing industry, 1980 through 1988". *American Journal of Public Health* 83 (1993): 685–688.

Schlick, Cornelia; Joachin, Manuela; Briceno, Leonardo; Moraga, Daniel; Radon, Katja. "Occupational injuries among children and adolescents in Cusco Province: a cross-sectional study". *BMC Public Health* 14 (2014): 766.

Schmier, Jordana K.; Jones, Mechelle L.; Halpern, Michael T. "Cost of obesity in the workplace". *Scandinavian Journal of Work, Environment & Health* 32 (2006): 5–11.

Schoech, Lauren; Allie, Kyleigh; Salvador, Paolo; Martinez, Mauricio; Rivas, Eric. "Sex differences in thermal comfort, perception, feeling, stress and focus during exercise hyperthermia". *Perceptual and Motor Skills* 128 (2021): 969–987.

Schubert, Ulrich; Dijkstra, Jaap J. "Working safely with foreign contractors and personnel". *Safety Science* 47 (2009): 786–793.

Schulte, Paul A.; Pandalai, Sudha; Wulsin, Victoria; Chun, HeeKyoung. "Interaction of occupational and personal risk factors in workforce health and safety". *American Journal of Public Health* 102 (2012): 434–448.

Schwatka, Natalie V.; Butler, Lesley M.; Rosecrance, John R. "An aging workforce and injury in the construction industry". *Epidemiologic Reviews* 34 (2012): 156–167.

Shaikh, Masood Ali; Shaikh, Irshad Ali. "Occupational injuries in welders – results from a six month follow-up study". *Journal of Ayub Medical College Abbottabad* 17 (2005): 9–11.

Shepherd, G.; Kahler, R. "Pattern analysis of drill and blast incidents in the open-cut mining industry". *Journal of Occupational Health and Safety – Australia and New Zealand* 20 (2004): 547–554.

Shi, Junxin; Gardner, Stephen; Wheeler, Krista K.; Thompson, Meghan C.; Lu, Bo; Stallones, Lorann; Xiang, Huiyun. "Characteristics of nonfatal occupational injuries among U.S. workers with and without disabilities". *American Journal of Industrial Medicine* 58 (2015): 168–177.

Scott, Douglas F. "A study of logger fatalities from 1992–2000". *Injury Prevention* 10 (2004): 239–243.

Seppälä, Anne. 1992. *Turvallisuustoiminta, sen kehittäminen ja yhteydet työtapaturmiin* (Evaluation of safety measures, their improvement and connections to occupational accidents). Helsinki: Työterveyslaitos.

Seppälä, Anne. 1993. "Industrial accidents of women in Finland". In *OECD panel group on women, work and health*, edited by Kaisa Kauppinen-Toropainen, 127–135. Helsinki: Ministry of Social Affairs and Health.

Shepherd, G.W.; Kahler, R.J.; Cross, J. "Crane fatalities – a taxonomic analysis". *Safety Science* 36 (2000): 83–93.

Shi, Junxin; Wheeler, Krista K.; Lu, Bo; Bishai, David M.; Stallones, Lorann; Xiang, Huiyun. "Medical expenditures associated with nonfatal occupational injuries among U.S. workers reporting persistent disabilities". *Disability and Health Journal* 8 (2015): 397–406.

Shibuya, Hitomi; Hannerz, Harald; Mikkelsen, Kim Lyngby; Cleal, Bryan; Gubba, Lotte. "Hospital contacts due to injuries among male drivers working for road goods-transport contractors in Denmark". *International Journal of Occupational Medicine and Environmental Health* 21 (2008): 59–66.

Shipp, Eva M.; Tortolero, Susan R.; Cooper, Sharon P.; Baumler, Elizabeth G.; Weller, Nancy F. "Substance use and occupational injuries among high school students in South Texas". *American Journal of Drug and Alcohol Abuse* 31 (2005): 253–265.

Shiri, Rahman; Turunen, J.; Karhula, K.; Koskinen, A.; Sallinen, M.; Ropponen, A.; Ervasti, J.; Härmä, M. "The association between the use of shift schedule evaluation tool with ergonomics recommendations and occupational injuries: A 4-year prospective cohort study among healthcare workers". *Scandinavian Journal of Work, Environment & Health* 49 (2023): 108–116.

Sincavage, Jessica R. "Fatal occupational injuries among Asian workers". *Monthly Labor Review* 128 (2005): 49–55.

Sinclair, Sara A.; Smith, Gary A.; Xiang, Huiyun. "A comparison of nonfatal unintentional injuries in the United States among U.S.-born and foreign-born persons". *Journal of Community Health* 31 (2006): 303–325.

Sinikumpu, Juha-Jaakko; Pokka, Tytti; Sirniö, Kai; Ruuhela, Reija; Serlo, Willy. "Population-based research on the relationship between summer weather and paediatric forearm shaft fractures". *Injury* 44 (2013): 1569–1573.

Slappendel, Carol; Laird, Ian; Kawachi, Ichiro; Marshall, Stephen; Cryer, Colin. "Factors affecting work-related injury among forestry workers: a review". *Journal of Safety Research* 24 (1999): 19–32.

Smith, Gordon S.; Kraus, Jess F. "Alcohol and residential and occupational injuries: A review of the epidemiologic incidence". *Annual Review of Public Health* 9 (1988): 99–121.

Smith, L.; Folkard, S.; Poole, C.J.M. "Increased injuries on night shift". *Lancet* 344 (1994): 1137–1139.

Smith, Michael J.; Anger, W. Kent; Uslan, S. Stephen. "Behavioral modification applied to occupational safety". *Journal of Safety Research* 10 (1978): 87–88.

Smith, Peter M.; Berecki-Gisolf, Janneke. "Age, occupational demands and the risk of serious work injury". *Occupational Medicine* 64 (2014): 571–576.

Smith, Peter; Bielecky, Amber; Mustard, Cam; Beaton, Dorcas; Hogg-Johnson, Sheilah; Ibrahim, Selahadin; Koehoorn, Mieke; McLeod, Chris; Saunders, Ron; Scott-Marshall, Heather. "The relationship between age and work injury in British Columbia: Examining differences across time and nature of injury". *Journal of Occupational Health* 55 (2013): 98–107.

Smith, Peter; Bielecky, Amber; Ibrahim, Selahadin; Mustard, Cameron; Saunders, Ron; Beaton, Dorcas; Koehoorn, Mieke; McLeod, Chris; Scott-Marshall Heather; Hogg-Johnson Sheilah. "Impact of pre-existing chronic conditions on age differences in sickness absence after a musculoskeletal work injury: A path analysis approach". *Scandinavian Journal of Work, Environment and Health* 40 (2014): 167–175.

Smith, Peter M.; Ibrahim-Dost, Jihan; Keegel, Tessa; MacFarlane, Ewan. "Gender differences in the relationship between shiftwork and work injury: examining the influence of dependent children". *Journal of Occupational and Environmental Medicine* 55 (2013): 932–936.

Smith, Peter M.; Mustard, Cameron A. "The unequal distribution of occupational health and safety risks among immigrants to Canada compared to Canadian-born labour market participants: 1993–2005". *Safety Science* 48 (2010): 1296–1303.

Soori, H.; Rahimi, M.; Mohseni, H. "Occupational stress and work-related unintentional injuries among Iranian car manufacturing workers". *Eastern Mediterranean Health Journal* 14 (2008): 697–703.

Souza, José Carlos; Paiva, Teresa; Reimão, Rubens. "Sleep habits, sleepiness and accidents among truck drivers". *Arquivos de Neuro-Psiquiatria* 63 (2005): 925–930.

Spangenberg, S.; Mikkelsen, K.L.; Kines, P.; Dyreborg, J.; Baarts, C. "The construction of the Oresund Link between Denmark and Sweden: the effect of a multi-faceted safety campaign". *Safety Science* 40 (2002): 457–465.

Spicer, Rebecca S.; Miller, Ted R.; Smith, Gordon S. "Worker substance use, workplace problems and the risk of occupational injury: A matched case-control study". *Journal of Studies on Alcohol* 64 (2003): 570–578.

Sprince, Nancy L.; Pospisil, Shirley; Peek-Asa, Corinne; Whitten, Paul S.; Zwerling, Craig. "Occupational injuries among workers with diabetes: The National Health Interview Survey, 1997–2005". *Journal of Occupational and Environmental Medicine* 50 (2008): 804–808.

Stallones, Lorann; Kraus, Jess F. "The occurrence and epidemiologic features of alcohol-related occupational injuries". *Addiction* 88 (1993): 945–951.

Starren, Annick; Hornikx, Jos; Luijters, Kyra. "Occupational safety in multicultural teams and organizations: A research agenda". *Safety Science* 52 (2013): 43–49.

Statistics Finland. "Palkansaajien työpaikkatapaturmat" (Workplace injuries among wage earners)". Accessed May 6, 2018. https://www.stat.fi/til/ttap/2015/ttap_2015_2017-11-30_kat_001_fi.html.Statistics Finland.

Statistics Finland. "Palkansaajien jatkuvat ja määräaikaiset työsuhteet, 15–74 vuotiaat" (Permanent and fixed-term work contracts, age 15–74). Accessed November 11, 2020. https://pxdata.stat.fi/PXWeb/pxweb/fi/StatFin/StatFin__tyti/statfin_tyti_pxt_12bt.px.

Stevens, A.; Minton, R. "In-vehicle distraction and fatal accidents in England and Wales". *Accident Analysis and Prevention* 33 (2001): 539–545.

Stirbu, I.; Kunst, A.E.; Bos, V.; van Beeck, E.F. "Injury mortality among ethnic minority groups in the Netherlands". *Journal of Epidemiology and Community Health* 60 (2006): 249–255.

Stojadinovic, Sasa; Svrkota, Igor; Petrovic, Dejan; Denic, Miodrag; Pantovic, Radoje; Milic, Vitomir. "Mining injuries in Serbian underground coal mines – A 10-year study". *Injury, International Journal of the Care of the Injured* 43 (2012): 2001–2005.

Stout-Wiegand, Nancy. "Characteristics of work-related injuries involving forklift trucks". *Journal of Safety Research* 18 (1987): 179–190.

Strahan, Clint; Watson, Barry; Lennon, Alexia. "Can organisational safety climate and occupational stress predict work-related driver fatigue?".

Transportation Research, Part F: Traffic Psychology and Behaviour 11 (2008): 418–426.

Strauch, Barry. "Can cultural differences lead to accidents? Team cultural differences and sociotechnical system operations". *Human Factors* 52 (2010): 246–263.

Strunin, L.; Boden, L.I. "Paths of reentry: Employment experiences of injured workers". *American Journal of Industrial Medicine* 38 (2000): 373–384.Strömnes, Frode J. 2006. *The fall of the world and the rise of the mental model*. Frankfurt am Main: Peter Lang.

Størseth, Fred. "Changes at work and employee reactions: Organizational elements, job insecurity, and short-term stress as predictors for employee health and safety". *Scandinavian Journal of Psychology* 47 (2006): 541–550.

Stuart, James C.; Brown, Beverly M. "The relationship of stress and coping ability to incidence of diseases and accidents". *Journal of Psychosomatic Research* 25 (1981): 255–260.

Stuckey, Rwth; Glass, Deborah C; LaMontagne, Anthony D; Wolfe, Rory; Sim, Malcolm R. "Risk factors for worker injury and death from occupational light vehicles crashes in New South Wales (Australia)". *American Journal of Industrial Medicine* 53 (2010): 931–939.

Stutts, Jane C.; Wilkins, Jean W.; Osberg, J. Scott; Vaughn, Bradley V. "Driver risk factors for sleep-related crashes". *Accident Analysis & Prevention* 35 (2003): 321–331.

Sullman, M.J.M.; Kirk, P.M.; Parker, R.J.; Gaskin, J.E. "New Zealand logging industry accident reporting scheme: Focus for a human factors research programme". *Journal of Safety Research* 30 (1999): 123–131.

Sundström-Frisk, Carin. "Varför tar skogsarbetaren risker in arbetet?". *Socialmedicinsk Tidskrift* 52 (1975): 179–183.

Sundström-Frisk, Carin. "Behavioural control through piece-rate wages". *Journal of Occupational Accidents* 6 (1984): 49–59.

Suokas, Jouko. "Evaluation of the effect of safety regulations. Case studies on press and conveyor regulations". *Safety Science* 16 (1993): 307–324.

Suominen, Sakari B.; Välimaa, Raili S.; Tynjälä, Jorma A.; Kannas, Lasse K. "Minority status and perceived health: a comparative study of Finnish- and Swedish-speaking schoolchildren in Finland". *Scandinavian Journal of Public Health* 28 (2000): 179–187.

Suruda, Anthony J. "Work-related deaths in construction painting". *Scandinavian Journal of Work, Environment and Health* 18 (1992): 30–33.

Suruda, Anthony; Smith, Gordon; Baker, Susan P. "Deaths from trench cave-in in the construction industry". *Journal of Occupational Medicine* 30 (1988): 552–555.

Suzuki, Kenshu; Ohida, Takashi; Kaneita, Yoshitaka; Yokoyama, Eise; Uchiyama, Makoto. "Daytime sleepiness, sleep habits and occupational accidents among hospital nurses". *Journal of Advanced Nursing* 52 (2005): 445–453.

Swanberg, Jennifer E.; Clouser, Jessica M.; Westneat, Susan C.; Marsh, Mary W.; Reed, Deborah B. "Occupational injuries on thoroughbred horse farms: A description of Latino and non-Latino workers' experiences". *International Journal of Environmental Research and Public Health* 10 (2013): 6500–6516.

Swartz, George. "Forklift tipover: A detailed analysis". *Professional Safety* 43 (1998): 20–24.

Swartz, George. "Danger zone: The industrial dock". *Professional Safety* 45 (2000): 30–35.

Swedler, David I.; Pollack, Keshia M.; Agnew, Jacqueline. "Safety climate and the distracted driving experiences of truck drivers". *American Journal of Industrial Medicine* 58 (2015): 746–755.

Sysi-Aho, Janne. "Nuorilla suurin tapaturmariski (The risk of occupational injury highest among young employees)". *Tapaturmavakuutus* 85 (2013): 12–21.

Taggart, Robert W. "Results of the drug testing program at Southern Pacific Railroad". *Research monograph series/National Institute of Drug Abuse* 2 (1989–1990): 97–108.

Takala, Jukka. "Global estimates of fatal occupational accidents". *Epidemiology* 10 (1999): 640–646.

Tarvainen, Hannu. 1999. "Tel-alan (alle 6 kk) pätkätyösuhteiden työtapaturmat v. 1995–1996 (Occupational injuries among employees with an employment contract of less than 6 months in 1995–1996)". Helsinki: Tapaturmavakuutuslaitosten Liitto.

Tessier-Sherman, Baylah; Cantley, Linda F.; Galusha, Deron; Slade, Martin D.; Taiwo, Oyebode A.; Cullen, Mark R. "Occupational injury risk by sex in a manufacturing cohort". *Occupational and Environmental Medicine* 71(2014): 605–610.

Thompson, G.J.; Mollan, S.P. "Occupational eye injuries: a continuing problem". *Occupational Medicine* 59 (2009): 123–125.

Thuret, Anne; Geoffroy-Perez, Beatrice; Luce, Daniele; Goldberg, Marcel; Imbernon, E. "A 26-year cohort mortality study of French construction workers aged 20 to 64 years". *Journal of Occupational and Environmental Medicine* 49 (2007): 546–556.

Thurston, Wilfreda; Verhoef, Marja. "Occupational injury among immigrants". *Journal of International Migration and Integration* 4 (2003): 105–123.

Tiagi, Raaj. "Are immigrants in Canada over-represented in riskier jobs relative to Canadian-born labor market participants?". *American Journal of Industrial Medicine* 58 (2015): 933–942.

Tilastokeskus (Statistics Finland). 2007. "*Vaaka vaaterissa? Sukupuolten tasa-arvo Suomessa 2006* (Scales in balance? The equality between genders in Finland in 2006)". Helsinki: Multiprint.

Tong, Michael; Wondmagegn, Berhanu; Xiang, Jianjun; Bi, Peng. "Hospitalization costs of respiratory diseases attributable to temperature in Australia and projection for future costs in the 2030s and 2050s under climate change". *International Journal of Environmental Research and Public Health* 19 (2022): https://doi.org/10.3390/ijerph19159706.

Toppila, Esko; Pyykkö, Ilmari; Pääkkönen, Rauno. "Evaluation of the increased accident risk from workplace noise". *International Journal of Occupational Safety and Ergonomics* 15 (2009): 155–162.

Torzsa, Peter; Keszei, Andras; Kalabay, Laszlo; Vamos, Eszter Pauna; Zoller, Rezso; Mucsi, Istvan; Novak, Marta; Kopp, Maria S. "Socio-demographic characteristics, health behaviour, co-morbidity and accidents in snorers: a population survey". *Sleep and Breathing* 15 (2011): 809–818.

Toscano, G.; Windau, J. "The changing character of fatal work injuries". *Monthly Labor Review* 117 (1994): 17–28.

Trent, Roger B. "Emergency room evidence on the role of alcohol intoxication in injury at work in the U.S". *Safety Science* 14 (1991): 241–252.

Tricco, Andrea C.; Colantonio, Angela; Chipman, Mary; Liss, Gary; McLellan, Barry. "Work-related deaths and traumatic brain injury". *Brain Injury* 20 (2006): 719–724.

Tucker, Philip; Folkard, Simon; Macdonald, I. "Rest breaks and accident risk". *Lancet* 361 (2003): 680.

Tucker, Philip; Lombardi, David; Smith, Lawrence; Folkard, Simon. "The impact of rest breaks on temporal trends in injury risk". *Chronobiology International* 23 (2006): 1423–1434.

Turner, Cathy; McClure, Rod. "Quantifying the role of risk-taking behaviour in causation of serious road crash-related injury". *Accident Analysis & Prevention* 36 (2004): 383–389.

Turner, Cathy; McClure, Rod; Pirozzo, Sandi. "Injury and risk-taking behaviour – a systematic review". *Accident Analysis & Prevention* 36(2004): 93–101.

Turner, Nick; Deng, Connie; Granger, Steve; Wingate, Timothy G.; Sahfqat, Rabeel; Dueck, Paul M. "Young workers and safety: A critical review and future research agenda". *Journal of Safety Research* 83 (2022): 79–95.

Turner, Nick; Tucker, Sean; Kelloway, E. Kevin. "Prevalence and demographic differences in microaccidents and safety behaviors among young workers in Canada". *Journal of Safety Research* 53 (2015): 39–43.

Tüchsen, F.; Hannerz, H. "Building camps and work related injuries". *Occupational and Environmental Medicine* 61 (2004): 370–371.

Tynkkynen, Mika. "Tapaturmataajudet laskivat (Decrease in injury frequencies)". Accessed November 4, 2019. https://www.kivirock.fi/uutiset.html?a1500=4928.

Tzamalouka, Georgia; Papadakaki, Maria; Chliaoutakis, Joannes El. "Freight transport and non-driving work duties as predictors of falling asleep at the wheel in urban areas of Crete". *Journal of Safety Research* 36 (2002): 75–84.

Uehli, Katrin; Mehta, Amar J.; Miedinger, David; Hug, Kerstin; Schindler, Christian; Holsboer-Trachsler, Edith; Leuppi, Jörg D.; Künzli, Nino. "Sleep problems and work injuries: A systematic review and meta-analysis". *Sleep Medicine Reviews* 18 (2013): 61–73 (a)

Uehli, Katrin; Miedinger, David; Bingisser, Roland; Dürr, Selina; Holsboer-Trachsler, Edith; Maier, Sabrina; Mehta, Amar J.: Müller, Roland; Schindler, Christian; Zogg, Stefanie; Künzli, Nino; Leuppi, Jörg D. "Sleep problems and work injury types: a study of 180 patients in a Swiss emergency department". *Swiss Medical Weekly* 143 (2013): https://doi.org/10.4414/smw.2013.13902. (b)

Vegso, S.; Cantley, L.; Slade, M.: Taiwo, O.; Sircar, K.; Rabinowitz, P.; Fiellin, M.; Russi, M.B.; Cullen, M.R. "Extended work hours and risk of acute occupational injury: A case-crossover study of workers in manufacturing". *American Journal of Industrial Medicine* 50 (2007): 597–603.

Vela Acosta, M.S.; Sechrest, L.; Chen, M.-K. "Farmworkers at the border: A bilingual initiative for occupational health and safety". *Public Health Reports* 124 (2009): Suppl. 1, 143–151.

Vennelle, Marjorie; Engleman, Heather M.; Douglas, Neil J. "Sleepiness and sleep-related accidents in commercial bus drivers". *Sleep and Breathing* 14 (2010): 39–42.

Viikari-Juntura, E.; Kausto, J.; Shiri, R.; Kaila-Kangas, L.; Takala, E.-P.; Karppinen, J.; Miranda, H.; Luukkonen, R.; Martimo, K.-P. "Return to work after early part-time sick leave due to musculoskeletal disorders: a randomized controlled trial". *Scandinavian Journal of Work, Environment & Health* 38 (2012): 134–143.

Violanti, J.M. "Cellular phones and fatal traffic collisions". *Accident Analysis and Prevention* 30 (1998): 519–524.

Violanti, John M.; Fekedulegn, Desta; Andrew, Michael E.; Charles, Luenda E.; Hartley, Tara A.; Vila, Bryan; Burchfiel, Cecil M. "Shift work and long-term injury among police officers". *Scandinavian Journal of Work, Environment & Health* 39 (2013): 361–368.

Violanti, J.M.; Marshall, J.R. "Cellular phones and traffic accidents: An epidemiological approach". *Accident Analysis and Prevention* 28 (1996): 265–270.

Virtanen, Marianna; Kivimäki; Mika; Joensuu, Matti; Virtanen, Pekka; Elovainio, Marko; Vahtera, Jussi. "Temporary employment and health: a review". *International Journal of Epidemiology* 34 (2005): 610–622.

Väyrynen, Seppo; Könönen, Unto. "Short and long-term effects of a training programme on work postures in rehabilitees: A pilot study of loggers suffering from back troubles". *International Journal of Industrial Ergonomics* 7 (1991): 103–109.

Wadsworth, E.J.K.; Moss, S.C.; Simpson, S.A.; Smith, A.P. "Psychotropic medication use and accidents, injuries and cognitive failures". *Human Psychopharmacology and Clinical Experiment* 20 (2005): 391–400

Waehrer, Geetha M.; Miller, Ted R.; Hendrie, Delia; Galvin, Deborah M. "Employee assistance programs, drug testing, and workplace injury". *Journal of Safety Research* 57 (2016): 53–60.

Wagner, Brandt. "Safety and health in the fishing industry". *International Maritime Health* 54 (2003): 151–163.

Wagstaff, Anthony Sverre; Sigstad Lie, Jenny-Anne. "Shift and night work and long working hours – a systematic review of safety implications". *Scandinavian Journal of Work, Environment & Health* 37 (2011): 173–185.

Waldron, I.; McCloskey, C.; Earle, I. "Trends in gender differences in accidents mortality: Relationships to changing gender roles and other societal trends". *Demographic Research* 13 (2005): 415–454.

Wang, Bing; Li, Dinglin; Wu, Chao. "Characteristics of hazardous chemical accidents during hot season in China from 1989 to 2019: A statistical investigation". *Safety Science* 129 (2020): https://doi.org/10.1016/j.ssci.2020.104788.

Wang, Jingxin; Bell, Jennifer L.; Grushecky, Shawn T. "Logging injuries for a 10-year period in Jilin Province of the People's Republic of China". *Journal of Safety Research* 34 (2003): 273–279.

Wang, Limin; Wheeler, Krista; Bai, Li; Stallones, Lorann; Dong, Yanmei; Ge, Jie; Xiang, Huiyun. "Alcohol consumption and work-related injuries among farmers in Heilongjiang province, People's Republic of China". *American Journal of Industrial Medicine* 53 (2010): 825–835.

Watt, Kerrianne; Purdie, David M.; Roche, Anne M.; McClure, Roderick J. "Risk of injury from acute alcohol consumption and the influence of confounders". *Addiction* 99 (2004): 1262–1273.

Webb, Gloria; Fresta, Joseph. "Alcohol and other drug problems at the workplace: Is drug testing an appropriate solution?". *Journal of Occupational Health and Safety – Australia and New Zealand* 10 (1994): 95–106.

Webb, Gloria R.; Redman, Selina; Sanson-Fisher, Robert W. "Work injury experience at an industrial worksite". *Journal of Occupational Health and Safety – Australia and New Zealand* 8 (1992): 143–153.

Webb, Gloria R.; Redman, Selina; Hennrikus, Deborah J.; Kelman, G. Richard; Gibberd, Robert W.; Sanson-Fisher, Robert W. "The relationships between high-risk and problem drinking and the occurrence of work injuries and related absences". *Journal of Studies on Alcohol* 55 (1994): 434–446.

Wehbe F.; Al Hattab M.; Hamzeh F. "Exploring associations between resilience and construction safety performance in safety networks". *Safety Science* 82 (2016): 338–351.

Wells, Samantha; Macdonald, Scott. "The relationship between alcohol consumption patterns and car, work, sports and home accidents for different age groups". *Accident Analysis & Prevention* 31 (1999): 663–665.

Welsh, Dianne H.B.; Luthans, Fred; Sommer, Steven M. "Managing Russian factory workers: The impact of U.S.-based behavioral and participative techniques". *Academy of Management Journal* 36 (1993): 58–79.

Westaby, James D.; Lowe, J. Krister. "Risk-taking orientation and injury among youth workers: examining the social influence of supervisors, coworkers, and parents". *Journal of Applied Psychology* 90(2005): 1027–1035.

White, A.C. "The relationship between alcohol and industrial accidents". *British Journal on Alcohol and Alcoholism* 12 (1977): 165–166.

Wickizer, Thomas M.; Kopjar, B.; Franklin, G.; Joesch, J. "Do drug-free workplace programs prevent occupational injuries? Evidence from Washington State". *Health Services Research* 39 (2004): 91–110.

Wilkins, P.A.; Acton, W.I. "Noise and accidents – a review". *Annual Occupational Hygiene* 25 (1982): 249–260.Wilkins, Kathryn; Beaudet, M.P. "Work stress and health". *Health Reports* 10 (1998): 47–62.

Wilkins, Kathryn; Mackenzie, Susan G. "Work injuries". *Health Reports* 18 (2007): 3: 1–18.

Williams, E.A.; Priestley, S.E. "Forklift truck injuries". *Journal of the Society of Occupational Medicine* 30 (1980): 149–152.

Williamson, Ann; Boufous, Soufiane. "A data-matching study of the role of fatigue in work-related crashes". *Transportation Research* F 10 (2007): 242–253.

Williamson, Ann M.; Feyer, Anne-Marie. "Causes of accidents and the time of day". *Work & Stress* 9 (1995): 158–164.

Wills, Andrew; Watson, Barry; Biggs, Herbert. "An exploratory investigation into safety climate and work-related driving". *Work* 32 (2009): 81–94.

Wirtz, Anna; Lombardi, David A.; Willetts, Joanna L.; Folkard, Simon; Christiani, David C. "Gender differences in the effect of weekly working hours on occupational injury risk in the United States working population". *Scandinavian Journal of Work, Environment & Health* 38 (2012): 349–357.

Wojtczak-Jaroszowa, J.; Jarosz, D. "Time-related distribution of occupational accidents". *Journal of Safety Research* 18 (1987): 33–41.

Wong, Imelda S.; McLeod Christopher B.; Demers, Paul A. "Shift work trends and risk of work injury among Canadian workers". *Scandinavian Journal of Work, Environment & Health* 37 (2011): 54–61.

Wong, Imelda S.; Smith, Peter M.; Mustard, Cameron A.; Gignac, Monique A.M. "For better or worse? Changing shift schedules and the risk of work injury among men and women". *Scandinavian Journal of Work, Environment & Health* 40 (2014): 621–630.

Wong, Imelda S.; Smith, Peter M.; Mustard, Cameron A.; Gignac, Monique A.M. "Health and occupational outcomes among injured, nonstandard shift workers". *Journal of Occupational and Environmental Medicine* 57 (2015): 1244–1249.

Wong, Tze-Wai. "Occupational injuries among construction workers in Hong Kong". *Occupational Medicine* 44 (1994): 247–252.

Wong, Tze-Wai; Chen, Wei-Qing; Yu, Tak-Sun; Lin, Yan-Zu; Cooper, Gary L. "Perceived sources of occupational stress among Chinese off-shore oil installation workers". *Stress and Health* 18 (2002): 217–226.

Woo, J.-H.; Sundar, G. "Eye injuries in Singapore – don't risk it. Do more. A prospective study". *Annals Academy of Medicine Singapore* 35 (2006): 706–718.

Wrench, John; Lee, Gloria. “Piecework and industrial accidents: two contemporary case studies”. *Sociology* 16 (1982): 512–525.

Wu, Trong-Neng; Liou, Saou-Hsing; Hsu, Chao-Chun; Chao, Show-Lin; Liou, Shu-Fen; Ko, Kquei-Nu; Yeh, Wen-Yu; Chang, Po-Ya. “Epidemiologic study of occupational injuries among foreign and native workers in Taiwan”. *American Journal of Industrial Medicine* 31 (1997): 623–630.

Wuellner, S.E.; Walters, J.K.; St. Louis, T.; Leinenkugel, K.; Rogers, P.F.; Lefkowitz, D.; Davis, L.K.; Gelberg, K.; Zak, M.J.; Castillo, D.N. “Nonfatal occupational injuries and illnesses among older workers – United States, 2009”. *Morbidity and Mortality Weekly Report* 60 (2011): 503–508.

Xia, Zhao-lin; Sorock, Gary S.; Zhu, Jin-liang; Courtney, Theodore K.; Fu, Hua; Liang, You-xin; Christiani, David C. “Fatal occupational injuries in the construction industry of a new development area in East China, 1991 to 1997”. *American Industrial Hygiene Association Journal* 61 (2000): 733–737.

Xiang, Jianjun; Bi, Peng; Pisaniello, Dino; Hansen, Alana; Sullivan, Thomas. “Association between high temperature and work-related injuries in Adelaide, South Australia, 2001–2010”. *Occupational and Environment Medicine* 71 (2014): 246–252.

Xiang, Jianjun X.; Bi, Peng; Pisaniello, Dino; Hansen, Alana. “The association between heat exposure and work-related injuries in South Australia, 2001–2010”. *Occupational and Environmental Medicine* 72 (2015): 580–586.

Xianglong, Sun; Hu, Zhao; Shumin, Feng; Zhenning, Li. “Bus drivers’ mood states and reaction abilities at high temperature”. *Transportation Research Part F: Traffic psychology and behaviour* 59 (2018): 436–444.

Yamamoto, Kazuhiko; Matsusue, Yumiko; Murakami, Kazuhiro; Horita, Satoshi; Matsubara, Yuri; Sugiura, Tsutomu; Kirita, Tadaaki. “Maxillofacial fractures due to work-related accidents”. *Journal of Cranio-Maxillo-Facial Surgery* 39 (2011): 182–186.

Yanai, Ornit; Goldin, Lev; Kugel, Chen; Hiss, Jehuda. “Occupational fatalities in Israel”. *Journal of Clinical Forensic Medicine* 6 (1999): 129–132.

Yang, Liu; Branscum, Adam; Smit, Ellen; Dreher, David; Howard, Karen; Kincl, Laurel. “Work-related injuries and illnesses and their association with hour of work: Analysis of the Oregon construction industry in the US using workers’ compensation accepted disabling claims, 2007–2013”. *Journal of Occupational Health* 62 (2020): e12118.

Yu, Haimiao; Chen, Hong. "Production output pressure and coal mine fatality seasonal variations in China, 2002–2011". *Journal of Safety Research* 47 (2013): 39–46.

Yu, T.S.I.; Liu, H.; Hui, K. "A case-control study of eye injuries in the workplace in Hong Kong". *Ophthalmology* 111 (2004): 70–74

Zaloshnja, Eduard; Miller, Ted R.; Hendrie, Delia; Galvin, Deborah. "Employer costs of alcohol-involved injuries". *American Journal of Industrial Medicine* 50 (2007): 136–142.

Zghal-Mokni, Imen; Nacef, Leila; Kaoueche, Mourad; Letaief, Imen; Bouguila, Hedi; Jeddi, Amed; Ayed, Saida. "Epidémiologie des Accidentes Oculaires du Travail". *La Tunisie Medicale* 85 (2007): 576–579.

Zhang, Tingru; Chan, Alan H.S. "Sleepiness and the risk of road accidents for professional drivers: A systematic review and meta-analysis of retrospective studies". *Safety Science* 70 (2014): 180–188.

Zhang, Yingyu; Shao, Wei; Zhang, Mengjia; Li, Hejun; Yin, Shijiu; Xu, Yingjun. "Analysis 320 coal mine accidents using structural equation modelling with unsafe conditions of the rules and regulations as exogenous variables". *Accident Analysis & Prevention* 92 (2016): 189–201.

Zhang, Xiaofei; Yu, Songlin; Wheeler, Krista; Kelleher, Kelly; Stallones, Lorann; Xiang, Huiyun. "Work-related non-fatal injuries among foreign-born and US-born workers: Findings from the National Health Interview Survey, 1997–2005". *American Journal of Industrial Medicine* 52 (2009): 25–36.

Zheng, Lei; Xiang, Huiyun; Song, Xiaoqin; Wang, Zengchen. "Nonfatal unintentional injuries and related factors among male construction workers in Central China". *American Journal of Industrial Medicine* 53 (2010): 588–595.

Zierold, K.M.; Anderson, H.A. "Racial and ethnic disparities in work-related injuries among teenagers". *Journal of Adolescent Health* 39 (2006) 422–426.

Zwerling, Craig. "Current practice and experience in drug and alcohol testing in the workplace". *Bulletin on Narcotics* 45 (1993): 155–196.

Zwerling, Craig; Ryan, James; Orav, Endel John. "The efficacy of preemployment drug screening for marijuana and cocaine in predicting employment outcome". *Journal of American Medical Association* 264 (1990): 2639–2643.

Zwerling, Craig; Sprince, Nancy L.; Davis, Charles S.; Whitten, Paul S.; Wallace, Robert R.; Heeringa, Stephen G. "Occupational injuries among older workers with disabilities: A prospective cohort study of the Health and Retirement Survey, 1992 to 1994". *American Journal of Public Health* 88 (1998): 1691–1695.

Zwerling, Craig; Sprince, Nancy L.; Ryan, James; Jones, Michael P. "Occupational injuries: Comparing the rates of male and female postal employees". *American Journal of Epidemiology* 138 (1993): 46–55.

Zwerling, Craig; Sprince, Nancy L.; Wallace, Robert B.; Davis, Charles S.; Whitten, Paul S.; Heeringa, Steven G. "Risk factors for occupational injuries among older workers: An analysis of the Health and Retirement Study". *American Journal of Public Health* 86 (1996): 1306–1309. (a)

Zwerling, Craig; Sprince, Nancy L.; Wallace, Robert B.; Davis, Charles S.; Whitten, Paul S.; Heeringa, Steven G. "Alcohol and occupational injuries among older workers". *Accident Analysis & Prevention* 28 (1996): 371–376. (b)

Zwerling, Craig; Whitten, Paul S.; Davis, Charles S.; Sprince, Nancy L. "Occupational injuries among workers with disabilities. The National Health Interview Survey, 1985–1994". *Journal of American Medical Association (JAMA)* 278 (1997): 2163–2166.

Zytoon, Mohamed A. "Occupational injuries and health problems in the Egyptian Mediterranean fisheries". *Safety Science* 50 (2012): 113–122.